# THE JOY OF MOTORCYCLES

## More Scraping Pegs

Michael Stewart

**Beaten Stick Books**

NONFICTION BEATEN WITH A STICK

ISBN 978-1-7774436-3-4 paperback
ISBN 978-1-7774436-4-1 eBook
ISBN 978-1-7774436-5-8 hardcover

# CONTENTS

# PREFACE

The Scraping Pegs books encourage readers to reflect on the motorcycle experience and what happens when riders climb on. The books do not teach specific skills, nor do they explore the mechanics of the machines.

# WARNING!

I'm not living like I should. Increasingly bitter, I may launch a vendetta, like in the movies *Kill Bill* or *True Grit.* Revenge and loathing are my companions.

Ride friends.

Find J O Y .

I cannot.

DO NOT READ if you are not open to what lies down the trail, along the highway, or around the bend. With motorcycles, life, and this book, there are no guarantees. Like riding, words can lead anywhere. But never lose hope.

I believe,

**J O Y will find a way.**

# PART ONE: ON-SCOOTER

*Dr. Tire told me, "I couldn't repair your brakes, so I made your horn louder." - Steven Wright*

# CHAPTER 1 – ATTEMPTED MURDER

The garage door closed. Under jubilant skies, I rolled down the street uncaged. Travel tickled my neurotransmitters the way a lick of cream lick triggers a tastebud explosion.

I had not smoked crystal meth, eaten dark chocolate, or otherwise chemically induced bliss. Neurologically, I was at the embryonic Motorcycle JOY stage. A state of mind riders nurture, similar to Jerry Lee Lewis or Wolfgang Amadeus Mozart tickling the ivories.

I think.

Take nothing I say for granted, especially on the subjects of piano playing and neurology. Motorcycles? My friends say, "the wheels are round and they roll." This is what I know.

*You & Your Motorcycle: there is MAGIC in your machine. Have you discovered it?*

The front tires hopped onto the sidewalk. I nudged

the bar to turn—mobility scooters do not respond to countersteering.

Big Terry spotted me. Ex-military, he blocked the sidewalk like it was a Kabul checkpoint. Marta had filled me in on his disturbing motorcycle dilemma.

"Shit."

Confined for months to my basement hospital bed, I longed to ride. "Please don't bog me down, big guy. Not a good time," I said to Pearl, my dog, who was checking out the human barrier ahead. "It's important I focus solely on myself. The things I must do, to climb back on."

There are times you must,

Scrape your pegs.

Wish others well and do your own thing.

I had to stop. Unlike two-wheel escape machines, mobility scooters cannot outrun or otherwise evade. On-scooter, I was a sitting duck.

Terry asked, "What the fuck should I do?" the way a customer pleads with the dealership service manager, after being told his pride and joy is an expensive hunk of junk. "About my motorcycle? There must be something I can do?"

I restrained a shrug, afraid the exMarine was about to leak tears the way oil drips from a sketchy amateur engine rebuild. Sure didn't want moisture landing on my new loaner mobility scooter, Scout. My dog Pearl wanted to skedaddle down the sidewalk. I longed to twist the throttle, see what Scout's made of, like Valentino Rossi, ripping down the ribbon of cement toward endless possibilities and grand adventures while giving society's laws and norms the biker salute. Or, perhaps as far as the local strip mall to refill my prescriptions and buy peanut M&M's.

"Don't know what to do." Terry looked like he should be on the Pul-e Sukhta bridge, looking down at the moldy Kabul River, in the tuck position, set to jump.

"Sure you'll figure something out, Terry." How about a shove? Hang my old bike frame around your neck. Don't drive like a Blockhead SQUID going into a corner. What to do? Step up and jump! Football player size, I could visualize Terry's splash—similar to a depth charge in *The Enemy Below* movie.

In the absence of a better solution, why not jump? We all end up in the river.

*Truth About Motorcycles: bikers know —indecision is a killer.*

If Shelly showed up, it'd be a repeat of the Second Punic War (when Hannibal, riding his elephant like a biker, crossed the Pyrenees and Alps, intent on kicking ass and raising hell. Or like Grendel Putin directing his Russian army to destroy Ukraine). The couple met and married in Idaho. Shell was "just passing through." Later she asked, "why the fuck did I stop?"

Acquaintances dismissed her bluntness and rudeness until she attacked Brenda, Terry's beloved Softail. "Unforgiveable," my Guzzi riding friend Marta said. "Motorcycles are innocents."

Terry and Shelly were physically joined but divided by divergent concepts of what is necessary to live a good life —a life filled with J O Y .

Terry spent six years in the Marine Corps and then rode his Harley to forget four of them. From soldier to fighting financial wars with Theisen and Nakamura

Wealth Management (thanks to Shelly's uncle in Victoria, on Vancouver Island).

"Just don't know what to do." The unspoken words—about Shelly's plan to murder Brenda.

*You have a bike, right, Terry? For fuck's sake, get on it and ride*! Escape is one of the joys of motorcycles.

When I'm lost, my wife Dori asks, "Don't know what to do with yourself? Want to clean the gutters?" Immediately I'm inspired to check oil, polish forks, or dick around with my motorcycle GPS. Nowadays, I'd love to clean the gutters, but I can't.

Terry was in danger of becoming motorcycle-less, so he blocked my way, thinking *he has answers because he has more experience.* A neuroscience fact: we all suffer from brain atrophy, losing cells over time. Based on age, I had the more significant deficit. Plus, I had the "possibility of motorcycle accident cerebral dysfunction" (thanks to Horace the Horrible, who took my sports touring bike down. More about that fucker later).

"Don't know what to do." Terry persisted, staring down at Scout's small tires, expecting a response. The soldier acted more like a rider-in-distress than a kick ISIS in the ass to bring peace and freedom to a part of the world that didn't want it, exMarine.

Terry fiddled with the emergency cane I'd strapped behind Scout's seat. I thought he might take it off and flog himself, attempt to pound in a solution. "I'm the one who suffered a traumatic accident, my friend," I wanted to say. *So why are you going on about Brenda? Man-up Marine! And get the hell out of my way!*

"Whatta'ya' think," Terry persisted? "I should do... to save Brenda?"

We were motorcycle acquaintances, not friends, and I

barely knew Brenda. "It's a tough one." My dog, Pearly, ran out of patience. I patted her head. *I know Pearl. I know.* Here's the thing: because I was visibly injured but didn't look gruesome, Terry treated me as if I'd morphed into a caring and wise motorcycle sage. He felt at ease because I'd been through an ordeal, survived, learned a thing or two (he believed), and was nonthreatening, sitting on a mobility scooter looking up. *It's like the bolt of lightning phenomenon Pearly, where electricity turns an ordinary person into a superhero.* There I was, trying to enjoy my second ever scooter outing, and big Terry thought I had answers. Never asked "what should I do?" when I could evade him.

"Do you think I should…" Terry's phone beeped. A large hand formed the do-not-move signal.

Pearl barked, *now's our chance to get the hell out of here, while the dude's on the phone!* Dogs don't hide urges well.

I may carry the mongrel gene—based on behavioral observations, not DNA analysis. For example, if a dog wants to hump the neighbor's poodle, pee on a car tire, maul a delivery person, they get on with it—no floating trial balloons or adjusting preload. Dogs practice Direct Honesty; people must be discreet and hide behind words. Of course, on-motorcycle, you can always ride away from jabber. It's one of the joys of motorcycles.

"Tact, it's called," my deceased motorcycle friend Bob advised. "You should trade in some blunt for tact." Why bother, I used to think? On-motorcycle, discretion is not required. You climb on, bugger off, disconnect, and do whatever you like (adhering to your riding rules, of course. We'll review mine shortly). My new loaner mobility scooter, Scout, was a different paradigm. Motorcyclists are at liberty to behave like mutts, but on-scooter, decorum is essential. Ever try to outrun intrusions on a scooter—can't be done. Getaways are always on sport or dual-purpose bikes; you never see robbers fleeing on mobility scooters.

Terry needed to escape and owned a motorcycle he called Brenda. It's a magic carpet—ride, Terry ride!

On a scooter, you're trapped and must learn to be tactful. It sucks! When I took Scout out on our maiden cruise (seated with my disability props, boot cast, and arm sling), the curious stopped to judge me. "What happened to you, fella?"

"Motorcycle."

"Were you driving like a biker-idiot?"

"Stag. Horace the Horrible... my number came up, and I went bang."

They shake their heads—no doubt driving like a wild man.

I wasn't.

Motorcycles don't judge; like dogs, they remain loyal, even to Blockheads (riders who choose not to develop a Motorcycle State of Mind) prone to abuse them. "And they detach you from those who do," Marta says.

*Truth About Motorcycles: unlike people,*
*bikes never criticize or condemn.*

Terry shook his head in disgust while putting his phone in his pocket.

I looked up, smiling like a nutter. A running shoe tapped Scout's tire, demanding, tell me, tell me, tell me.

"You'll figure something out. I'm sure, Terry." *Good luck with that. Of course, you could just ride away. USE YOUR MOTORCYCLE TERRY!*

Again, his phone beeped. Up went the halt sign.

Pearl gave up. Dogs don't dwell on dilemmas. The urge to murder a delivery person lingers, but in a few minutes, it's gone. Pearl stayed put on her belly. She can nap anytime, anywhere. My mongrel gene implored me to join her on the grass, but I could not.

Psychologists took Napping Therapy out of their rate book because even coated in academia, it's challenging to monetize, but snoozing is very effective for mild cases of uneasiness (for severe problems, jump off a bridge). Stretch out on the green grass beside your motorcycle or best friend. Then wait for life to settle down and sunshine to warm your cockles—stimulate new brain cells as life giving rays cause plants to grow. It seems logical, but sunlight cultivates skin cancer, so not at all like recharging a battery, more like Mother Nature tricking you with false joy while she drains you. Nasty, nasty bitch.

*You & Your Motorcycle: may Life borrow your magical machine? It needs more J O Y .*

*Truth About Motorcycles: there is more Life, the Beautiful and less Life, the Bully on the Road to JOY. Ride, friends, ride! Do not jump! You'll miss your motorcycle.*

Motorcycles exist in a state of mechanical bliss. Born of engineers and technicians, their care passes to riders, the way puppies pass to owners. If respected with reverence, the machines remain forever faithful and devoted.

*Mutt JOY and Motorcycle JOY are kindred spirits.*

Life is the opposite, constantly up to no good: "What pestilence shall I unleash today? A new cancer? Virus? Have one of my boas swallow Fluffy alive? What tomfoolery tickles your poison ivy, Mother Nature? Or have you had your Nap Therapy and feel mellow?

To be fair, it's a two-way street: Mom cannot take Humanity for granted—we're constantly kicking her in the poles or causing chewing on her surface like termites. Except when on-motorcycle when we cause Mom to smile. She nods and thinks—the wheels are round and they roll.

The answer to Terry's motorcycle dilemma is obvious: hop on and move until J O Y blows Warhammer Shelly's angst away. Wind therapy, like napping, is not included in the counseling industry rate book.

*You & Your Motorcycle: have you ridden to escape or just to clear your head? Have you experimented with the nap-ride combo? Or Nap-Ride-Nap Mega Therapy?*

Terry needed to ride until a moment of Absolute Clarity answered the question; how to save Brenda from being expelled? But, in a way, Terry, like me, was motorcycle-less. His motorcycle sanctity was under attack. We were like a couple of soldiers stripped of our rifles, neutralized while the battle raged.

Wellness professionals who ride flip out perceptive gems of wisdom without hesitation. Is Life being a bully? No problem. Get an appointment with Dr. Phil. Phil's answers are super legitimate because he has stellar credentials: a doctorate in clinical psychiatry, but more importantly, dirt bike rash.

My wife's doctor friend Peggy is the opposite. She's diagnosed me with biker-idiot syndrome and would like to smarten me. "To make things easier for Dori." Doctor Peggy has never been on-motorcycle and couldn't clip a toenail to save herself, but the word doctor is in with her *Ode to a Daisy* recital—it only rattles my demons. Her brain's so lopsided she can't walk straight; constantly trips over mom and mum. A doctor? Direct Honesty: Pearly has more common sense and way more healing power, but I don't call her Dr. Pearl. Dr. Daisy couldn't pee on a tire for all the classic Brit bike, electric repair jobs in the world. Let's clear up title confusion. I'm Zen Jackass Mike (a reformed Curmudgeonly Jackass). Nice to meet you. Dr. Phil is a certified medical doctor. Dr. Peggy does a beautiful job reciting *Ode to a Daisy*, but no one gives a worn sprocket; remember, if you need your brain fixed, see a motorcycle qualified professional, like Dr. Phil, not a phony-baloney doctor, like Dr. Daisy.

Or nap. Then ride. If you're dealing with a hopeless dilemma, don't rule out jumping (in the absence of a suitable bridge, do a one and a half twister off a tall building, being careful not to land on a motorcycle). Go down shouting, "Hello, Life Part II." Based on the collective portrait theologians paint of heaven, it will of course include motorcycles.

The counseling industry turns a blind eye to gearheads. "They're a dismal revenue stream. Have this thing they call J O Y . A cure all. Just ride, they say."

"Do you ride a motorcycle?" crisis center agents ask, screening calls. "Yes, then go ahead and jump," they sing. Sometimes they put bikers on hold and play Van Halen.

I slumped forward, giving Terry my irritated pissed-off signal, but he was lost in phone world. My attempt was as effective as glaring at Dori, *can't Pissy stay home!* The two words, doctor plus Peggy, boil my blood. Service doesn't pass the kid who fixes flats off as a doctor because he can recite *Ode to a Tire*. "Hello, I'm Dr. Tire. Would you like me to re-tune your very sophisticated engine while I rap *Ode to a Tire* like Dr. Dre? By the way, is your bike gray or grey?"

I wondered about linking Terry up with Dr. Daisy. Could a poem about a flower focus his mind away from a troubling motorcycle dilemma? *Oh, bellis perennis...* "Not tactful," Bob would warn. "Possibly even mean." I smirked and thought, Dr. Phil. Dr. Phil. Help me out here, Dr. Phil. What to do? We're all members of the motorcycle community. What have you got for me, Philip? Transfer your knowledge so I can assist his rider-in-distress.

"Sorry," Terry said, and put his phone away.

Using my good arm, I scratched Brain. Without hesitation or thought, out came, "What do you think you should do, Terry?" WHOOP DE DOO! I was channeling Dr. Phil. Holy matching side cases! Watching the doc on TV with Bunny (our cat) wasn't a complete waste of time,

Dori!

I could see my question had Terry's brain cells racing around the way Sir Isaac Newton's did when he came up with r2n = nRλ. Two riders experiencing Disconnectedness off-motorcycle. Three, if you count Dr. Phil's spiritual presence. For emphasis, I added, "What do you think you should do to save Brenda?"

When bikers connect, there is a shared moment of JOY.

*You & Your Motorcycle: have you experienced off-motorcycle JOY?*

Terry did not have his helmet on the ground (the universal help signal), so I was not technically obligated to assist. Still, it's gratifying to aid a brother in anguish, even when you should be skedaddling. It was gratifying to observe a glimmer of optimism in Terry's eyes, even if it meant forgoing an *Enemy Below*-sized splash and a tremendous deal on a second hand motorbike.

◆◆◆

The exMarine's military training kicked-in. Terry analyzed all factors, risks, and probable outcomes. Or was he stalling, supposing I would offer a comprehensive solution?

I hope not, because truth be told, I'd drifted to thoughts of a recent meeting at Beaten Stick Books. My two-book deal was hanging on the assumption I'd be willing to punch up content.

I'm not.

Romance, erotica, fantasy, and thrillers sell. "We'll spice up *Joy.* Give Marta a secret gang life," Dolores, my advisor, said.

"No spice."

Dolores paid no attention. "Add Terry war flashbacks... an ex-Marine with exotic girlfriends... and a jealous psycho wife. The bikes add flair but don't get carried away. Maybe add one closet gay biker dude for the LGBTQ market."

"Sorry, Dolores, *Pegs* is about motorcycle Truth, MAGIC, and JOY. Creative, but absolutely nonfiction. There are already a gazillion biker romance books. Why would you want another?"

"It's what readers want. Romance sells. Run-of-the-mill truth is hard to give away. At least open your book with a proper Introduction for the sake of those who haven't read Book One... or have forgotten your fuzzy facts. Readers expect order, not a book with an Introduction buried on page fifty-three. Your books will be return stamped, Defective."

I nodded because I'm a biker, not a book guy. What do I know? If Marta hadn't been acquainted with someone with influence, I wouldn't have a publisher. If I weren't decrepit, I'd be riding or hiking with Pearl, not worrying about commas, for apostrophe's sake. I'd like to help Dolores climb her corporate ladder, but I'm sorry, I cannot write Marta and Earl making out behind an Indian with a battered pickle.

According to online opinion, "motorcycle culture gives the finger to society's laws and norms." I'm doing my bit by giving the finger to the Book Introduction and Beaten

Stick Book's list guidelines. "My Introduction won't be on page one. And there will be eleven rules in my updated list of motorcycle rules." I'm not out to harm anyone: promoters, political scientists, literary traditionalists, the counseling industry, the jerk cop who gave me a speeding ticket... perhaps the cager who T boned Dori's hybrid, but that's it. My thinking is, why cater to readers who can't be bothered to read book one before book two? Why adjust valves for a biker who doesn't take the time to change their oil?

"Readers won't get it. May as well call your book *The Road to Mumbo Jumbo and Other Foolishness*," Dolores told me.

"It's not exactly Sir Isaac's *Mathematical Principles of Natural Philosophy*, Dolores. I'm sure readers will sort it out. Bikers are a hell of a lot smarter than they look."

"It's like putting the front entrance of a house in the backyard. Look at me! I don't follow convention! I'm an outlaw! There's a reason front entrances are always at the front... even at Hells Angels' hangouts."

Watching Dolores fret about books amuses me. Dori says, "You're being childish. Just because Dolores drives a car, and works with words like Peg, don't dismiss her."

"Don't be Mr. Jackass," Bob might say if he wasn't dead (that story is in book one, *Scraping Pegs*.)

Marta, a volunteer at MRR Labs (my garage and clubhouse), rides an old Moto Guzzi and is very good at translating to a language I comprehend. "Think about renting a motorcycle. You go to check the mirror, but Dr. Tire stuck it behind the seat. Not on the handlebar where it belongs."

"I get it, Marta, but we're talking books. Everyone is trying to kill riders, not readers," but to prove I'm a team player and to help Dolores out with her publishing norms, I wrote *Scrape Your Lists.* It's cheap and includes a dictionary of the capitalized words used in *Joy*, my Motorcycle Riding Rules, and much more. Will it be enough to avoid a State of California warning label on the cover of *Joy* (warning: this book may cause confusion)?

California should use these labels:

WARNING
Forget About It.
Just Ride!

"I know you'll sell a ton of books, even if my Introduction is not on page one, the content is not on-trend, and my list contains eleven rules," I told Marketing (Pete, a part-time ex-appliance salesperson). "You're extremely good at what you do. The Valentino Rossi of booksellers. You get sidecars of crap, books without motorcycles, on bestseller lists."

Pete smiled, *appliances or books, it's all the same.* "I do my best."

I hope to be on-motorcycle by the time *Joy* hits the shelves. Why read if you can ride (unless you're camping, stuck on a ferry, the weather is shitty, or you have a copy of *Pegs* or *Joy*). That's my position. "JOY hangs out on motorbikes, not in bookstores, Dolores."

Surely Terry will buy a copy? "Did you know I probably have a new book coming out, Terry? It's all about J O Y ?"

◆◆◆

Terry stared at me. I recognized the gaze; it is the one

desperate customers form when they spot the genius mechanic straying from the dealership's backroom. *I must have answers! It's the second coming of Christ! All will be revealed.* Affordable ideas flipped out while the service adviser glares. "Your bike just needs a bit of our secret sauce. Only take a second. Then Dr. Tire will check your pressure and do other unnecessary stuff... it'll all be on your humongous bill. Or you could easily do it yourself."

Terry looked at me, like I was the genius mechanic. I'm far from it. "So, what'd ya think?"

My motorcycle acquaintance had himself a humdinger of a dilemma, which made me think of Feeble. Jorge Jorgensen regularly knocked the stuffing out of my classmate in elementary school (seemed hilarious at the time, now it bugs me). Terry regret was not something I wanted to add to Feeble regret. "I'm sure we can come up with something, Terry." I had nothing better than *murder Shelly before Warhammer kills Brenda.*

Terry nodded and smiled.

I rubbed my forehead—Brain was beginning to hurt.

Motorcycle Murder is a head-scratcher because it's unfathomable, like when you see a wonderful person slaughtered on the TV show *Dateline*. It's almost always motivated by finances, and Shelly liked to say, "what a gigantic waste of money your fuckin' toys are."

*Truth About Motorcycles: there are Killer Bikes (Rule #4) and people who want to kill bikes.*

Never! Never! Never assume your motorcycle is safe.

Ask Terry.

Thanks to Marta, I had all the nuts and bolts needed to

review my Motorcycle Friend's full story.

### *Terry's Dilemma*

The yard, the weeds in the grass, the crack in the driveway, the bird resting on the eave, everything surrounding Big Terry was drenched in deception as if both bravery and fraud dripped from the crankcase of his bike as it rolled under the garage door. He felt like a combatant again. Heading out on a mission, but betrayal, not anticipation, hung in the air. No witnesses: Shelly and son Matt were off to ball practice in the Leaf. *Never tell a lie?* "Bullshit," Terry snapped at a squirrel. "Whoever said that doesn't know Shelly." And does not own a motorcycle.

Never tell a lie is pure, horseshit.

The squirrel pranced and signaled, I Don't Care. Squirrels possess natural joy.

Saddlebags loaded, Terry drove over to Adam's Storage on the west side of town. The rent was prepaid six months in advance. The manager, Sergio got a little extra to ensure "confidentiality." It wasn't necessary: the storage business works on the Q.T. Sergio never asked, "Why do you need a storage unit, fella?" nor would he advertise the fact that Terry was Adam's newest customer. At out-of-the-way Adam's Storage, the policy was: no questions asked-exactly what is needed when treachery is locked behind storage unit doors.

Stabilizer in the tank would maintain the Softail's gas for six months. Time enough to stabilize a life? Come out of the closet; a silly notion that made Terry smirk —world, I love my motorcycle! Forbidden man-machine lust. A ludicrous lock-him-up-and-throwaway-the-key concept to NimRods like Shelly. Maybe if she read the *Zen* motorcycle book? Or *Scraping Pegs*? Or booked a session with Dr. Phil. Then she would learn to appreciate two-wheelers?

Terry felt terrible lying to Shelly. Even worse, about abandoning Brenda inside a gloomy, cobweb infested cell. *No offense, Adam, but your rooms aren't fit for motorcycles.*

It was like giving a family pet up for adoption or dropping a child off at a strange out-of-town college, but for Terry, there was no alternative. Life can be spiteful; it enjoys painting complexity black and white and having it face-off, from the two Koreas down to dueling banjos. It stomps on riders and turns motorcycles from art to junk. Like a bowl of cherries with sour, rotten fruit hiding in the bottom, Motorcycle JOY and Motorcycle Misery coexist. Love and hate. Life and death. Sir Isaac nailed it: "equal and opposite reactions." Yin and Yang.

To get his mind off murder and Warhammer Shelly, Terry liked to sing the old blue eyes song:

♫ That's life,
You're riding high in April, flat tire in June,
But I know I'm gonna get it changed
And be back on my bike, back on the road real soon ♫.

Terry and Brenda (his Harley) had been a couple for six years and formed a bond, like the one Mr. Pirsig described in the best-selling motorcycle book of all time, *Zen and the Art of Motorcycle Maintenance.*

Shelly and Terry met three years before Terry bought his first motorcycle. At the time, there was no need to check for Motorcycle Compatibility. They got along. Brenda wasn't in the picture, and Terry was used to occasional battlefield explosions.

Shelly, a Canadian, didn't have a clue about the MAGIC

in the machines. When the Harley arrived, it was a mistake. Wasted money better spent on curtains, a new roof, or Matt's college fund. She's blunt and crude: "Dump the fucking bike and move on. Grow the fuck up, Terry! You're not playing soldier anymore."

"That's life," Terry sang to drown his wife out. “One Jihad after another.” Then he and Brenda would flee the battle zone.

To keep the peace, Terry hid his bike at Adam's. A ceasefire, providing time to build a plan. Big Terry regularly snuck over to check on Brenda. "Brenda" because a Softail's name must be feminine, Terry believed. Shelly called her husband "a little bent" for wasting "all that time and money on a toy." Bent. Brent. Brenda. A natural naming, twisted from bad to good, a resurrection of hope.

The sound of the word "Brenda," for Terry, came with a smirk of pride and contentment. It’s the power of J O Y .

I'll never abandon you, is what Terry's touch said. We'll ride again one day, my friend. Travel and Disconnect. Can you guess what the unspoken words were? ...far away from Shelly because she wants to murder you.

Terry once loved his wife; but can love exist for a rider denied J O Y ?

"Life shouldn't be static," my departed friend Bob used to say. "That's why there are motorcycles. Something doesn't work out; hop on. Get the hell out of Dodge." Bob never married. But he was right: ride is always the answer.

Terry often drove the family's Nissan Leaf over to have coffee with the gang at Tony's Deli. He told them his Softail needed to go to Service, but he hadn't had time to talk to Gus, the service adviser. He'd "get on it before long."

Fooling the gang was easier than lying to Shelly because they understood.

Shelly believed the lie. The toy was sold to an out-of-town buyer. She hadn't seen or heard the damn thing for a month. "How much money did we lose?"

Shelly doesn't understand—it's not about money.

"How much did we get back?"

"Enough." *How do you put a price on a friend? No one left behind.*

"Yeah. Yeah. Yeah," the gang would say, but didn't because they'd heard Shelly's advice: "Why you all so attached to expensive toys? Grow the fuck up! Moronic for men with families and mortgages. Dangerous. Noisy. Terry's got rid of his toy." The unstated words: and so should all you jackasses. Grow the fuck up!

Poor Terry, but what could his buddies do? They were not one of those intimidating gangs with "neo" or "hell" in their name. They were not up to dishing out rough justice or retribution, more of a coffee club, really.

Terry lost hope that his wife would come around. A wall divided them.

*You & Your Motorcycle: have you noticed,*
*three can be a crowd? Or are you lucky and*
*enjoy Motorcycle Compatibility?*

One rider plus one motorcycle. After that, the math is sketchy. But hope springs eternal.

Terry couldn't dismiss the thought. *Maybe Shelly will soften? She did eventually agree to upgrade to a 75" TV. Or maybe I can change?*

Can a Marine ride away from war? Can Brenda be abandoned?

Soon there was a lounge chair and a small sound system in the spruced-up storage unit, along with a floor lamp, an HD poster, and a few kitchen utensils. Terry's riding gear was there, in two boxes sitting on a plank, perched on the concrete blocks lugged over from the lumberyard next door. Shelly would get mad if the Leaf got messed up. It's important to have a nice electric car, but fuck "obnoxious motorbikes." Everything necessary to climb on and ride away was at Adam's. Terry was tempted. Back to Idaho? Patagonia? Alaska?

*Will I be a deserter?*

Against regulations, a small electric heater was added to the unit. Bikers bend the rules, living outside society's norms. *Fire regulation this, Adam!*

To avoid Shelly's questions, Terry often took his lunch and drove to the storage unit from work, Theisen and Nakamura Wealth Management (learning to paint "investment pictures." Shelly insisted it was an opportunity to move up). He thought about bringing his son, Matt; he'd understand, but Shelly had a way of shaking secrets out of their son—blunt moms intimidate kids, and Shelly could be a Warhammer. Then sweet a minute later, like a skilled interrogator.

On nice days, Terry raised the cargo door to let in natural light, keeping it low to avoid prying eyes. He sat in silence, thinking of what could be and what is. Sometimes, he listened to country music. "Your Cheatin' Heart" was a favorite with Brenda.

Dr. Phil might ask, "Does paranoia live in the storage unit, Terry?" The suspicion that Shelly was on to the deception crept under the crack in the garage door, like a Stephen King omen. Up goes the unlocked door. There is Shelly, looking to confront the despicable cheater with his curvy, blond slut, but there is only the big, expensive machine, a space heater, and a stunned husband holding a bottle of lite beer. Lame, Terry knew. He could picture it unfolding on SNL, humorously, with Leonardo DiCaprio as Terry.

"You dug yourself a hole," Dr. Phil would say. "What do you think you should do to resolve it, Terry?"

"Maybe tell Shell; I've bought a new bike? Same model as the one I used to own. She'd never know the difference. Doesn't have a clue. Be mad as hell. *Facing the barbarian enemy again would be less stressful.*

The gang at Tony's Deli had seen it: "Lookout! Mount Etna's about to blow." Shelly doesn't hold back. NimRod blunt! Terry's the gentle one. His blunt was gutted on the battlefield, but he could be deceptive. Crooked as a wheel bashed against a curb.

Terry kept his gas cap locked tight. There's no explaining to an outraged motorcycle hater (a NimRod. Definitions of capitalized words and much more can be found in included in *Scrape Your Lists*). Canadians, like Shelly, don't know full-on PTSD, he believed. Keep your mouth shut, your ears closed, and move your bike to Adam's.

Terry pulled the cargo door up every second week, unplugged the battery tender, wrapped his legs around Brenda, and started the engine. Once the Harley warmed up, he pulled out and turned left, proudly parading between the long row of rental units. The big man rumbled along, helmet-less. He waved when other customers spotted him. On-motorcycle, Terry was in charge. His own man. Marine tough. Able to give his dilemma the finger. There was JOY on the asphalt at Adam's.

Sometimes it was all he could do to keep from riding away, the way he should have fled the Marines. Victory and peace in Afghanistan were horseshit.

*Truth About Motorcycles: motorcycle bonds are solid. Human relationships are fragile.*

Inevitably, motorcycle fuel tanks run dry. They're easy to refill. Again and again. No problem. Have you tried refueling a relationship?

Storage customers talk little but share a common purpose. Each has a secret. Life behind the security fence is nonjudgmental, like motorcycles. No one asks, "why you hide'n stuff here, buddy? What you got in there, anyway?"

When Brenda was switched off, Terry hid the key in a cardboard box before sitting to dream of the day he would roll out the gate. Disappear down the endless highway of possibilities. Brenda was excellent company. The relationship could go on, in secret, indefinitely. Terry could tell the guys he dumped his bike to keep the peace. They'd understand.

*Truth About Motorcycles: motorcycles can be selfish.*

Hello! Machines are not family, not even the way a pet is or the Marine Corps. Owning a bike is an indulgent, narcissistic, spoiled, unnecessary act. Little wonder NimRods exist—they know the facts.

"Horseshit," Bob would say (he owned both a sport-tourer and a cruiser and planned to buy a small dual-purpose bike). "Ever hear of Motorcycle JOY?"

"Many haven't," Marta said. "And never will."

Let's face facts. There is a line too far, like a crap bike bought instead of braces for the kid. Or spending the prescription money on new tires.

*Truth About Motorcycles: there is a line,*
*cross it and bikes weigh on you.*

*You & Your Motorcycle: does your bike ever make*
*you wonder, am I being responsible?*

At least riders are devoted to magical. Not something stupid, like a Dr. Daisy poem. You won't have an adventure reading *Ode to a Flower.* Jog and develop runner's knee. Golf is a pleasant walk gone bad. Drugs take you down the wrong bend in the road.

Terry turned up the volume. *Your cheatin' heart will tell on you...* Sneaking off to Adam's was like shooting up, a compulsion impossible to shake. The needle goes in; the family is abandoned. No matter how loathsome, the ritual must continue. Terry knew he could not survive without Brenda. Not as Big Terry, ex-Marine. Perhaps as Terrance, financial adviser?

There were days Terry believed he could walk away. For Shelly and Matt—they deserved better. Find a devoted owner for his Softail, return to normality, and work on life the way Shelly wanted him to. Become motorcycle-less, but with new curtains.

It's an achievable state, like taking a devoted pet to be

put down—you hate to do it, but it's demanded of you. Life, the Bully often calls the shots.

It's a selfish act, falling in love with a machine. Marta left her marriage after she met Guzzi. “We weren’t Motorcycle Compatible.”

Terry knew his co-workers at Theisen and Nakamura Wealth Management would snicker if his secret got out. Parents would instruct their children to stay away from Matt's weirdo dad, the guy who hid his motorcycle. He would have to survive on his own, like in the movie *Rebel Without a Cause*. Become a lone rider.

The folks at Tony's Deli would say, "Understandable because Shelly intended to murder Brenda. Ride away, friend."

Terry dreamt of pulling his helmet on. Checking wallet and passport. Set GPS for a distant destination, hop on, gas up, and ride away from war and Shelly. Brenda waited, always ready. Like a secret escape hatch. On-standby. *Might save my life one day. Should we go?*

*Truth About Motorcycles: motorcycles are patient.*

*Ride away. Itchy Boots.* The notion always brought J O Y especially when Terry daydreamed about Matt. A little older. Riding together like the father and son in the *Zen* book.

Terry loved sitting in the easy chair, in the storage unit, beside Brenda, at times even more than he enjoyed riding. It's not necessary to be on-motorcycle to experience J O Y .

◆◆◆

Rather than throw an apoplectic fit like Shelly, Pearl slept. Terry and Shelly should try napping, I thought. Along with Israel, nestled between Iran and Palestine. "What do you think you should do, Terry?" I repeated, trying to move things along.

I looked up at my motorcycle acquaintance and continued as Dr. Phil. "Acknowledge your purpose, Terry. Is it helping you deal with anxiety and stress? Understand, at a subconscious level, your addiction is unhealthy. Motorcycles are not a replacement for family." Kidding! I'm not really Dr. Phil or his smart, handsome assistant. What I did was reach into my motorcycle tank bag in Scout's mobility scooter basket, and pull out a Tupperware container. "Battered pickle," I offered? "From Tony's Deli."

We crunched our pickles.

Battered pickles are like a makeup kiss; they return normality to most situations.

Consider the two Koreas; political science has deployed every trick in its arsenal, including sanctions and basketball star Dennis Rodman, without a crumb of success. It's unlikely the responsible parties will kiss and make up, but battered pickles could clear the decks. There is no need to spend billions developing another doomed strategy. Drop by Tony's Deli. Communicate If the Battered Pickle Initiative isn't successful, give the crunchy delights to the starving North Koreans. At least some good would come of it. Use the diplomacy time saved to declare an official Motorcycle Day. If there are no days available, motorcycles are treasured, like children, so adapt November 20th to be Official Children's and

Motorcycle Day. If the General Assembly gets stuck, send in motorcycle engineers.

I understood what Terry was going through, having put my GT down thanks to an insurance write-off. I miss many of my old bikes, but, like if you had a large family, some more than others. Tactless, but Life, the Bully makes many of the rules, not me.

After a motorcycle mourning period, I've always made it back to the showroom. "More motorcycle, please." If Shelly prevailed, Terry would never make another trip to the sales floor. Permanently motorcycle-less, the key comes out, and your best friends are gone.

Brainwave! My battered pickles worked their magic. I had a moment of Absolute Clarity. "Terry," I began, "What do you think of this? You could really help me out."

We had a plan. A peace treaty.

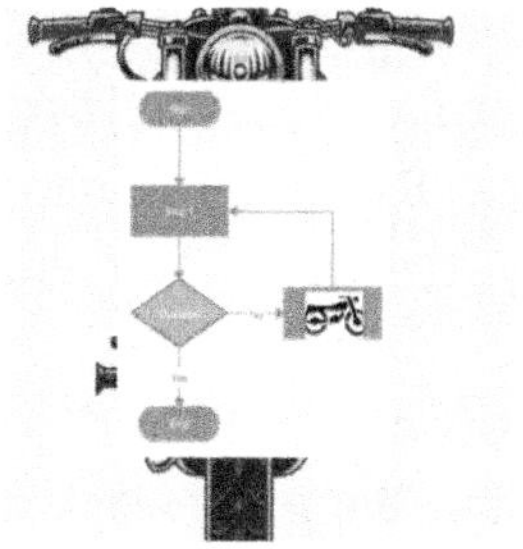

◆◆◆

Pearl and I were off. We proceeded to the Panama Flats Trail (on Vancouver Island, not Central America). Scout doesn't like gravel. If the scooter weren't an insurance loaner, a suspension upgrade would be in order. Also, a custom paint job, larger tires, a better seat, and an air horn. Do they make a battery supercharger? Elon would know.

Terry was on his way to share the good news with

Brenda. Here's the question and the solution I put to my motorcycle acquaintance: "Why not sell your Softail to MRR Labs? Become a lab volunteer and take her out whenever you like? It'll be there, waiting, just for you. Repurchase it anytime... after you've signed a nonaggression pact with Shelly. Meanwhile, you'll be free and clear. No deception. Technically, you won't be a bike owner. No lies. Shell doesn't have to know what's going on behind the garage door." Yes, I said it, "What goes on in the lab, stays in the lab."

If you drop by, you'll see Brenda parked at the back of our garage.

"Another toy?" Dori was not impressed, but at least she didn't behave like a flakey Howitzer. I trust she likes me more than she dislikes bikes. I suppose you could say I'm like a wine sommelier for both motorcycles and women.

"That's two full loads of horseshit," Bob would say.

"Just doin' a favour for a friend," I told Dori. Motorcycle acquaintance, really. Rider in distress. I wonder if it made Dori proudly think of her husband as a giver? Gearhead Mahatma Gandhi? Despite my misfortune and challenges, stepping up to aid other down-and-out bikers? Valued like Dr. Peggy's work at the soup kitchen (she does poetry readings, Tuesday afternoons).

The club gave Terry $8,925 for his Harley using money Bob left in his will to continue our "good motorcycle work." Terry may repurchase Brenda anytime within five years for the same amount.

"You're doing me a huge favor," I told Terry the day he dropped Brenda off. "It's lonely without a bike sitting in the garage. I'm not used to being motorcycle-less." The Softail is nothing like the nimble Beemer Horace targeted in his jihad, but we get along fine. I call the Harley, Softy.

"Hey, Softy, one of these days I'll climb on. We'll share an adventure." I'm respectful of motorcycle space. Terry's a big man, a trained killer, suffers from PTSD and is not decrepit. I wouldn't want him to have an episode, like when he hears, "the war on terrorism is terrorism."

At Marta's insistence, the lab will deduct $35 per month as a "storage fee," much less than Terry was paying at Adam's. "We're playing with the big boys now," she boasts about the club's reoccurring revenue stream. "On sound financial footing. Thirty-five bucks plus book royalties from *Scraping Pegs* nudging twenty bucks on a good month."

"Battered pickle, Marta?"

It took a minute for my brainwave to sink in, but when it did, POW! Terry grinned like a Marine scoring a direct hit on an enemy encampment. A moment of pure JOY. Brenda saved!

All is well.

For the time being.

It was wonderful to watch JOY overcome my motorcycle acquaintance. The experience made me understand, "It's better to give than to receive." It's a statement that needs beefing up. It should read, "It's better to give than to receive unless you're receiving a motorcycle." I was about to receive one, at least temporarily—it felt like the first time I scrambled to the top of Impossible Hill on TS-125.

I wish I'd taken a picture the day Terry asked, "What should I do?" Another of the Harley arriving at the lab. A day later, Terry relaxing beside Brenda, holding a beer. "See," I would point and say, "The shift from might-as-well-jump to pure JOY."

◆◆◆

Life interrupts: JOY is not a constant; riders must do time on Nothingness Highway and travel down Misery Miles. There will be no glory if Terry doesn't resolve his dilemma before my tell-all book comes out and becomes food for gossip.

"Terry, *Joy's* all about truth. I can't screw with the facts. You must find a solution before the book comes out." The unspoken words? Or Shelly will learn the facts and Brenda will die.

Shelly and Terry could always do a tandem dive. *Couldn't agree on a solution, but we're committed to staying together.* Give two fingers to the rehabilitation industry. Make an exciting dual splash and leave me with an expensive bike for cheap (especially if Terry was considerate enough to return the $8,925 payment with interest, drop it in the lab mailbox on their way to the bridge).

An innocent child is involved, but I'd be willing to pass Softy on to Matt (once he's matured and has wedged riding rules in his back pocket). Thoughtful, don't you think? I'd explain why jumping is a smart, honest, no-nonsense solution for irreconcilable motorcycle differences. "Heard your dad singing, *That's Life*, on the way down, Matty."

*Yes, Bunny, I'm kidding.*

*For Shelly, Matt, Terry, and Softy, I trust,* ***JOY will find a way.***

"You kicked the can down the road," Marta texted.

"Gave us time to figure something out. Good job! *smiley face*"

I was exhausted, so I lay on my hospital bed with Bunny (our cat) to watch an episode of Dr. Phil.

# CHAPTER 2 – SCOOTING

Following my accident, Good Insurance Company sprang for Scout. I discovered: there is JOY in the slow lane.

Scooters are uncaged and just one wheel away from being one of those three-wheelers. I'd love to try a trike when I'm able. Trikes would make great Therapy Bikes and I have a debilitating case of agrizoophobia—never take animals not crossing the road, at the exact moment you're zooming down one, for granted!

Scout is red, the #1 choice amongst Mobilities. There are no chopped scooters or classic restorations. A few basket ornaments. Lots of flags on floppy poles. Not a single sound system. A loud pipe speaker may be a good idea? Clear the sidewalk! Get the hell out of my way!

Some bikers swear loud pipe racket adds safety. The mean streets by the strip mall can be a chaotic hell hole for a newbie scooter driver.

If you've watched *Escape from Devil's Island* or *Prison Break*, you know there's no chance feeble, busted up convicts will breakout unassisted. But hop on a scooter and the road to freedom is within reach. Scout gave me the ability to fly the coop, my hospital bed. Step one on my return to JOY plan.

First big surprise: dogs and scooters get along! Pearly has a thing about most small-wheeled transportation options like skateboards and baby buggies, but Scout didn't trigger her canine urge. Match a delivery person with a cargo cart and it's mayhem; in Pearl's mind, it's the assassination of Archduke Franz Ferdinand all over again. A noble reason to kick off World War I, except Pearly doesn't care about the decline of the Ottoman Empire, the way it annoyed many European leaders and got young Gavrilo Princip thinking.

As Scout rolled along, I wondered why my best friend hates wheels the way Gavrilo hated Franz? Rather than military alliances, imperialism, or ethnicity, rotation seems to get Pearl's goat. Thankfully she hasn't started a *war to end all wheel rotation.* If only you'd known Motorcycle JOY Gavrilo, humanity would have been spared the *war to end all wars.*

"Oh well," the people-in-charge said when the next world war broke out. "Back to the drawing board."

Why do you attack prams, strollers, and skateboards, Pearly? Why do we need *Ode to a Daisy*, box jellyfish, evil deer, world wars, Brussels sprouts, what does the UN Second Committee on Disarmament do, and what makes politics a science? Life can be so damn mysterious. That is where JOY comes in—it facilitates Disconnectedness allowing you to say, I Don't Care.

*You & Your Motorcycle: can your motorcycle disconnect you from the madness of life?*

I don't want to leave the impression Pearl is a killer like Gavrilo and should be put down.

WRONG!

Ask any Copley Park Dog Mom. They'll all vouch for Pearly. She's a sweetheart. Take small-wheeled transportation options, delivery people, and toddlers off the table, and she's practically Shirley Temple; Pearl even loves Dr. Peggy. The bizarre thing is, despite the size of its wheels, Pearl and Scout took to one another right out of the gate. Like North Korea and Texas bumping into one another and hitting it off. The unexpected happens: Scout and Pearl, ex-Dallas Mavericks, Dennis Rodman, and dictator Kim Jong-il, a Harley and a BMW.

Scout, Pearl, and I turned off the sidewalk onto the Copley Park compacted gravel and dirt trail. Good thing Scout's seat is way better than any motorcycle seat; at least any motorcycle seat my bottom has touched.

Thanks to Scout, once again, I enjoyed Travel.

Mr. Pirsig wrote in his much lauded *Zen* book, "it's a little better to travel than to arrive." His statement referred to the spiritualism bikers feel when on-motorcycle, with Buddha tagging along nestled in the electrics. There is truth to Mr. Pirsig's observation. When you arrive, you're reconnected and things can get messy. "You're late! Why can't you be productive like Gavrilo? Take out an archduke instead of playing with your toy?" POW! Goodbye Disconnectedness. "Now that you've Arrived, late, as usual, take the stinkin' trash out. Clean the gutters to end all gutter cleaning."

*Truth About Motorcycles: step down. J O Y ends. Your reality may suck. That's life off-motorcycle.*

Off-motorcycle, Mother Nature may bite you with one of her venomous monsters. You discover someone ate the piece of carrot cake with extra cream cheese icing you hid at the back of the fridge. Arrival can be pure,

Horseshit.

So much for riding the endless ribbon of asphalt because you've Arrived, and it's leaking oil. Step off your bike and everyone wants a piece of you. There is no separation: off-motorcycle, life can smoother you. Marta says, "Arriving is like finishing a battered pickle." So true. No wonder it's better to keep rolling along on-motorcycle, with J O Y flowing and more of it down the road. Riding allows you to:

Rejoice.

But Traveling is not absolute.

Let's face it, the *Zen and the Art of Motorcycle Maintenance* author is more Dr. Daisy than Sir Isaac Newton or Dr. Phil.

Mr. Pirsig's analysis is selective and woefully incomplete. To start with, Robert doesn't even mention Departure. Not a peep. "It's philosophy, no need for facts," he explained to his editor. Just keep traveling forever."

Departure, on-motorcycle, unleashes eager anticipation. Does it get any better? NO! Things may go downhill after Departure. Clearly, it may be better to Depart than to Travel. When I Departed my recovery bed to Travel on Scout, I was ecstatic. It was like the *Great Escape*. The moment you're released is mind blowing.

Before and after, not so much.

Traveling beside Copley Creek was great, but I can't say it trumped the glory of departing my garage. Preparing for a motorcycle trip always made me feel like I had a new set of plugs. No need for wonderful drugs, Motorcycle Departure Anticipation cranks JOY up. "On The Road Again," I'd sing Willie Nelson's song for days before I left. "Just can't wait to get on my bike again." Why did Mr. Pirsig ignore Departure (which logically includes the first miles, the first hour of Traveling)? Is it okay to skip logic and a medically verifiable state of mind? Proceed directly to pie-in-the-sky musings if you're a philosopher?

"Tiddle-tattle," Sir Isaac called it. Words without substance.

Many riders have known long, ass-pounding days spent Traveling. Boy, are they ecstatic to Arrive! No matter what Mr. Pirsig's book states, it may not be better to Travel than to Arrive. After a miserable day in the saddle, Arrival can't be beat. Well, maybe by Departure, but not by Traveling. Finally, well-deserved relaxation. A chance to review Traveling and be glad you're not doing it. Sip a beverage. Chit chat. Move your body. Arrival allows you to do all the stuff you couldn't do while Traveling.

Why didn't you go on forever, Robert, if Travel is so great? Down the Never-ending Highway? Skip Arrival altogether? The way you forgot to include repair information in your useless maintenance book.

On August 18, 2019, Conrad and I Departed our motel, bound for Omak, Washington. We never Arrived. I crashed (Book One). Is it better to Travel than to Arrive? Come on, Robert! Boy, do I wish I had Arrived in Omak rather than Traveling by ambulance to Ferry Memorial

Hospital.

Let's face it—sometimes it's best not to go at all—the Motorcycle Stay Put. Leave the kickstand down. Re-read *Scraping Pegs*. On rare occasions, it's better to Stay Put than it is to Travel, but again, not a peep from Mr. Pirsig. It's philosophy. Why mess things up with reality? Marta said it best. "Sometimes motorcycles suck, and sometimes they don't."

Motorcycle JOY is not a constant. Depart. Travel. Scrape Pegs. Arrive. Stay Put. It's complicated—JOY must be nurtured.

"Remarkable," Dolores said. "The *Zen* book hasn't a single babe in it. No hunks pulling wheelies with their tee shirts off. Yet it sold like the *Valley of the Dolls*."

"I could take my shirt off and try to pull a wheelie on Scout... if you think it would help sell books, Dolores?"

◆◆◆

We got back on the sidewalk to Travel home. No sign of Big Terry. He was likely hugging Brenda, feeling Relief JOY. "Found you a good home, buddy! Until I sort things out. No more hiding out at Adam's to avoid Shelly's murderous intentions."

What next, Terry? My solution was like wrapping tape around a busted fender—it wouldn't hold forever. Shelly remained locked and loaded.

Pearl seemed eager to stop Traveling and Arrive at her food bowl (she's familiar with mealtime joy).

Bunny prefers a permanent Stay Put, hates Travel, but then Bunny can't ride a motorcycle. Sometimes I look at Bunny and ask myself: do cats experience a natural form

MICHAEL STEWART

# of Disconnectedness?

# CHAPTER 3 - INTRODUCTION

*Truth About Motorcycles: the highway is not endless; we each get a finite number of rides.*

There comes a time to push kickstands up. Move on before tires become bogged down in worn-out prose. To keep my literary nuts screwed tight and to calm my publishing waters, I'm happy to call this section the Introduction. Let's clear a few things up.

## ***The Truth About Publishing***

"I thought the book business would be different than Dr. Tire's attempt to sell me new age cleaning products," I told Marta. "It's not."

Publishers wouldn't consider *War and Peace* today unless rolled out as a series and punched up. Prince Bagration would be multiracial and gay. Anna Pavlova would have a secret superpower, a refined social conscience, a secret vulnerability, and struggle with nymphomania. Sure, it would be way more exciting and make a compelling movie—especially if the prince rode a chopper or superbike, wore an old Russian army helmet, and had a gun like Punisher's, but it would stink of pandering.

"A hunk or a bikini babe, on a larger bike in motion, would be a much better cover," Dolores advised.

The Truth About Publishing: it is like one of those velvet paintings sold as art (I have one in my garage, *Motorcycle on Velvet*).

## ***The Truth About Introductions***

I skip or skim introductions because they're the Nothingness Highway of books. Read and you're soon off the road and up to your knees in Complacency Word Swamp. "Is that another publishing industry rule," I asked Dolores? "Rule #3: Introductions Must Suck."

Introductions are like It'll Do Bikes. Ho-hum. Publishers often agree to farm them out as Forewords (Dolores suggested Tom Cruise write one for *Joy* to spur sales).

"Just because Tom rode a bike in one of the *Mission Impossible* movies doesn't mean we're Motorcycle Friends, Dolores. I'm more worried about the ending. *Pegs* finished with a crash. Got nothing for *Joy*."

Dolores nodded. "Crashes make excellent endings... as part of a hospital romance story."

"But not great for nonfiction authors."

"A large percentage of Nascar and Daytona 500 audiences watch specifically to see crashes. Preferably with a nice fireball," Dolores informed me. "No one's watching to see truth or joy. You could easily toss in another accident."

Hopefully, one of the other motorcycle book endings will come to pass. Finding yourself after a long ride is extremely popular. Coming from behind to win a track event? An escape following a robbery? Maybe throw them all into the mix... or would that be pandering and not truthful?

I asked Marta to check *Zen and the Art of Motorcycle Maintenance* to see how it ended, but she said, "That'd be like trying to find the end of the beginning."

"Just the end part," I repeated. "Don't have to read the entire book."

"Everything's connected. There is no end. Or beginning."

Why can't she just say, "No?" I worry about Marta; she refuses to move on from Guzzi and get a mainstream brand.

Dolores asked, "Will your ending be at the end of your book? Or are you planning to shove it in at the beginning?"

She's turning out to be quite the smart ass.

## ***The Scraping Pegs Books***

*Scraping Pegs* is a series of related books. I really had a serious motorcycle accident: healing doesn't happen overnight. Going down hard changes your perspective. It's a tedious business, like riding through the flatlands, just after you stopped at the Flat Earth Cafe and Truck Stop to drink weak coffee. Why bog readers down in a single fat volume, droning on about the monotony of off-motorcycle change?

"Often life isn't interesting, and truth isn't very profound," Marta says.

That's for sure. "It's why we ride, Marta. To strip out mundane and add intrigue." Separate books are like building a café racer—the unnecessary boring parts can be stripped off.

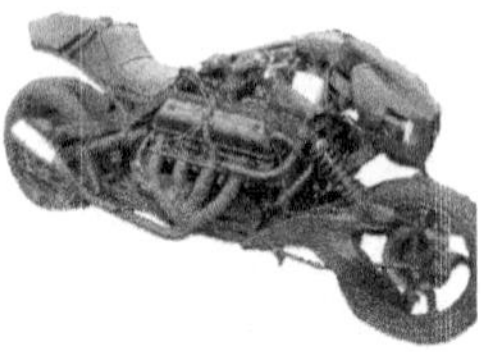

Have you seen that custom Russian bike? Like that other Russian creation, *War and Peace*, both are intimidatingly obese. *Scraping Pegs* is about motorcycles; the books must be manageable and handle well, rather than a single fatty that looks like a Soviet Blockhead created it. Each *Scraping Pegs* book will work as a unicycle, but remember, there is a reason the front wheel leads the way.

"Nonfiction that sells is about solving a problem," Dolores advised. "What problem are you solving?" She headed down the hall without waiting for a response.

*The truth about motorcycles, Dolores. An inquiry into joy.* Dolores is a NimRod. Attempting an explanation would be pointless.

## ***The History of Scraping Pegs***

On August 18, 2019, I was ambushed by a hideous, vile, giant rat named Horace (a "stag" the Republic, Washington police called him). After decades of riding adventures, I was in the hospital with an acute case of Motorcycle Misery. My J O Y ended.

Being motorcycle-less is like losing a dog you loved,

you're left to wander best friend-less in the vast emptiness that life can be. Motorcycle-less is far worse than losing touch with most humans. I've found very few people rise to the level of the Joy of Motorcycles.

*You & Your Motorcycle: where do you place motorcycle-less on the scale of traumatic life events?*

Motorcycle-less, bitter, and uneasy, I wallowed in self-pity. "Not feeling like I should," I whined.

"Try writing your feeling down," Dr. Peggy suggested. "He can write, can't he, Dori?"

Pissy looks like the 2003 *Uglystrada —yes, bikers write, heard of a guy named Bob Dylan? Try changing a tire, doc. You can fix a flat, can't you?*

Writing refocused me, like turning onto Curvy Road. Marta knew someone who knew someone and got *Scraping Pegs* into the hands of Beaten Stick Books.

Again Dolores asked: "Sorry, but I don't get it. What exactly is the problem your book is solving?".

"J O Y through Truth... the MAGIC of motorcycles. Understanding Truth opens the door to J O Y ."

Dolores shook her head—I don't blame her; it's complicated and sounded a lot like something Mr. Pirsig would write.

I tried again. "Motorcycles have been my friends, Dolores. I'm trying to explain why."

*Truth about Motorcycles: motorcycles can be far better friends than drugs, alcohol, or NimRods.*

There's almost always been a bike parked in my garage. I don't leave my friends standing outside.

*Truth about Motorcycles: motorcycles can comfort, like teddy bears.*

*You & Your Motorcycle: have you owned a Motorcycle Teddy?*

## Reference

Should your mind start to ping, nagging for more definition about the odd words you'll encounter in this book, like Blockhead or Disconnectedness, check out *Scrape Your Lists.* It contains a word list, my Motorcycle Riding Rules, and much more. It's the motorcycle experience expressed in point form.

## Climb Back On?

After my accident, the #1 question was: will you climb back on? Seeing the aftermath of my accident made other riders wonder: what will I do if my number comes up? Of course I'd ride again. Stupid question. Man up! Climb on! Don't be a weenie!

It'd be silly of me to say, "I may buy a bike, park it in my garage and never ride." I'd have to explain my Teddy Bear Theory, which would make me sound like a pussy. "Possibly. Be kinda stupid, though... right? My number'd go back in the Motorcycle Lottery." Get banged up twice, and it's hello morgue or handicap parking and pee bag.

Every year, over 7,000 riders in the United States do not climb back on because they're dead, killed in a bike accident. 55% of motorcycle accidents cause significant injuries, many of those riders do not climb back on. They learn a lesson, are scared shit-less and stop riding. Accidents of any nature are a deterrent. They scream, "do not repeat this dumb, harmful action!" But, for addicts, after rehab, the needle goes in.

*You & Your Motorcycle: are you hopelessly addicted?*

"What'd you mean... you may climb back on?" Dori asked.

"Could have been worse," I answered. Did the crash leak all the amyloid-beta proteins from my brain?

*Truth About Motorcycles: it can always be worse.*

I can't stop thinking about riding because of this:

beyond the trauma, there is JOY, and you must have a motorcycle to reach it. But I have doubts, like the fear the Great Plains, Flat Earth Society members confess: "I'd like to take the kids to Hawaii, but it's awfully close to the edge."

*Truth About Motorcycles: JOY requires a motorcycle.*

Bob used to say: "Life works best as a series of bikes."

I was back at Step One in the JOY Formula: Buy a Motorcycle.

For most circumstances, the industry manufactures products; why nothing specific to accident recovery? Why the glaring hole in manufacturers' lineups? Has to do with marketing, I suppose. Engineering could quickly whip up a Therapy Bike, given the green light from Finance. Something along the lines of a Cam-Am Spyder, but with a roll cage.

On TV, Dr. Phil talked about the mental wrestling match that followed his motorcycle accident. When Oprah called, he admitted to being nervous about climbing back on. "Sounds like the making of a TV segment," Oprah said. "Have your handsome assistant pop round. We'll massage it into shape."

I spent many hours online trying to solve my motorcycle-less dilemma, wondering about Truth and searching for an elusive Therapy Bike, one that's wildlife resistant. Serious accidents change your perspective: appearance, specifications, size, number of wheels, etc. were no longer important to me. Horace turned me into an honest to God motorcycle agnostic. Fuck brands and what's on-trend. The capability to resume my Ride to JOY was my only objective.

"A full-time Motorcycle Teddy," Marta asked? "Remember, you're not obligated to climb on."

Would nightmares prevent me from climbing on? Giant rats waiting around every bend? Crouching, concealed, on straight stretches where high banks and woods sit close to the road?

"Why not buy a car?" Dori, my wife, asked. "One of those cute electric ones with a sunroof, like Peg's? We could park it in our garage."

"Huh?" A cage is no substitute. A car waiting in the garage is not a teddy. I drive automobiles but have never achieved Disconnectedness inside a cage. Maybe a smidgen of joy, but nothing like Motorcycle JOY. Because, my dear, I think, but don't say. Cars are for losers like your ugly friend, Pissy.

WHOOPS—that would have been inappropriate, untrue, and certainly not tactful. Zen Jackass-ism teaches —try not to let things get your goat. Sorry, doc. Hugs and kisses! "Maybe a bike with an extra wheel," I said.

Therapy Bike must have styling and a feel nothing like my last bike. GT was a terrific machine, but it, and similar bikes, will forever be antler apparition generators. I must not climb on and see the ghost of Horace or hear a replay of a Stephen King horror soundtrack. A brute like Softy is enticing, but I am busted up, and, as Bob and I agreed, we're getting older, not stronger. As part of my search criteria, I've set a 600lb weight limit, ruling out many strong, glorious, comfortable possibilities. Three-wheelers are exempt.

"You say you're getting weaker," Marta said when I told her about the weight criteria. "Add cerebral atrophy to the mix... we're both getting dimmer." She didn't mention my debilitating case of agrizoophobia. “You'd better factor that in.”

"Age brings wisdom. I may lose brain cells, but the ones I have work better." Marta is half a decade younger than me.

"Experienced, yes, but physically weaker and mentally suspect. Biological facts." Marta winked.

"Thanks for pointing that out, Marta."

“Make JOY your secret sauce... it'll keep you strong and wise. Never give up. Climb back on.” Marta suggested the perfect Therapy Bike would be an old Guzzi. "Ridden slowly."

"Remember," I answered. "Comfort is my #2, after avoiding wildlife."

I would not be riding off anytime soon, so I had plenty of time to find Therapy Bike and finish this book. Meanwhile, Scout and I had a mission: get in with Scooter Crowd. Scooters force the socially lazy to remain plugged in—there's no pulling a wheelie and ripping off, like a Born to be Wild outlaw or hiding behind a visor. Mobilities must linger out in the open. "Being sociable," Marta calls it. "It's not that difficult."

I teased Marta, suggesting, "How 'bout we turn MRR Labs into a Scooter Truth research facility? I could recruit volunteers at morning coffee, starting with my new friend, Hans."

"Does Guzzi make a scooter?"

She's so loyal. Not me. The field is wide open for Therapy Bike.

I worry about Marta; too much, Guzzi? I think Marta and Hans might hit it off? They're both a tad eccentric, and Marta isn't put off by neurodegenerative diseases.

## *JOY Clues*

Transport Motorcycles are about getting from A to B. Buddha is not on board. There is no expectation of JOY.

*Truth About Motorcycles: some bikes are strictly business; there is nothing magical about them.*

*Truth About Motorcycles: any bike can do duty as a Transport Motorcycle.*

*You & Your Motorcycle: while riding, do you ever think—I'd rather not be riding? If yes, you may be sitting on a Transport Bike.*

Trout fishers tell me, "Catching rainbows and cutthroats ain't easy. They're not always around."

*Truth About Motorcycles: MAGIC and JOY are like trout.*

Trout nibble at the bait. Many bite and end up panfried.

JOY clues are buried in this book, but riders must bite. They must ride to discover their machine's MAGIC.

"Sounds like a cop-out to me," Dolores said. "You're not really solving the problem."

NimRod, I thought.

## *An Important Note*

🙏 You may not ride but comprehend the MAGIC in the machines. If this is you, please disregard the brutal truth about NimRods in the pages to follow. There are cager Saints. Thank you for not trying to run bikers down.

# CHAPTER 4 – ABOUT WORDS

Dolores returned with two new releases. "These motorcycle books will sell. Study them." She placed Seduction of the Heart on my lap in my wheelchair. The cover showed a bikini babe on a flashy sports bike and said the book was "bewitching" and included "cheating." The second book Snakes, Songbirds, and Secrets, promised "a vanishing boyfriend." Apparently, he vanished shirtless on a chopper. "Learn," Dolores said. "These authors know how to sell motorcycle books."

"Written by AI?" Dolores frowned. It's a touchy subject. Knowledge workers can be replaced. AI cannot replace Motorcycle Joy.

Visiting Beaten Stick Books always made me think about words. That's what they sell. They're everywhere, being mulled over, polished, market-tested, and sorted into genres, like bike models. I peeked to see if I could find authentic words lying around like hardtail, high side, rat bike, or boxer. I searched for a biker word Dr. Peggy said was "offensive" but found only popular culture: hunk, devil's riders, gun-toting hotties.

According to Dr. Peggy, "words make us who we are," and bikers are in a world of trouble because of one "inflammatory disgusting word."

I enjoy the doctor's rants because Pissy's face transforms as her blood pressure soars—two hundred years ago, she could have earned a comfortable living working at a freak show. Rage turns her skin blotchy red. Then a warped world map forms on her face (her nose is the eastern edge of Brazil, where it juts into the Atlantic Ocean. Greenland is the witch's mole by her right eye). She's quite a talented freak, from Uglystrata to a distorted map—her performance always impresses.

I remember Pissy telling me about young Selma and Freddie, dad Haru, and mom Alana. The family was on its way to Samson's Ice Cream Emporium on a pleasant Sunday afternoon, with the windows down and laughter in the air. They debated: one scoop or two; licorice or blueberry; waffle or stubby sugar cone. They were enjoying ice cream anticipation joy.

*You & Your Motorcycle: can you recognize the distinction between ice cream pleasure and Motorcycle Anticipation JOY? One is MAGIC, and the other is chemically induced, an assault on your brain.*

Alana turned the Honda CRV onto Laurel Street, not their usual route, but on that Sunday, they had time to meander. "My friends weren't bothering a soul," Dr. Peggy assured me.

*Cager family bonding. Nice.* It's one thing cars are better at than motorbikes.

Three men and one woman were on the lawn (if a lawn can be dirt and weeds) of a shabby rancher, drinking beer and smoking dope. Bored, jacked-up outlaws get a kick out of role-playing. The Motorcycle Cunts bombarded the CRV and its occupants as it passed. "Hey, fuck'in cagers! Ya, you bitch. Get the fuck off our street. Die cagers die!" They presented a unified one-finger salute, tossed beer cans, and pretended to rev throttle controls, threatening to chase.

Shaken, Alana hit windows up and sped away. "What did we do?"

Haru shrugged, ready to dial 911. "Not a thing." The CRV turned onto Oak Avenue.

What they did was drive a car. The event outraged Peggy. "I do not understand bikers." *Like you.* Her blood pressure soared. *Biker-idiots.*

*Ode to a Daisy*, this, Dr. Peggy. Motorcyclists also use words to express themselves. "Assholes are assholes. Got nothing to do with bikes."

"What's a cager," Dori asked?

Following my explanation, Dr. Daisy said, "It's a derogatory word, Dori. I researched its use." She looked at me. "Vehicle racism used by your Neanderthal pals. A word designed to be hurtful. No different from shouting: Wop, raghead, honkie, Eskimo, Hymie, or that other word that's even more frowned upon. You and your biker friends ought to be ashamed! Using a word designed to ridicule and hate."

Dori shrugged, "Cager. Certainly, nowhere near as horrific as the N-word. Or even the C-word."

*Thank you, Dori!*

"Alana wouldn't agree," Dr. Peggy warned. "Cager was used to single her family out. It's intolerable with the potential to wreak havoc."

Can a word squeeze JOY out of motorcycling? I never considered it, but Dr. Peggy made me think, don't take language for granted.

"We absorb words into mainstream usage." I listened while Argentina pulsated on the phony baloney doctor's face. "Some become neutralized, while others run amuck. The way your biker friends use cager, it's sure to become poison."

There wasn't enough blood pressure to locate Sir Lanka. "Cager," I barked, trying to flush the tiny island out. The doctor didn't use this example, but I think she meant a word like "cunt," while it may be jarring, is harmless. The C word has been absorbed into general usage, is universal and gender-neutral; regardless of sex or ethnicity, anyone may be a "cunt." You may be a Motorcycle Cunt, or a fisher cunt, or a real cunt. Like "asshole," it pisses people off to be called a "cunt," but it does not single them out.

"Cager." Peggy said, "Puts a derogatory label on a specific category of people." You can have a motorcycle preference and be a cunt but are not a cager. My friends, Alana and Haru, were traumatized.

*So who's responsible, doctor?* Engineers test for structural defects and accept accountability. They develop mitigation strategies and replacement projects. Why is language treated differently? Why are word PhDs at liberty to focus on their salary reclassifications? Should they not be battling bad words?

"We can't have censorship," Dori said.

I nodded.

"Bikers must choose to use socially acceptable language. Like responsible people."

What Peggy meant is we may continue to use non-discriminatory harsh words like "motherfucker," and "cocksucker," but must stop using cager in public. Bikers must learn from the history of language racism and be proactive.

Despite its vile connotation, "cager" is not yet a top priority bad word. "Make no mistake, its day will come," Dr. Peggy warned as Latvia sunk into a wrinkle.

Are bikers doomed to be despised by woke progressives and labeled pure evil? Will the C-word become a JOY killer?

No! We have the MAGIC.

Climb on.

Ride away from the horseshit.

Get the hell out of Word Hell Hole town.

"Why not be proactive," Peg suggested? "Get out in front of your language issue?"

It wouldn't be a big deal to strike the word "cager" from public discourse. Embrace all forms of transportation, including fully loaded hay trucks (the speed cornering standard used by risk mitigation departments worldwide). Let's be pre-emptive—don't allow vehicle preference to fan the flames of bigotry and kick off a civil rights-car club anti-motorcycle coalition.

Kidding!

Dr. Peggy is full of cager academic horseshit. Fuck NimRods!

"Cars are not an all-or-nothing proposition," Dr. Peggy continued. "Drive to a national park using a motorcycle or a car, step away from the vehicle, and the drivers are equals. Neither one is locked in a cage, as you like to say. Your premise is faulty. "

True. Undressed, without clodhopper boots and brain buckets, we're all the same, some more repulsive than others, but the same in terms of basic anatomy. For example, a car driver may exit their vehicle, drag a kayak off the roof, and become one with nature by floating on a body of water. Try accomplishing that on a motorbike. Cagers take cross-country skis out of their trunks and slide across the snow through pristine environments.

"There is no difference, right?" Dr. Peggy asked, using her holier-than-thou tone of voice while picking at a Mongolian blackhead?

"It's complicated." There's no chance a NimRod incapable of changing a tire will understand the nature of MAGIC and JOY, but nevertheless I attempted an explanation. Riders take in a hell of a lot more environment running over it on a motorcycle than cagers kayaking, cross-country skiing, or hiking. On a bike, nature whizzes by, bombarding you with everything it's got. In a kayak, the paddler barely moves. Might as well be a turtle. Crawling along. How much of the world does a turtle see? Not much. You won't understand the Cosmos if you don't cover more ground. Even if you get out of your car and do a slow activity, you're still caged. "Car drivers and motorcycle riders are radically different. Using 'cager' is totally justified, doctor."

"History shows, words are a problem when they suggest one group is superior to another." Peggy's spittle was flooding Zambia. "When words degrade a category of people, they become poison."

"Even if there actually is a difference?" Motorcycles allow you to tailor your outdoor experience in ways skydiving or snorkeling do not. For example, if a cager skydives, they pull on drab overalls, jump out of a plane, and go more or less straight down. No diverting to check out that neat thing over there. Skydivers go down. Down. Down. Straight down. If they descend at motorcycle speeds, they die. Once down, they're stuck on the ground beside a turtle as a dirt bike streaks by to experience J O Y further along the trail. Skydivers cannot go up the mountain pass or scoot over to Joy Canyon. No vast array of stylish clothing. No adding loud pipes for an extra bit of stimulation. Skydivers and snorkelers are not in traditional cages, but the narrow confines of their activities hem them in, and then they climb back into their cars.

Thanks to *Zen and the Art of Motorcycle Maintenance*, we know Buddha likes to hang out in motorbike circuitry. No one has found Him stretched out on the bottom of their kayak or holding His nose inside a ski boot. Having Buddha with you makes it easier to climb out of metaphysical cages as you speed through the world. "There is a difference," I stated proudly. "Using a word to express the difference makes perfect sense."

"How about using automobile driver, rather than a word chosen to be derogatory? Your justification does not excuse the use of a vile word hurled with hate at my friends, Alana and Haru."

Motorcycle Cunts. Not all bikers are saints. I didn't try to explain. Pointless.

Thanks to a vein on Pissy's forehead, Russia's Volga River looked like it was about to breach its banks. "Bikers are not linguists. Many," Dr. Peggy said, "I suspect, are barely literate and impossible to deal with."

Motorcyclists are a diverse, proud bunch, connected to Earth and a Zen world, in a way cagers and phony-baloney doctors cannot comprehend. "Some people overreact. Caged simply means sealed off. With climate controls, listening to yacht rock, sipping a cappuccino, in a seat with lumbar support, cushioned by a superb suspension system while the kids play Super Mario Allstars and eat chips in the back seat. Riders enjoy none of these comforts. Get caught in a rainstorm, and car drivers are smug. Many purposely spray puddle water at us. They call us biker-idiots, implying we're low-life forms. Cager-cunts, we scream back! Tit for tat."

I continued, trying to explain the motorcycle-automobile divide. On-motorcycle, weather can beat on weary souls. Cooler as you drive toward the ocean. Freezing at the top of a mountain pass. Hot as hell crossing the desert. Raindrops can be projectiles. It's not always pleasant, but it is the nature of exploration. "Cagers and bikers are radically different; it's not just terminology."

Follow a garbage truck on a hot day, in slow-moving traffic, on a motorcycle, and you can be sure Buddha is pinching His nose. Drive past miles of fresh manure sprayed on a field, and you'll wish you had a window to roll up.

There are many miles of Earth where Mother Nature wasn't inspired. Endless stretches of shoddy work. Miles where a distraction, even *Ode to a Daisy*, would be welcome—adjust the sound system, inflate the seat support, or chat with your partner. But motorcyclists must hunker down and grind it out. Fed up with discomfort and the endless dull landscape, they may lash out at a distracted driver who tried to kill them.

"Cager-cunt!"

"Biker-idiot!"

"Cager-cunt!"

"Biker-idiot!"

The exchange is childish, but then the throttle twists. The biker waves, so long, idiot! We ride away until JOY flows.

Two Wheels, Not Four!

Make no mistake; cagers will continue to kill bikers, but not all four-wheelers are bloodthirsty. While stretched out on Highway 20, west of Republic, Washington, I met Cager Saints. They were my saviors.

Our chat was over when Dr. Peggy excused herself to use the washroom.

I smiled at Dori and thought, your friend can be such a cunt.

◆◆◆

I offered *Seduction of the Heart* to Marta. She added it to the lab's stack of Unreadable Books, the books we used to block our bikes when doing maintenance. The Readable Bits stack includes *Zen and the Art of Motorcycle Maintenance.* We stuck *Philosophiae Naturalis Principia Mathematica* in the Shop Manual pile. Also a graphic novel Manny was reading.

"Piles of words," I said. "Funny how they affect people differently."

Marta won't even peek at *Seduction of the Heart,* "destined to become a best-seller," according to Dolores.

"They say it's good to read a wide variety of books."

“Disgraceful," Marta said, "Labeling books like *Seduction*, motorcycle books.”

I shrugged. Perhaps I'll read *Seduction*—absorb a few tips to pass on to Marta and Hans.

I'll suggest Terry read *Snakes, Songbirds, and Secrets*; it has a boyfriend vanishing on a chopper, so will contain insights the big Marine can use. We're full-on Motorcycle Friends now.

"What should I do... before your book comes out?"

Terry asks.

"What do you think you should do, Terry?" Sometimes I offered a battered pickle.

Alone in the garage with Pearl and Bunny, I pushed the stacks of lab books over on the shelf and started a new pile, beginning with *Seduction of the Heart*. Dr. Peggy will donate a copy of the volume containing *Ode to a Daisy* for the new pile—*Books Riders Should Study to Better Understand the NimRods.*

When Marta saw it, she said, "At the end of the day, life is unfathomable. It's why I ride."

*Truth About Motorcycles: words connect.*
*Motorcycles Disconnect.*

There is a Zen saying, "No thought. No Problem." It's tough having no thoughts when reading a book, watching a movie, listening to the news, or fill in the blank. On-motorcycle riders can Disconnect. Explore. Escape words. It explains the Joy of Motorcycles.

# CHAPTER 5 – ABOUT DECISIONS

Motorcycles and scooters share a proud history. Both are eco-friendly soldiers. They should revel in righteous praise, but crusaders ignore us. Why do you turn your backs? Why do you refuse to blow your ecological and equality trumpets in honor of scooters and motorbikes? As a Mobility, I was stunned to find myself in the bigotry of exclusion. "They're just annoying old kooks and the infirm clogging sidewalks. Forget about them," anti-discrimination discriminators say.

Never assume the self-righteous are righteous!

Why is there no *World Scooter Day*? Because the UN limo crowd filed the scooter nomination under the *UN Doesn't Give a Shit Day*, along with *Motorcycles.* "We can't assign days willy-nilly," I heard an official explain to Dr. Phil on *World Television Day* (November 21st).

When Scout turned onto the Mann Avenue sidewalk, I wondered, would it have killed the UN to add a scooter apostrophe to *International Wheelchair Day* (March 1st)? Would it have messed up *World Statistic Day* October 2)?

If I wasn't socially lazy and laser-focused on *Project Climb Back On*, I'd lobby on behalf of my new scooter friends, at the very least, collect petition signatures demanding a dedicated lane to the strip mall. "Why only bicycles lanes?" I'd challenge Major Dumbass. Maybe I'd start a YouTube Channel with Hans as a co-host. **The Power of Scooters**, featuring Pearl and Bunny. Invite Dr. Phil with musical guests Taylor Swift and Justin Bieber. The virtuous would be taken to task for failing to acknowledge Scooter equality and greenness. "Why aren't you riding a scooter, Greta?" I'd demand answers. "Did you know scooters have always been zero emission vehicles? And nonbinary?"

Kidding!

I don't want to get shot like Martin Luther King or Medgar Evers. Standing up for the oppressed is a dangerous business, and I suffer from a touch of hoplophobia (the fear of weapons and being gunned down).

Tooting Scout's pitifully weak horn in honor of my mobility friends would have to suffice.

Like Mobilities, there are plenty of ladies on low emission bikes these days. Marta was a weirdo when she purchased her first Guzzi, but today, more women than young men replace aging-out bad boys. The equation is shifting. Abusive relationship—bugger off on your bike. Harassed on the job—bugger off on your bike. Underrepresented at the Academy Awards—bugger off on your bike. Women are discovering the Road to Joy.

"Look to motorcycle engineers," Marta says. "Not to the Woman's Right's Council. Scooters, motorcycles, token cabinet appointments, next the world. All part of our domination plan."

"It's a clever approach, Marta. My cousin Tish is a Girlie Rider." I'm not supposed to call her that, but I do because it gets her goat, which amuses me."

"Girlie Rider? Makes you sound like a dinosaur," Marta

said. "A Neanderthal. Maybe Dr. Peggy is right about you?"

I do feel a little Cro-Magnon at times.

Male bikers can get away with acting like fossils. Folks don't bat an eye when they encounter male biker vulgarity. Popular culture portrays us as insensitive remnants of the Paleolithic era. Crudeness is not only tolerated, it's expected. Bikers are victims of a stereotype reinforced by trashy novels, B-movies (like *Werewolves on Wheels*), video games, and undercover TV exposés. Despite Mr. Pirsig's contemplative characters in his Zen book, we're labeled a dim-witted and vulgar bunch.

Motorcycling is changing. According to a recent gender survey, the under 800cc SQUID category is now gender neutral. The percentage of bikers who identify as female is soaring. It's encouraging ladies are discovering JOY. Someone has to keep the industry afloat.

Hans approached. He drives an EV Rider with one of those tall orange flags waving around at the back, flapping, "Don't hit me. Please don't hit me! Please don't hit me." In the same way, some people look like they shouldn't be on a motorcycle, Hans doesn't fit the scooter stereotype. "Too lazy to walk, buddy? Get off that toy! Man up!" Nothing's broken and my friend's disease isn't apparent. People see Hans as a sloth, not a Poor Dear. "Scooters are just a lazy ass excuse to clog sidewalks."

The reason I like Hans is, he never wallows in self-pity. "I like that you're accountable. Life handed you Huntington's Disease, but you make the best of it."

Hans is a bit of a kook, but super friendly and smart. He edged EV Rider alongside, like an expert mariner docking an enormous yacht.

"Want to go trout fishing Tuesday?" Hans must pick activities that accept his affliction and limitations.

"Can't... doctor appointment. How about Marta? She likes trout." I reached into my tank bag, wedged into Scout's wire basket, and offered, "Care for a battered pickle, Hans? Marta helped Tony make them at the deli. She's quite the little cook."

Is there such a thing as pickled trout, I wondered?

◆◆◆

It was a real shaker when my young cousin Tish hit the Decision Wall, an unavoidable bump on the Road to Joy. Pre-Horace, my walls were all low, but eventually, I ran smack into the Great Motorcycle Decision Wall. Many bump up against the wall and call it quits—never take open roads and trails for granted.

*You & Your Motorcycle: how many bumps in the road have you encountered on-motorcycle?*

An event happens, and we think—two wheels is stupid and avoidable by driving a car. Time to quit? Any minor incident can trigger the idea: money, family pressure, physical discomfort, dropped bike, mechanical issue, weather.

Tish hit a Decision Wall seven months after she began riding. Growing up, Theresa looked more like a water skier than a biker. Her dad introduced her to riding (if a 35cc canary yellow kid's toy bought on eBay can be called a motorbike). Tish rode cautiously on the family toy. Her older brother, Sid, tried intimidation: "It's not a girlie toy. Stay off my bike," but Tish paid no attention. She had her allotment, and annoying her brother amused her. Sid sulked, waiting to hear, "Your turn, Siddy."

Like me, being told what to do rubs Tish the wrong way. "Stubborn, but not a Lenny," Auntie Minnie proclaimed whenever her daughter dug in her heels.

Tish was eleven years old when Siddy, pretending to be Valentino Rossi, did something stupid. He drove the toy bike into the creek that ran alongside the field behind their suburban home. Tish thought, Sid's done us a favor and was happy when eBay bike refused all revival attempts—no more parading around on the stupid, noisy contraption to keep Itty-Bitty Siddy in his place. No more aimless figure eights in the backfield, on a toy that had become undersized. "Stupid bike. I'm glad Siddy broke it," she said to her dad, who worried about driving his future Goldwing into a creek.

Uncle Tarter (as we affectionately nicknamed him after the sauce he liked to lather on fried fish) owned a copy of the book *Zen and the Art of Motorcycle Maintenance.* "The bible of motorcycle thinking. A way to live your life, even if you don't own a bike," which was perfect because Arthur never owned a motorcycle. Every so often, he'd sit in the big, cloth-covered, dark-green easy chair, often with a substantial Scotch on the rocks, and read random pages of the "wise book." "Preparing for retirement," Art would declare, the day he'd be on-motorcycle, rolling down the endless highway, a lone rider (except for Buddha who would tag along and, of course, his best friend, Stu). Uncle Arthur was a Motorcycle Dreamer.

"A Goldwing will make you rejoice," Henry Foster, a relative of Stu's and former British Biker Boy, assured Arthur. Art and Stu liked to drop by Cherished Waters Retirement Living for complimentary snacks and Biker

Boy stories (we'll get back to Henry later).

Tish thought her dad's motorcycle book must be magical. It seemed to transform her father when he sat in the big chair. She took a sip of his drink and knew it couldn't be the Scotch.

When Tish was twenty, she pulled *Zen* off the shelf and sat down in the easy chair with a tall glass of orange juice and soda. "I flipped through the pages, stopping to read bits as I went," she told me. "It would be nice to have a way to live my life, I thought. My family is so lucky to have a wise book." Tish admired her dad's respect for Mr. Pirsig's work, so, when Dad walked into the room and asked, "Well, what'd you think?" Tish replied, "It's okay." Truthfully, she wanted to say; why do you think it's so great? I don't get it. She didn't want to call her father's devotion into question, pull a Siddy, and drown his retirement dream.

To prove he wasn't all talk, uncle started a Goldwing fund. One hundred dollars a month. I donated twenty bucks at Christmas get-togethers. "One more bolt," I'd say, adding to uncle's Anticipation Motorcycle JOY.

When the family's Sears lawnmower died, uncle met his Decision Wall. Bike or lawn tractor like Stu's? He gave up on his Goldwing dream. "One day, I'll drive my Craftsman* over to Stu's," he'd say. Stu lived four blocks away and also owned a Craftsman*. "Perhaps we'll roll onto Brady's Fish and Chips." The Wing was forgotten. Instead, Uncle Tarter rattled on about making an epic overland tractor trek to Stu's, "One of these days."

"Put my contributions toward the bagger attachment," I said when Tarter offered to refund my donations. "Or fish and chips."

◆◆◆

Here's a definition from *Scrape Your Lists*:

Motorcycle Dreamer

Self-explanatory. Mostly middle age men who talk about wanting a motorcycle, but never take the next step. They enjoy chatting about their dream at rest stops, gas stations, and on ferries.

◆◆◆

At age twenty-four, out of the blue, Tish bought a Honda CB 500 (eight years after her mother, my Auntie Minnie, totaled Lenny's blue Yamaha 500 and left her nephew with a stump).

"A very poor decision," she scolded her daughter. *And extremely insensitive.* Auntie Minnie had been on antidepressants since the Lenny incident.

My aunt and uncle asked me to reason with their daughter. "Tish looks up to you." I was to "scare her off her dangerous motorcycle notion."

“An old man on a Goldwing is one thing,” Uncle Tarter said. “My daughter ... no damn way!”

"Everyone will try to kill you, Tish," I pointed out. "Is that what you want?"

"Don't be stupid," she replied. "I'm the careful one." Tish was young, and most kids believe they are invincible. I know I did.

*You & Your Motorcycle: were you fearful when you began riding?*

I tried to dissuade Tish, but some things are inexplicable. You must find out for yourself, like the *Zen* book. You get it, or you don't.

Or *Ode to a Daisy*?

Lawn tractor or bike?

Three wheels or two?

Peek, peak, or pique?

"Ride," Bob used to say, "It'll all make sense. And if it doesn't, you won't care."

Tish landed an excellent foot-in-the-door job as a scheduler at Baker-Jones. She had a bachelor apartment in a pleasant part of town and an on-again, off-again relationship with Brad, who wanted to get married. Tish bought a motorcycle instead.

Before CB 500, Theresa often felt trapped, a prisoner at Baker-Jones, hemmed in by an industrial park. The Honda liberated her. "I'm an experienced rider," she told her father, recalling her eBay bike days. "How hard can it be to ride a larger one?."

Girlie Biker wore a yellow backpack over her old white and blue volleyball team jacket. She attracted attention and didn't mind being the industrial park sweetheart biker chick. "Just a practical way to get around," Tish assured people who imagined she led a wild life outside of work.

CB made Tish the master of her domain. *I call the shots now!*

*Truth About Motorcycles: motorcycles are empowering.*

"Commander Gal," I'd say.

Route, schedules, what music not to listen to, all up to The Commander. Commute time slashed in half compared to taking the #10 bus. On-time for work instead of fifty minutes early or ten minutes late. Going home, Tish was no longer stuck, pretending to be busy to discourage Paul, the weirdo she dated once six years earlier. She told her dad, "I may buy a Goldwing and drive across the continent. Before I turn thirty." Tarter had yet to complete his Craftsman* overlander to Stu's, but they often made plans over lunch at Brady's Fish and Chips. Sometimes they talked about buying motorcycles.

*Truth About Motorcycles: motorcycles encourage dreams.*

Tish rode sensibly. She didn't get angry when cagers tried to kill her. She always remained Aware and Accountable.

*Hello there, motorcycle momma!* Sometimes she waved when a driver took a second look.

I assured Auntie Minnie, "Tish is no Lenny. She'll be fine." But I worried because everyone would try to kill my cousin (Motorcycle Riding Rule 1).

The Honda commute became routine, and months went by without incident. The family settled down and assumed, "Tish knows what she's doing. She's the careful one. Not a Lenny." Lenny rode like a Born to be Wild Blockhead smack into his Decision Wall.

Tish contemplated borrowing the wise book from her

father and having another crack at it. "Now that I'm a rider, it's bound to make sense," she told me.

"Don't count on it."

Every night Tish covered CB the way a mom tucks her children into bed. Every weekend, she cleaned and inspected the machine as one tends to surgical instruments or a treasured saxophone. Tish said she felt guilty if she skipped any part of the ritual.

In late October, Mother Nature signaled a change. Motorcycles hate the Dark Season. They are not like Skidoos, those motorized sled contraptions that wait patiently for cold weather. Tish assumed better outerwear would solve the approaching problem. She asked for my advice.

"Easy. Don't ride. It's stupid. Winter's coming. Put your bike away."

"Lots of people ride... for much of the winter."

"It's not fun. Take the bus. Ride on the best days only, if you must ride at all. And be extra careful."

Tish thought I was being a lazy, timid old fart, even though I was young and undamaged at the time. Except for a few weeks of extremely shitty weather, it's possible to ride year-round in Vancouver, and Tish was determined to be an all-season rider. Claim the biker dedication badge of honor. Conquer Motorcycle Misery, the way Sir Edmund conquered Mount Everest.

*Truth About Motorcycles: motorcycles don't like shitty weather.*

I'll admit it: I'm a winter cager.

On a Thursday afternoon, late in October, Tish was on

her way home. Later than usual, thanks to Mr. Nirvan and his mandatory Operations Safety Meeting. *What an utter waste of time! I work at a desk.* It teed Tish off, but she repeated, "Everyone wants to kill me," before CB headed out of the industrial park.

The route was congested—vehicles glued to asphalt like snails stuck in slime. Road Vomit soon hemmed the Honda in. The truth is: on a bike, mostly stationary, in terrible weather, motorcycles connect you to your environment in a way that is both unpleasant and joyless or, as Marta says, "In a way that makes you want to carjack the Tesla next to you."

Traffic ground to a halt. Tish could only sit tight and pray for a break. First, drizzle, the type of rain her jacket could fend off. Next, a warning shot: *get ready, Girlie Rider!* "Thanks for being an exposed, free spirit," Mother Nature spat. "Not tucked out of harm's way, hidden inside one of those dry, protective, sensible shells you like to ridicule. You make a lovely target, Girlie Biker!"

*Truth about Motorcycles: Life, the Bully likes to torment bikers. Mother Nature can be a nasty cunt.*

Unlike playing ball, there is no *motorcycling called on account of rain.* Baseball and cricket players are ushered under cover when it sprinkles. Riders shrink into themselves and hold on. Like being stuck in a WW I trench, there is no choice but to hunker down.

Maybe I'm more of a ballplayer, riders stuck in shitty weather, think? Not cut out to be a biker, at war with the elements. *I belong in the lounge with the baseball and cricket players.*

*You & Your Motorcycle: are you tougher than ball players?*

A torrential downpour let loose on my cousin. In the distance, thunder boomed. Maybe lightning; Tish's visor fogged up; she rode blind. Water torrents poured off her helmet. Unseen, a kid in the back seat of a Prius pointed and laughed. What a joke! *Can't afford a car, lady? Ever heard of the bus... biker-idiot?*

*You & Your Motorcycle: have Mother Nature and a cager ganged up on you (at the same time)?*

To Fall Storm, the investment Tish had made in wick-able, breathable summer riding pants and water-resistant gloves was a joke. *You expect those to protect you? Hah! You make me laugh, Girlie Rider.*

Fall Storm increased its bombardment. Take that, sitting duck! Duck going down! Drowned duck! I will make you wish you were dead. Or at least, sitting in a car. Storms are always on Team Cagers' side.

A driver, relaxing in a truck, sipping a hot drink, and fiddling with his lumbar support, glanced down at CB and thought, biker-idiot!

*You & Your Motorcycle: have you ever thought—going nowhere is so much better in a car?*

Stationary on a motorcycle multiplies frustration, causing the Decision Wall to pop up. Motorcycles must move. When they are forced to crawl, trapped by Road Vomit, bikers think, I'd rather be in a car.

"I was so pissed off," Tish told me. "What idiotic notion made me buy a motorcycle?"

She wiped her visor with a soggy glove and spotted the #10 bus barely moving in the far lane. Weirdo Paul waved from the back seat. *Nice in here. Warm and cozy. Come? Join me? Dump Brad?*

Tish would gladly have traded CB for a seat next to Paul.

"I've never been so fed up. I felt like driving CB off a bridge... or into a creek, as Siddy did. It was hell on two wheels."

"Part of the package," I said. "Motorcycle Payback." It's the equal and opposite reaction to Motorcycle JOY. Sir Isaac does a marvelous job explaining the phenomenon in his physics book, a must-read for all riders.

Kidding!

Read *Scraping Pegs* instead.

"It's a question every biker asks, eventually," Marta says. "What am I doing riding this horrible piece of junk? Fortunately, Guzzi understands when my nose gets bent out of shape. Always forgives me."

*Truth About Motorcycles: motorcycles don't hold grudges.*

Deadeye Dick polished his rifle. "A few ducks out tonight," he said. "Thanks to Fall Storm. Let's see if I can bag one or two."

"I give," Tish told the Wall. "No more bikes. Just let me get home. It'll be my last ride."

Good old simple Motorcycle Misery, I thought. It can

drive riders smack into the Decision Wall.

Thy rod and Thy staff, they comfort me. No, they don't! No rod! No Staff! No comfort! Only Payback. "Where the fuck is Buddha, Mr. Pirsig?"

Bob used to say, "If Buddha has any common sense, He's in a car because the weather's extraordinarily shitty."

Barely moving, there was nothing to do but shiver. Socks, wet. Water-resistant gloves hung like dish rags. Fingertips were white and numb. Tish had become a shrunken, dismal, pissed-off ex-biker. Her JOY experience was not deep and Misery quickly overwhelmed her. *Make it home. Dump the bike. It's better to Travel than to Arrive—stupid Zen book.*

By the time the Honda pulled into its parking space, Tish was hypothermic, forty-five minutes late, and disgusted. She replaced "stupid" with stronger words.

Mother Nature mocked, not so tough, are you, girlie biker? Why don't you take up baseball or cricket?

Tish didn't bother covering CB and didn't pull the key out of the ignition. "I hope someone steals you!" *Tomorrow you'll be listed for sale.* She hurried inside and ran a hot bath. *Brad is right about motorcycles.* She fell asleep on the far side of the Wall, dreaming about buying a car. *Maybe an EV? With a rebate.*

By morning, Fall Storm had moved to the east. The sky was clear. "Warming trend," said the weather channel metrologist. Tish looked out her bedroom window. No one had stolen CB. A bird sang, "Hello, beautiful day." Theresa grabbed the key on her way to catch the #10 bus. Weirdo Paul sat next to her. The guy behind her blasted Linkin Park. When she walked in, Mr. Nirwan shot the look, twenty minutes late for work.

"All day long, it bothered me." Poor CB, abandoned.

Uncovered. Waiting without complaint. The Wall was sinking. CB had not conceded to Fall Storm. No tantrums; if you want me, I'll be here, waiting. Business as usual... if you still want me?

*Truth about Motorcycles: except for Killer Bikes, motorcycles are incredibly loyal.*

"Couldn't wait to get home," Tish told me. "To say sorry. Forgive me? Please?"

*You & Your Motorcycle: has a bike ever flipped your thinking?*

"In hindsight, it's kinda funny. The next day, I rode to work. Couldn't wait to tell my storm story."

Tish had earned the right. She carried on beyond her Decision Wall and gained her first Motorcycle Misery Tale: the worst rides make the best stories.

J O Y waits down the road for Girlie Rider.

*Truth About Motorcycles: J O Y rewards those who ride past their Decision Wall.*

*You & Your Motorcycle: do you have Motorcycle Misery tales?*

◆◆◆

Uncle Tartar never completed his Craftsman*

overlander to Stu's, let alone the second leg to Brady's Fish and Chips. He may have, but his number came up in the Death Lottery: brain aneurysm. All that tartar sauce? One minute upright, the next horizontal, which is why it is never a good idea to put off buying a motorcycle. If you, or someone close to you, recommends delay, tell yourself this: at any moment, it could be tits up, so why wait?

*BUY a motorcycle! Ride the Road to Joy.*
*Don't be a Motorcycle Dreamer.*

And BUY a couple of copies of *Scraping Pegs* to go with your new bike.

"Atta boy," Dolores said when she read that sentence.

* My editor-in-training suggested replacing *Craftsman* with an inclusive word like *Artisan, Craftworker, or Technician* tractor.

 I drew a finger next to the note and wrote, "include this," which elevated my office persona to a rude Neanderthal who doesn't take direction well.

Inclusivity does not extend to bikers (or Mobilities).

# CHAPTER 6 – SO LONG SCOUT

They arrived in a black Transit van—an ominous, unwashed, soulless machine. Grave Digger Joe and Young Muscular stepped out of the hearse. No announcement was necessary. The weary Gestapo chief and his blood-thirsty lieutenant had come for Scout.

I surrendered without protest; handed over the key. "The charger's in the lab; the garage. Just in there."

Young Muscular quickened his pace.

*Where's my Zatoichi sword? Howitzer? Grease gun?* I stood in silence—a mute sympathizer watching as they rounded my friend up. They came for Scout, but Scooter Crowd was not there to bar the way.

I raised my right crutch in a silent salute, so long friend, and motioned, haul the four wheeled machine away. It means nothing to me. Force it into your coffin.

The wicked shatter bonds with ease—you must be cold-hearted to survive in the machine recovery business.

Poor Scout, shuffled between homes, never allowed to stay and become family. *Bunny will miss you! So will I, my friend.*

On-scooter I'd traveled exposed. Fell in with Scooter Crowd. Found a buddy Hans. Enjoyed the benefits of being a Poor Dear. Now the Gestapo was ripping part of my identity from me. Did the two SS officers plan to strip Scout down? Conduct crude experiments?

Kidding!

The gentlemen actually worked for Island Mobility, not Hermann Goering. Grave Digger Joe smiled when he handed me a "20% off your next rental coupon. "In case you get busted up again."

Scooter Crowd had turned their backs. I had been labeled an interloper. You will forsake us, their looks said. "Always the same with you healers, so fuck off, asshole! Become a show-off, a Constant Walker, and then a dancer."

Kidding again!

Scooter Crowd was always accepting and polite.

They organized a going away party with carrot cake, the healthiest of cakes, topped with cream cheese, the protein king of icings, perfect for someone training to be a Constant Walker. Marsha brought coffee in a big stainless-steel Thermos. Clarence passed napkins. There was a card, and a picture of me wearing my stallion tee shirt, sitting on Scout, sandwiched between eight scooters in Copley Park. Hans was there. I introduced him to Marta.

"Mare," Hans asked, pointing at my tee-shirt?

"Stallion?" My sister Joan would know.

"Lame ass would be more appropriate," Marta said, which caused Hans to erupt.

My scooter send-off was better than any motorcycle farewell I've attended. Riders grunt a few times, then everyone buggers off to disconnect. Scooter Crowd was intimate and difficult to move on from, although I promised Hans, "we'll stay in touch," which is unlikely unless staying in touch means bumping into one another by coincidence and then pulling the got-an-appointment excuse.

I'm kidding, again.

Hans and I had become pals, more than just scooter acquaintances.

When I spot Hans on EZ Rider I, rejoice.

If Hans can do stuff and enjoy life, it would be pathetic for me not to climb back on and find the Road to Joy.

Banished to no-man's-land, I watched the Gestapo load Scout into the hearse. I was no longer frail enough to be a Mobility, but still too compromised for a motorcycle. Good enough to have coffee with Hans, but no longer would Scout and EZ Rider hit the sidewalk and roll toward the strip mall like a couple of kids with bursting bladders.

Constant walking is not in the cards for Hans. He has a neurodegenerative genetic disorder called Huntington's ("a mild case," Hans says). My scooter friend will never know Motorcycle JOY, but he is happy. When I see Hans, the neuroscientist in me wonders: what is the source of his JOY? He should be miserable. But Hans won the lottery, born pumped full of natural JOY. I got UNEASY, but God also gave me a prescription: *you will discover the MAGIC in motorcycles.*

"Walk," Hans ordered!

"I will. "

"Constantly. No frequent stops."

"I'll do my best."

"Nice that you don't need the scooter anymore," Grave Digger said. "Won't be long. You'll be off and running."

"Yes." I took care not to reveal my anxiety as the door of the hearse slammed shut. Like lukewarm engine oil, the conversation was easy, an honest verbal exchange: no weather, sports, poetry, or political lectures. Joe appeared to be interested in my thoughts on modifications and how I'd come to require a loaner.

Here's what he said after my Horace story: "Look at you. Could have been worse, am I right?"

I nodded. Had Joe read my brothers Ron and Lance's stories in *Scraping Pegs?* They know it can be a hell of a lot worse.

"You're comin' along."

Yes. Four months after the accident, I had permission to apply full weight on my left leg and commence serious rehabilitation.

"Think you'll climb on again?"

I offered the pat "depends" answer without mentioning my exhaustive Therapy Bike search, agrizoophobia, or how Bunny like to tap my head with his paw as if to say, smarten up. *You're under no obligation to climb on.*

It was business as usual for Joe and Muscular. They would soon be off to their next assignment, dumping Scout with a new decrepit, one without an adventurous dog, like Pearl, or an enlightened cat, like Bunny.

"Every few months, there's a scooter accident. Haven't had one that involved a deer yet." Grave Digger and Muscular laughed. "Mostly, they tip over, get hung up, or run into a lamppost, sometimes into each other." Young Muscular drove a fist into the palm of his opposite hand. "POW!"

The ridicule turned my stomach, but I remained silent. *So long, Scout. I'll miss you. Until I get a Therapy Bike.* Supported by crutches, I went into the garage and closed the door.

Bunny leapt off of Softy. I worried Big Terry would drop

by and catch Bunny catnapping—*why am I paying the lab thirty-five bucks a month? Keep your furball off of Brenda!* It's tough being in the motorcycle customer service business.

*You & Your Motorcycle: are you overly protective of your bike?*

Who knows what cats think when they knead your lap? They keep their emotions close to their paws. My motorcycles have all been like that, but sometimes they purr like Bunny and fill me with J O Y .

◆◆◆

Scout-less, I walked. Walking where each step requires thought. Each movement calculated. "Like going into a hairpin," I explained.

"Walking would be so much easier on Mars," Marta said, as if Elon and I planned to pop up for a visit. "Where gravity is 62% less."

"On Mars, everyone is a dancer," Dolores, who had crashed the get-together, added.

"Overweight? Decrepit? Parkinson's? Hans could dance on Mars," Anita said.

"On Mars, everyone's an Anna Pavlova, Rudolf Nureyev, or BBoy Crazy Legs," Earl said.

"There is one enormous outer space problem: no motorcycles," Cam pointed out.

"No Motorcycle JOY on Mars. Why do we want to colonize the red planet? A planet of motorcycle-less dancers? Is that a good idea? Does NASA think these things through?"

"What about an electric motorcycle on Mars?" Conrad suggested.

"Engineering could do it," Marta said.

I hope so. It'd be terrific to have a new planet to explore. Forget about touring Croatia or New Zealand, do Mars on a TS-125 or KTM! Have you seen pictures of the red planet? Off-road glorious! Plus, no speed traps or political scientists mucking things up. Definitely no Dr. Peggy types in outer space. No flowers, so no reciting *Ode to a Daisy*. Mobility scooters are unnecessary; even Hans rides an electric motorcycle and dances.

On Mars, where Life is Beautiful, everyone will, rejoice!

Why do people say, "There's nothing to look forward to?" Martian Motorcycle JOY, that's something worth dreaming about.

Terry stood. "Shelly's expecting me. Better skedaddle."

The garage door closed.

"No Shellys on Mars," Den said.

"That's where Terry should be," Tony said.

◆◆◆

When I lost Scout, I discovered: most able-bodies are kind to scooter-decrepits but leery of trainee Constant Walkers. I always kept my left leg in its cast prominently extended on-scooter and wore my arm sling for extra effect. I smiled. Able-bodies thought: he's not one of those dumbass, lazy posers. *Obviously, this guy's suffered a traumatic accident and isn't letting it get him down. It's so true: bad things happen to the nicest people? Poor, poor dear... what a trooper!*

On-scooter, my demeanor said, yes, it was awful, but

I'm determined to keep my chin up! Did you know I'm a Zen Jackass? Yes, please, a slice of carrot cake would be perfect... with extra cream cheese icing, of course... or just a bowl of the icing would be fine... if it's easier? Don't want to be a bother.

What a dear! Take another slice along with extra icing. Anything else, dear?

I portrayed a winning combo: Poor Dear + Trooper. People like to see a smile and persistence in the face of adversity. It brings a hint of joy to their day.

If the Gestapo is at your door, a pitiful, why me expression is understandable. If only the Jewish people had invented motorcycles and escaped the death camps. Instead, they sat around eating sufganiyot and rugelach, getting fat, making it easier for the Philistines and the Nazis to spot them. Had an Israelite stumbled on the Motorcycle Scrolls instead of those other ones, history wouldn't be so gruesome.

I'm neither Jewish, German, nor Arab, so the holocaust and the Palestine question never came up when Able-bodies spotted me. To them, I was a harmless, neutral Poor Dear. *Let me get the door. Please, go ahead. There's my good deed done!* They took products off grocery shelves and asked, "Anything else you need, dear?" Yes, a motorcycle and my old body back. "Take care now." *Poor dear.* The silent chorus: *what a trooper!*

When I became a trainee Constant Walker, strangers became leery. People aren't eager to assist decrepits sporting arm crutches. *Will he break if I help him up? Will I be liable? Is he contagious?* On Scout, I was harmless. As a struggling walker with a wonky left side, I was a looming disaster, unbalanced like Feeble and Hans. Beware! Steer clear! Decrepit going down!

The more I shed visible signs of my beat-up past, the more sympathy waned. I found myself in no-man's-land without icing, my Poor Dear days cherished but gone. Able-bodies gave me a wide berth. *Is he an addict? Got Huntington's? Parkinson's? Drinks? Homeless?*

Unable to move to Mars, I was like a bike with poor compression in one cylinder, struggling, in need of repair, but ignored, like Ann Frank, overlooked by the Gestapo.*

"Shifting from Poor Dear to Constant Walker sounds like a Buell sportbike trying to become a Harley," Conrad said.

* Legal insisted I add this note. For the record, Dr. Peggy, Dori, and Beaten Stick Books disapproved of all Gestapo, Nazi, Jewish, and Palestine references.

I understand. They've never suffered from motorcycle-less, transitioned from Poor Dear to Constant Walker, or witnessed the SS pushing a friend into a hearse. My apologies to those who find the references offensive

◆◆◆

GT. Bob. Walking. Scooter Crowd. Scout. All gone in less than a year. It's been one thing followed by another recently. Makes you wonder, what's next?

It turned out to be a global pandemic, a real JOY ball buster. "Sometimes I wonder if the people in charge of virus control aren't worse than the virus," my classic biker friend Pete said.

I had to adopt the classic biker (CBer) example. Rusting bikes ignored become junk. CBers rescue them—they transform old bikes into beautiful works of art. Projects are completed one step at a time, like soft tissue repair. You must refuse to say, "Good enough. Fuck it." Be Stubborn in a Good Way because there is a crossroad. Give up on a junk bike, and it gets wheeled back behind the shed to rust away. Take your body for granted, and it's a downhill slide into a coffin.

When a pandemic comes along, the authorities yank all support services away. "Fuck everyone who doesn't have COVID, especially decrepit biker-idiots! The greater good of society is a little more important than wind therapy." Rehabilitation, like classic bike builds, must continue with no outside resources. You must be Stubborn in a Good Way (Rule #7).

CBers unable to source a critical component reach the end of their ropes and contemplate throwing in their torque wrenches. *Fuck this! What were we thinking? Can't be done during a lockdown without Fabrication Expert.* But they regroup and persist: "Can this not-so-unique part be adapted?" They come up with what engineers call workarounds. More difficult to implement, but a way forward. Classic Bikers are always scraping pegs.

In my case, COVID-19 took away my massages, needling, in person doctors, sonic lasers, water walking, kinesiology, physiotherapy, sauna, steam room, fitness center, hot tub, and the morale that comes with group rehabilitation. Life, the Bully, kicked me in the camshaft. It pushed me down when I'd been ascending.

"Follow the CBer example," Conrad advised.

"I'll try."

Public Health orders forced Tony and others to shutter their businesses. Tony waited and wondered, is the pandemic my Deli Decision Wall? Time to walk away from pastrami and battered pickles?

Marta posted COVID protocols (suitably revised) on the lab walls and started making *The World's Battered and in a Pickle*, pickles at home.

The world fell into despair and became uneasy except for the people-who-run-things and public health bureaucrats, who thought *pandemics aren't so bad.*

Lockdowns are tough on free-spirited rebel bikers.

◆◆◆

Dori helped me turn the lab into a rehab center.

Bunny was my coach.

Pearl, my cheerleader.

Dr. Peggy spent a lot of time sheltering at home, disinfecting.

Hans rolled the dice and invited me to go fishing at Elk Lake. Fortunately, we never hooked a fish. Sitting beside the water with a friend can be fun. If you have a trout fisher state of mind, it's okay if nothing happens.

"No fish were harmed," I assured Dori before taking a nap.

I passed my rod onto Marta. "It's fun. Especially when the fish aren't biting, Hans will show you how not to catch trout."

Sitting beside a lake, with a best friend (or your motorcycle), eating battered pickles is Life being beautiful.

Scrape your pegs.

Take a nap.

Give pandemics the biker salute.*

* Legal insisted I add, "while respecting the safety of others and complying with all public health directives."

# PART TWO:
# THERAPY BIKE

*"Four wheels move the body, two wheels move the soul." – Anonymous*

# CHAPTER 7 – ESSENTIAL TRAVEL

9 AM. Wednesday, June 10, In the Year of COVID.

Like a rental bike with old gas, I lurched along making excellent progress.

I'd learned: never take walking for granted.

I swore I wouldn't.

But before long, I did. Walking does not bombard you the way driving a motorcycle does. It's easily dismissed.

Living is a constant state of forgetting not to take things for granted, I thought as I sat in Terry's Leaf. "Good morning." The exMarine wore a black COVID mask. He knew—life can flip as quickly as a cease-fire.

Five months into the pandemic, the NIAID Director (Dr. Fauci), the World Health Organization, many politicians, and much of the media advised, "we should not take breathing for granted!"

"Unless you're on-motorcycle," my friends replied. "Two Wheels, Not Four!"

"Don't be Chicken Little," Hans said bravely, even though he was lumped in with the "compromised group."

Hospitals were pleading—more ventilators, please! Shoppers hoarded disinfectant and toilet paper. Entrepreneurs sold counterfeits medical-grade masks. Donald Trump drank bleach (according to the media) and blasted the WHO.

It was a real shit show.

Marta nailed the solution: "Climb-on. Everyone ride! COVID can't catch hosts on open-air machines. Two Wheels, Not Four!" The WHO filed Marta's cure under No One Gives a Shit About Biker-Idiot Suggestions. The pandemic dragged on.

"Problem solved," Conrad said.

Not for me. I could not climb on.

◆◆◆

I started to put my mask on, but Terry took his off. "No Shelly, no mask." He looked me in the eye. "Shelly doesn't know I'm giving you a ride."

Renegade, I thought as we headed to Victoria International Airport. My friend was on hard lockdown. Warhammerred by Shelly. Poor, poor Terry, what's he to do? Which is stricter, Shelly's COVID rules or Marine rules, soldier? "It'll be over soon," I said. "Best to hunker down. Wait it out." *Unless you're uneasy and have motorcycle-lessness.*

I'll sneak over to your garage... to see Brenda. What happens in the lab stays in the lab."

"Absolutely." Until it's published in a tell-all book, which loomed as a Big Terry Decision Wall. Family or Brenda? J O Y or Complacency Swamp? People like Shelly force decisions. It rattled Marta, the optimist; always seeking perfect solutions.

What can a war-weary exMarine, trapped between a virus and a motorcycle hater, do? Brenda must die, many thought. I was fighting my own battle.

At Departures, I thanked Terry and said, "See you in a few days," wishing I had more to offer. "Take care, buddy."

Mask wearing was mandatory; our first line of defense against the army of tiny killer germs. Mine was white and blue.

Ten months earlier, at YYJ, I'd been in a wheelchair rolling toward Royal Jubilee Hospital. Now, at low revs, I was a slow dancer. On Mars, I'd be Mikhail Baryshnikov or Michael Jackson. On Earth, more like my scooter friend Hans, or classmate Feeble, with a gimpy leg and limited shoulder movement.

"Have you lost it?" Dori had asked. "Gone completely bonkers?"

Peggy gave a condescending nod of approval.

I grinned like a nutter. A couple of months after losing Scout, I bought a step-through, ebike. With little weight on my left side, riding proved easier than walking. Logically, driving a motorcycle would be a breeze and "I really need some wind therapy."

"You haven't heard, there's a pandemic?"

You haven't heard about JOY, I thought? *That it is stronger than COVID.* My explanation of medical-physics realities proved to pointless. I had to go. I had the itch.

It was June 2021 and I was one of a handful of essential travelers at YYJ. "Flushed out into the open," the fearful might say. "Prime viral targets." Walking toward check-in, I looked normal in the sense that my movements no longer caused people to give me a wide berth. My motorcycle jacket was neutral, not reflective lime green or leather with tassels, skull and crossbones. My look didn't scream biker dude, possibly a member of a hellion anti-masker gang on the verge of rebellion. It's easy to go unnoticed in an airport, especially one emptied by COVID-19. The few staff and travelers wouldn't have noticed a box jellyfish in Bermuda shorts returning to shelter at home in Australia.

I checked my boots and helmet with the airline. The attendant didn't ask why the motorcycle gear, mister? I nodded thanks, assuming she understood—I must venture where disinfectants fear to go, like Sir Edmund Hillary and Tenzing Norgay when they broke through the clouds to conquer Everest. Sir Ed told Tenzing on the way to their press briefing: "No need to mention how many times you've been so close to the summit, you could have pissed on it, Tenzing. No one's interested in your urination stories." I didn't elaborate on my essential travel situation.

"Have a good trip," the attendant said.

"Thanks." I smiled and continued toward Security.

Still wonky on the inside; my anatomy occasionally misfired. My Complainers, I called them, the invisible whiners—muscles, tissues, nerves, and joints who asked, why did you do this to us? They nagged: *we're not ready. Sheltering at home is the sensible thing to do, given we're compromised and vulnerable. We're on COVID's target list. Retreat! Back to our hospital bed in the basement with Bunny.*

"Silence, My Complainers! Don't make Security suspicious! Would you prefer the knife?" The prospect of surgery frightens body parts. "We're outlaws, remember? Wonky but capable of giving health authority rules and recommendations the finger."

"Best to duck and cover," My Complainers urged. "Follow all protocols. Let's turn around before Security... head back home."

I popped a pill—drugs make My Complainers think, All Is Well.

Think Motorcycle JOY!

For the first time, I walked unassisted. I missed the reassurance my cane gave me. They're a valuable safety tool, ensuring stability, but canes do nothing to prolong the Poor Dear persona. *Why the stick, buddy? You're not Zatoichi, the blind Japanese warrior concealing a sword, are you? Let me see you swing that thing. You look fine to me. Are you planning to beat a kid with that stick?* Canes generate the opposite of the Poor Dear Sympathetic Response.

"The image of a cross old man waving his walking stick in the air did canes in," Marta had explained. "There's no salvaging them."

"People see them as weapons," Dolores said.

At the time, it was academic—unless you had COVID, no one gave a fouled spark plug. It was, back of the line, if you could find a line for the nonCOVID but sickly. Some nurses and doctors called horse shit, bent the rules, and healed because they are Medical Saints with a touch of natural outlaw. Battling disease and bureaucracy brought them joy.

Cane-less, I blended in. Security was both bored and diligent, forcing me to summon my Zen Jackass-ism (a practice described in *Scraping Pegs*). *Security, shouldn't you be hunting COVID germs, not looking for weaponry in my shoes?*

"Go ahead," Security frowned, suspecting my travel wasn't really essential, but not granted enforcement powers. *If it were up to me, you'd be denied! Locked up and shamed, COVID rule breaker!*

"Have a good trip."

"Thanks," I smiled, put my belt on, and walked to my gate. Pandemics are primarily about waiting, not at all like the movie *Outbreak*, more like *House Arrest*.

The authorities had put the brakes on my initial therapy plan: fly to Arizona, pick up a used two-wheeler I'd tracked down outside of Phoenix, followed by a Grand Canyon or Death Valley route home. An Easy Rider trip, except with legal drugs. But the people-in-charge slammed the longest undefended border in the world shut. Thanks to microscopic bugs who don't respect boundaries, it had shown no signs of reopening. Illegal migrants okay, but we can't have the little COVID buggers crossing our borders, US strategists concurred, without considering the fact that their declaration impeded motorcycle flow, preventing freedom riders, isolated on open-air machines, from conducting scouting forays and seeking International Motorcycle JOY during a time when intelligence and distraction were critical.

Motorcyclists were casualties of war.

*Truth about Motorcycles: motorcycles love freedom.*

Just like Zorro, I put on my protective mask. At times I swung a bleach gun, which is more effective than a sword during a pandemic. **Disinfect Before Boarding**, a sign said. I spread goo on my hands. Outlaws must make allowances during global wars; modify their behavior to align with the greater good. It can be hard because:

*Riders never assume the people-in-charge are*

*in charge because they know what they're doing.*
*We understand, most don't have a clue.*

I found my therapy bike at a dealership in Kelowna, B.C. Newer and more expensive than the one in Arizona, but the same model. It checked all the boxes on my Climb Back On Checklist.

Marta asked: "How is it you qualified for a free scooter loaner, surgery, subsidized drugs, physio treatments galore, a free cane, government-provided drugs, but you can't get a dime toward a Therapy Bike?"

I shrugged. *Because life is not fair?*

"No shortage of clinical evidence," Marta continued. "Lots of motorcycle books were written by folks riding to get over something and heal themselves. Motorcycle Therapy is legit, much healthier and less costly than drug addiction."

True. We have several biker therapy books in the lab library, like *Ghost Rider*.

*Truth About Motorcycles: for bikers,*
*there are no free rides.*

"Few bikers vote," pundits point out. "Vote buying must focus on car drivers. In progressive cities, bicycles and transit, but never motorcycles or Mobilities!"

*Truth About Motorcycles: like cross old men*
*with canes, motorcycles face discrimination.*

Shunned by conservative think tanks and woke progressives alike, idealogues dole out money like overfilled gas tanks, trying to build perfect societies while ignoring the obvious solution—pour money into Motorcycle JOY. It would solve so many problems. Bob used to say, "Riding would be far more effective than gunboat or public diplomacy."

Shout it in front of the UN in New York:

"Two Wheels, Not Four!"

"Two Wheels, Not Four!"

"Two Wheels, Not Four!"

It's difficult to comprehend why humanity doesn't take advantage of the MAGIC and move to a world of JOY. Choose to live with Life, the Beautiful?

It's perplexing but,

*Truth About Motorcycles: despite injustice and discrimination, for bikers, JOY persists.*

The jet's door closed.

"Forward the Light Brigade," I said silently.

Ride on Hannibal!

Fasten your seat belts.

"Oh god," My Complainers moaned.

◆◆◆

The Airbus A329 went up, pointed to the northeast, and flew across the Salish Sea. "Prepare for landing," the five passengers were instructed. There'd been little time to unprepare in the minute since the plane leveled off. Victoria (on Vancouver Island) to Vancouver is a slow-mo version of high siding (going over the bars). Up and then down. Before you know it, you're on the ground, the

North American continent. No longer adrift, an islander.

Thanks to the essential travel decree and flight cancellations, I faced a five-and-one-half-hour wait for my connecting flight. Viral wars are mostly about washing your hands, being told what to do, and waiting for the world to end.

To kill time, I walked out of the secure area toward International Departures, where hordes of YVR travelers were fleeing to Asia dressed in full-body disposable jumpsuits—like motorcycle protective gear except no armor, skin protection, or humongous boots. A good thing about viruses is: unlike kamikaze stags, they don't break legs or trigger brain bleeds. Asia seemed an odd choice to lie low, so I logged it in my memory bank under Potentially Useful Intel, in case Marta quizzed me, "anything going on?"

It felt good to walk. Thank-you Legs! I have taken you for granted, but never again. Starting with purchasing better quality socks—no more marked-down ten to a bag imperfects.

Legs walked me back through security to Domestic and USA Departures. No queuing. Few travelers were rushing off to shelter in Toronto, Montreal, or Buffalo. All the action was in Asia.

I snapped a photo of planes, victims of the travel ban, waiting on the tarmac beyond the glass wall, and sent a WhatsApp pic to my family group. "On maneuvers," I wrote. "Scraping pegs."

Apart from those with a need to know, I traveled clandestinely. Stay low in the trenches, we were told! Keep your head down! The virus is like mustard gas, except invented by Life, the Bully instead of Humanity. Follow all rules! Shelter at home.

People interpret the word "essential" differently. Some can't grasp that collecting a Therapy Bike is a necessity; I had no choice. *Are you not familiar with Motorcycle Teddies? Motorcycle JOY? The pain of Motorcycle-lessness? Wind therapy? Are you a NimRod?*

It's pointless trying to explain, "it's important to ride during pandemics. How else can you escape the madness?

Marta was supportive, of course, as were Bunny and Pearl. It's good to have encouragement when you're on a quest to regain something, like Bilbo Baggins (with Gandalf's support) in *The Hobbit.*

Sending the WhatsApp message had felt selfish. Too much information? Like a recovering alcoholic uncle who declares, "Taken up with the devil again. Watching the drunken fun on TV made me yearn for the good times. The world's ending, so why not have a bit of a piss up before we run out of booze and it's lights out for humanity?" Uncle will wake up the next afternoon feeling like shit. "What, the world hasn't ended? The experts on TV were so convincing. Oh, well, maybe tomorrow... it'd be a shame to waste these bottles. There's no free booze."

*You & Your Motorcycle: have you ridden hungover and joyless?*

Never take the world ending for granted! The declarations of the Jehovah's Witness, the Aztecs, and Camille Flammarion (Halley's Comet will obliterate us) made them all look foolish. "Oh well," they shrugged afterward. "I'm sure Armageddon is around the corner. Let's pick a new date."

*Carry on riding—on top of the world and over the moon. Don't wait for the world to end.*

# CHAPTER 8 - KELOWNA

Kelowna, with its 150,000 inhabitants, is nestled on the shores of picturesque Okanagan Lake, a popular tree fruit, vineyard and summer tourism destination. David Furnish, the husband of Elton John, is from Kelowna. Or wife? I never know. It's a word conundrum. I should pay attention when Dr. Peggy explains the modern day use of pronouns and relationship terms. Significant other is a safe bet, I suppose? Pick the wrong word, and you're in the doghouse and on the news, accused of being an insensitive Neanderthal. Please simply the word rules, Dr. Daisy! Partner, may be the best bet? Sounds business-like, though. The partners enjoyed fresh Okanagan cherries during their visit to Kelowna. Or the significant others enjoyed fresh Okanagan fruits during their visit to Kelowna? Don't make things worse by tagging on the word "cagers." Either way, fresh cherries are hard to beat, don't you think? Put a few on carrot cake with extra icing. YUM! Guaranteed to make you grin from ear to ear.

Like Tony's Deli, pandemic bakeries had been shut down and in grocery stores, supplies dwindled. In place of dairy products, there were only those less healthy icings, like fondant and royal. No cream cheese. YUK! Buttercream is good, but not a protein star.

"Be steadfast like Bilbo Baggins," I told myself. Go directly to the dealership. Forget about hobnobbing with Rocket Man, eating tree fruits, or hoping to find carrot cake with extra cream cheese icing.

◆◆◆

I had considered going with a trike until I checked the price. Have you seen what they want to add a wheel? Along with a 600 lb. weight limit for Therapy Bike, I also set a low budget. "The bike may spend much of its time on teddy bear duty," I explained to Conrad.

Cost does not translate to J O Y .

*You & Your Motorcycle: have you found*
*J O Y on an inexpensive machine?*

The moment I stepped inside the store, my uneasiness went through the roof. *Is this how Feeble felt whenever he spotted Jorge Jorgensen?* What once was comforting felt foreign. "We should be at a mobility scooter shop," My Complainers whispered. "Kicking small tires with Hans."

The door closed. I downed a pill, then inched forward.

Many of the customers were off-road'ers. Nothing frightened them, certainly not a puny virus. The bravado made me long for Scooter Crowd and Bunny. If only Pearly was with me. She'd boldly lead the way. Do they give treats here? Where's this therapy bike? Want me to pee on some tires?

Memories of naps filled my head. Watching *The Sound of Music*... in the basement with Bunny... hunkered down.

♫ *The hills are alive with the sound of music. With songs they have sung for a thousand years* ♫ I imagined myself as Rocket Man, out on the road alone.

*Truth About Motorcycles: riders do not always feel they were born to be wild.*

I was like a member of Flying Wallenda high-wire act stepping back into the ring after a fall. Afraid to trust the cable strand. Timid. *The wire is so thin, and it's such a long way down. What am I doing here?*

The shoppers were all lions or warriors; I was the lone mouse. A therapy bike? This isn't a treatment center, buster! Get the fuck out of this motorcycle store!

"Feeble, you're going in," I heard my old gym teacher call. Sometimes there is no escape. Like being ordered to the front in WWII, retreat, and GI Joe shoots you in the back. Outlaws don't carry white flags. Instead, we honor the poem *Forward, the Light Brigade:*

Into the unknown.
Rode the bikers.
Forward, the Light Brigade!
Charge with MAGIC,
Into the Valley of JOY.

I heard Bunny singing from the shelter of my recovery bed: ♫ the hills fill my heart with the sound of music. My heart wants to sing every song it hears ♫.

Why didn't I listen to Conrad or Marta? They offered to meet me in Kelowna. "As a precaution. In case you need support."

"Did Tom have a buddy in any of the *Mission Impossibles*... besides his Scientology

Electropsychometer, which brings him joy?"

"Huh?"

"Motorcycle therapy is best as a solo endeavor, like a monk on retreat."

"Huh?"

"Essential travel only. But thanks for the offer." It's easy to fool yourself when you're browsing at home, doped up on medications, taking advice from a cat, and encouragement from a dog. It's different when you're in the ring, looking up at the high-wire, wearing marked-down imperfect socks.

Marta? Conrad? I expected a tap on my shoulder; friends often ignore my advice.

No one was there.

Would you accept my call, Dr. Phil?

Hans, do you think you could scoot you up to Kelowna?

Mother Mary in Heaven, what am I doing here?

"This is crazy," My Complainers said.

# CHAPTER 9 – AT THE DEALERSHIP

My phone rang. Hans asked, "Coffee?" Poured into disposable cups from a Thermos in Copley Park. "Or fishing at Elk Lake?"

"Maybe next week." Han's call bump started me—follow the arrows pasted on the floor of the Kelowna Powersports dealer. Linger and remain in No-Man's-Land, no Motorcycle JOY, no longer a part of Scooter Crowd, just trout.

Forward to the Proud Machines!

Charge for the bikes!

Steel horses worked their MAGIC, luring prospects, enticing customers with promises of life altering adventures and the means to reinvent themselves. They whispered, "go ahead, give the health authority's arrows the finger," in a polite, understated Honda voice. Free-spirited bikers contemplating farkle purchases were acting... well, free. Don't tell me about slow-speed maneuvering! Rode a beast, for fuck's sake. I'll wander around this store anyway I damn well please! Fuck your guide ropes!

A teenager wiped down fixtures. He fired one of our side's big guns, a jumbo-sized, scented disinfectant spray bottle. I wondered: doesn't Buddha, sheltering in showroom circuitry, value microscopic life as much as He does the life of the fat ass biker chick contemplating a bandanna purchase? Isn't that His mantra? All life is scared.

The teenager fired gobs of germicide and wiped-out trillions of organisms. *If only I had my bleach bottle handy. I'd join in. Slaughter the little pricks!*

Buddha shuddered. Shall I reincarnate them as trout? Everyone loves trout, especially Smokey Bear. He loves well-aged, decaying Dolly Vardens. And the trout can be reborn as Scientologists.

Unlike Tony's Deli, motorcycle shops had been declared Essential and remained open thanks to a loophole which lumped bikes in with cars. "Why is buying a car essential when travel is locked down? Worshipers can't attend church, and my customers can't buy a Cosmic Special," Tony demanded? In emergencies, deli operators must be made of "sterner stuff," Judy told him. "It's not up for debate. Do your part for the greater good, Tony" (more about Marc and Judy later).

It had been a real head scratcher when the authorities lumped places of devotion in with delis. "God belongs with pastrami?" You might think if there ever was a time for Supreme Being to step up and weigh in, this was it. "Hold on a dang moment. Let's think this through," but not a single omen because "I don't consider Myself a business. More of a Deity, really." Businesses use YouTube and bash people over the head to sell the Meaning of Life. Deities are spiritual; way more subtle. "Sure, some humans have turned Me into a business, but that's free will for you. Anyway, no more listening to those dreadful old hymns on Sunday mornings. I prefer throaty pipes, the sacred sound of J O Y ."

Five CBers (Classic Bikers) were lined up in front of the parts counter. They're always there, on quests, like Bilbo Baggins. Does the grease and oil residue embedded in CBer skin provide pandemic immunity? Can they touch Hands to Face without the fear of death?

*Truth About Motorcycles: classic bikers can do stuff others can't, like Gandalf in the Lord of the Rings.*

Motorcycle professionals know how to reassure timid shoppers. I couldn't tell how Colin, my sales consultant, assessed me. *Does this guy know motorcycles? Is he fresh out of Parking Lot Cone School? A Motorcycle Dreamer? After years of being lost, another dude buying the bullshit about finding himself on the open road?*

Colin is young enough to believe the marketing hype: we're selling a lifestyle son, not machines, but he had answers and raced. Impressive. I wondered, does Colin understand the truth about motorcycles?

Sometimes Truth is best left under the seat where it can't wriggle up backs, wrap around necks, poke its bony finger under helmets or down ear channels before injecting reality into gooey brain matter. I played it safe and stuck to bike chit-chat. "Why am I here buying this particular motorcycle? It's complicated. I need a ride that isn't like other bike I've owned," I explained after telling the story of Horace the Horrible. *A PTSD service bike. Already have a great dog, Pearl. And a cat, Bunny.* I liked Colin, and talking bikes fueled my confidence.

Colin mentioned he raced motocross.

"Amateurs can qualify for the Isle of Man TT. Did you

know, Colin? When I'm fully recovered, maybe..." An old dream that was a smelly load of horseshit.

My therapy bike choice: a Honda CTX 700. "A cross between a sports bike and a cruiser," YouTubers informed me, and I could see it. Mid-sized. Easy to handle. It looked comfortable and was unlike any other bike I'd owned. Thoroughbreds will scoff, but my bike vanity was embedded on Highway 20.

No bags. "Talk to Parts. You'll get five percent off."

I didn't—too many CBers lined up.

I don't recall seeing a Honda CTX before my therapy bike search. Honda discontinued the model in 2019. The one I bought in Kelowna was brand-new, leftover stock, unwanted until I came along. I liked the low center of gravity, lightweight, low cost, and unusual appearance. I assured myself it would not remind me of antler monsters. Excellent reviews, but one reviewer called the CTX "the man-bun of motorcycles," no doubt referring to the popular DCT automatic model (mine is manual). Is man-bun code for therapy bike, I wondered?

I expected questions: is that the man-bun you have? Do you drive a Miata? *No! See—shifter and clutch. Owned a Movie Bike once (that story's in Scraping Pegs). It was a selection error which turned it into a Killer Bike.* Had the Kelowna CTX been the man-bun DCT model, I would have purchased it. Why not? I was looking for different and easy to ride.

*You & Your Motorcycle: how do you feel about automatics? An extra wheel?*

"Not on a CTX, of course," I assured Colin, circling back to my Isle of Man TT comment. *Unless the organizers introduce a mobility scooter or CTX category.* I had no problem beating Hans to the strip mall. "Loser buys peanut M&M's!"

Familiar with seat removal, Colin took control and cinched my dry bag down on the pillion. *Should I ask him to ride behind, in sweeper position? Take Bob's place? No!* Riding solo is essential when you're on a mission to heal, find yourself, and reopen the door to JOY. I had a touch of autophobia (the fear of being alone), but Mr. Pirsig assured me: "Buddha will be with you in the circuitry."

I was out of the dealership quickly. Insured. Bag strapped on. Wearing my new, improved motorcycle boots (the old ones failed to prevent ankle breakage). My boots were comforting but stiff, forcing me to walk like Feeble after being blindsided and kicked in the crotch by Jorge Jorgensen.

Therapy Bike circled the lot, checking me out. Are you a SQUIB? You're very shaky. Heard your last bike ended up in a crusher? I've had it good, hanging around the showroom; sure don't want to end up as scrap metal. Why not stick to the lot? Until you're ready? Back to your old self. Capable of jumping berms. Climbing hills. Qualifying for the Isle of Man TT. Now you're just pathetic. Not road ready.

Limping around in endless circles wasn't an option.

*Truth About Motorcycles: bikes aren't fond of parking lots.*

Like a returning Flying Wallenda with acrophobia (an irrational fear of heights), CTX edged into city traffic.

Then Life, the Beautiful, stepped forward, and the hills came alive with the sound of music. "I'm doing it!" It was like witnessing the miracle of childbirth (without the disgusting parts). I glanced down and said, "Thank you, Buddha." Motorcycle-less no more. I had been reincarnated. It felt great. J O Y flowed.

♫It's lonely on the road on a timeless drive♫ I sang to settle myself and assured My Complainers, "No, we are not about to be torpedoed into the asphalt."

Ride with authority, like a Templar knight.

Always aware. Be accountable.

♫Rocket Man. Rocket Man. Out here on the road alone♫

I Rode to Joy.

# CHAPTER 10 – ON THE ROAD AGAIN

I stayed put in the HOV lane for twenty miles before it merged into a divided highway for the 140km/90mile run to my motel in Merritt, B.C. On to Vancouver and across the Salish Sea, home to Victoria the following day. My body fumbled with the bike's geometry, learning required positions. Especially lazy was Left Foot, which acted as if it had never been in charge of a gearshift. Not a clue. Brian had to talk Left Foot through each movement. "Don't give me, the I'm full of metal now, excuse!"

*Never take shifting for granted (unless you own an automatic).*

It was easy going and going easy on the freeway—loads of space and little essential traffic. CTX followed an SUV doing 70 mph or 115 kph. It was 82 Fahrenheit or 28 Celsius at 344 meters or 1129 feet. I wondered: what exactly the UN Committee of Experts on Standards did between meetings in Barcelona?

I worried about driving on the wrong side of the road. Why had other countries chosen left? Had a study concluded left is better for wildlife avoidance? Was choosing right an ill-informed political snub rather than fact-based?

CTX, being a therapy bike, is sensible; I didn't feel obligated to pass. Sportbikes embed aggression in their flowing bodywork, race-inspired seating, and powerfully tuned engines, sending a compelling message: climb on, twist the throttle, release the MAGIC, and become Rocket Man. Hope there is more skill, ability, and luck than bravado and fantasy.

*You & Your Motorcycle: have you noticed roads turning into race tracks?*

Cars passed, but I was thrilled just to be in motion. Everyone, and COVID-19, was trying to kill me, but sixty miles from the dealership, I was still going easy and easy going.

The hills were alive with the sound of music. Of course, it made me,

Rejoice!

Motorcycle-less no more.

Hallelujah!

Like my dog Pearl, CTX was welcoming. Pearly is perpetually on the job, in charge of hellos. Have you seen the movie *Old Yeller*? Or *Marley and Me*?

My dog, Pearl.

*Truth About Motorcycles: JOY is like the love of a devoted dog.*

◆◆◆

West toward the Pacific Ocean, the terrain changes from arid desert and dry grassland to scrub before becoming rain forest on the ocean side of the mountain divide. The temperature fell as Therapy Bike climbed toward the Coquihalla Pass. By how much? No idea. My GT had a temperature indicator, but CTX did not. I wish it did; not knowing the temperature made me feel uneasy.

Information is a critical input to Motorcycle Pullover Judgement and I didn't want to execute an unnecessary stop. We'll descend before long. It'll be fine, I decided. *Why waste time pulling over if it's likely to be unnecessary? Drive on! Damn the torpedoes!*

*Truth About Motorcycles: small things (like knowing the temperature) matter when you're in charge of a motorbike.*

I failed to factor temperature gauge into my search. Also, no gear indicator, which explained why Left Foot was behaving like a WHO investigator searching for a virus leak.

The CTX is part cruiser, sportbike, and MAGIC—a true melting potter. Some say it's plain weird. Doesn't know what it wants to be. Ugly or beautiful? That's an artistic question. Motorbike taste is like painting with calculus; there is no correct answer. CTX appealed to me because of its difference. It lacks a temperature gauge and a gear indicator, but those would have been icing on the cake.

I sang to my machine as we rolled along on a perfect day, ♫you are so beautiful to me. You're everything I wanted, everything I need♫.

The Honda seat was uncomfortable, but YouTubers exaggerated. I've ridden on stock seats from Hell—CTX isn't one of them. Or did My Complainers distract me from the severity of my Ass Problem? Left Foot continued to whine about shifting; why didn't you get the automatic, dumbass? Ever heard of common sense? Shifting is horseshit when you have a titanium leg!

"Shut the fuck-up and hang on," I warned. "Or no more pills!"

Hanging on, is a skill motorcyclist must learn.

*You & Your Motorcycle: has your motorcycle taught you patience? How to hunker down & grind it out?*

I squirmed, trying to relieve the pressure on my sore butt cheek, aware of Rule #9 (An Irritant May Get Your Goat).

# CHAPTER 11 – ABOUT SITTING

Let's pull onto a sideroad for a moment and add a fact about motorcycles.

E Coli is sneaky. Disguised as tasty food, it upsets Stomach before moving on to Ass to spray diarrhea, resulting in a very messy, smelly Emergency Pullover if it happens while on-motorcycle. Motorcycles seats don't mess around—they get straight to business working directly on your ass.

*Truth About Motorcycles: bike seats can be JOY killers.*

*You & Your Motorcycle: has a bike seat tortured your ass?*

Spectators sit on cheap planks to watch never-ending kids' sports games. They're in heaven compared to sitting on a motorcycle. Fans aren't confined. Spectators can stand and scream, "Go, little Hornets Go! Murder the Bees! Kill the ref!" They shake their booties, massage them (to be polite, don't be too aggressive with your finger) until rear-ends are again happy-go-lucky.

On-motorcycle, riders are in seat jail. Hunker down

or initiate an Emergency Ass Pullover. I'm not an Insensitive Asshole and have experienced rear-end agony —particular motorcycle seat-ass combinations just don't work.

In the beginning, motorcycle seats were like church pews coupled with nonexistent suspensions. Instead of a sermon, bums bounced. Up. Down. Up. Down. Up. Pound. Up. Pound. Pound. Never a complaint. Bums had to be troopers back in the day. Rear ends sucked it up, did their jobs without a fuss; a few even enjoyed their spankings. Hit me harder. Give me a sermon! Teach me a lesson! Today we do not discriminate. Ass is a respected part of new-age anatomy with pampering rights equal to Hands, Face, or Brain.

Harley and Davidson didn't contemplate an Emergency Ass Pullover following their famous wave. "Ass problem? Try our new motorcycles. They're bum lovers. Way better than horseback."

WW1 dispatch riders sat on molded pieces of metal without complaint. Soldiers volunteered to put Triumph Model Hs up against carrier pigeons, snipers, barbed wire, European mud, and constant breakdowns. For them, it was full-on Rule #1: Everyone Is Trying to Kill Us. "There'll be plenty of time to focus on the Ass Problem once we achieve peace on Earth thanks to our war-to-end-all-wars strategy," the geniuses-in-charge assured motorcycle engineers.

Today bikers sit longer, believe in equal anatomy rights, and expect immediate solutions. *Total nonsense! We can travel to Mars, yet the Ass Problem has us stumped? Pure horseshit!* It's astonishing, but engineers know the only viable solution is, add a third wheel to enlarge seat mass.

Sit for minutes on a magnificent machine in the dealer's showroom, and "the seat seems fine. Why do people grumble? Could be higher, but otherwise, fine."

"Higher?" The sales consultant perks up. "Our comfort seat will fix that. Optional, but well worth it." Who wants to go with the low-down uncomfortable seat? "Just $999. Raises you almost an inch. The extra cushioning... out of this world! Everyone gets one. I'll have Dr. Tire add a comfort seat... shall I?" Manufactures can move riders up or down an inch to make knees and legs happy, but seat height cannot eliminate the Emergency Ass Pullover.

In the showroom, the OEM comfort seat sounds like the ticket. "With tax, documentation fee, dealer prep, installation, tax, and safety check," the sales consultant says. "Well worth $2,837." Yes, you think, because it will bring me closer to JOY. But the comfort seat isn't at all like sitting in your SUV. On the highway, both your derrière and your pocketbook grumble. "Would have been much worse had I cheap-ed out and gone with the standard seat," riders console themselves after sitting on their barely tolerable comfort seat.

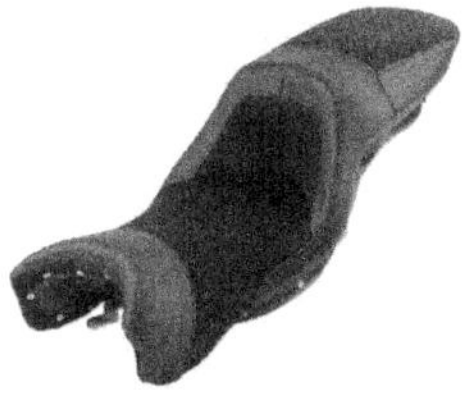

Motorcycle seats are simple—a small foam layer attached to a steel pan. Not like the large-framed, heated automobile La-Z-Boy that moves back and forth and up and down. Car seats are cozy; drivers can move around, sleep in one if they choose, dine, or have sex. On a motorcycle, Ass can shift an inch or two. After that, you're picking gravel out of your crack.

*Truth About Motorcycle: unlike cars, bikes are not motels.*

Hang a left at the Road to Fire and Brimstone and watch the Devil direct recruits to spend eternity on a motorcycle seat.

In Heaven, angels have solved the Ass Problem. "Has to do with light as a feather," they play on their harps. "Our cloud seat, plus a third wheel."

On Earth, riders may employ mitigation techniques. Use footpegs to boost their bums up, temporarily relieving pressure and pain. Standing or sliding around makes sense. Buttocks require circulation. Keep one compressed, with minimal shifting, and you'll develop Grumbling Anus. Follow the lead of care home attendants. "Time to flip comatose Helmetless Mary McGregor. She's grumbling."

Standing on road bikes is against the law in some jurisdictions—more four-wheel horseshit. "Let's keep the biker-idiots in ass hell," over-regulator-louts snicker.

Give Risk Mitigation Guy the middle finger!

Stand!

Raise your ass!

Scrape your pegs!

Two Wheels, Not Four (unless you suffer from hemorrhoids and rectal bleeding, in which case no JOY).

Add-ons (like memory foam, sheepskin, and air pads) may delay the onset of the Ass Problem, but they cannot overcome fundamental physics. Making a seat broader or longer, allowing the rider to shift helps but interferes with styling. Who wants a fat-ass seat on a crotch rocket? Not Marketing.

Riders of luxury tourers swear, "my ass is delighted." They're comparing their fat-ass seat to the one on their old naked bike, not to the recliner in their budget

SUV. A small fortune got them a seat nowhere near as comfortable as the beauty in the used Kia that cost much less. Still, by increasing mass, large touring machines are headed in the right direction—add a third wheel, even better. Ask a rider who's been on a luxury tourer for hours. They'll say "pretty damn nice, but I wouldn't say no to a good bum massage."

"It's like straddling a log," Marta says about her Guzzi. "But I like it." God blessed Marta with perfect Ass-Guzzi seat geometry. Let's call these elusive matches, Insensitive Assholes. Not only do Insensitives ride in bum bliss, they like to gloat. "Could go another four hours. Wanna do an Iron Butt?"

"Shut the fuck up! Where are my sore-ass pills, Insensitive Asshole?"

*You & Your Motorcycle: have you been forced to make an Emergency Ass Pullover? Standard, comfort, or custom seat?*

Engineers have backed away from the Ass Problem. "More upholstery than engineering," they say because they understand structural limitations. Like crocodiles as pets, it's not in the cards. Get off your bike. Move around. Exercise to improve blood flow. Lose weight. Get a three-wheeler with a fat-ass seat. Or, as Hannibal liked to say to his slaves, "fingers ready, girls?"

Upholstery can't overcome physics, but the attempt is a good money-maker. For a substantial sum, riders can buy a molded, sculptured, padded attractive seat that may improve weight distribution and reduce the severity of the Ass Problem, depending on what's going on down there. Custom seats mitigate but will not eliminate the

Ass Problem.

Soon, people will walk, dance, and sit on Mars. On Earth, the Ass Problem will persist. For an in-depth understanding of ass-seat structural limitations, read Sir Isaac's *Philosophiæ Naturalis Principia Mathematica.*

Kidding! Sir Isaac was an Insensitive Asshole like Marta.

No slave girls? Use different cushions to alter the seat-to-ass dynamics. Swallow pain medication. Try bum Botox injections. Pack a massage gun. Sign up for spanking sessions to harden Ass.

Brain asked, "can we go?"

Take Marta's advice: "My brain's in charge, not my rear end."

*Truth About Motorcycles: there are Emergency Ass Pullouts on the Road to Joy.*

# CHAPTER 12 – RIDING TO MERRITT

After a brief break, I rejoined the Coquihalla Highway, the largest of four routes connecting Vancouver to the interior of the province. Completed in 2006, the road defies nature.

*Truth About Motorcycles: most modern highways give riders the finger.*

"Build them straight and true," Risk Management instructs modern road builders.

"How about a Motorcycle JOY allowance," bikers plead?

"No J O Y ! Roads are for automobiles."

The Coquihalla (#5) isn't terrible as divided super highways go. Mother Nature's terrain made the No J O Y design principle tricky; there are many ups and downs and arounds. It's perfect for Constant Walkers driving therapy bikes.

The road builders cleared the strips between the highway and the forest extra-wide. Do as instructed, watch for wildlife, and chances are, you won't hit a bear, moose, stag, mountain lion.

Evil mole rats couldn't hide close to the road, so I sang. ♫ Get your motor running. Heading down the highway ♬.

*Truth About Motorcycles: on-motorcycle, everyone's a diva or a divo.*

Luciano Pavarotti, Whitney Houston, Snoop Dogg, Adele, Ed Sheeran, Johnny Cash ... take your pick—you can be anyone you want to be.

Here's the song I composed and sang on the Coquihalla:

♫ Climb back on; all is well,
An hour down the road and all is well,
Deer are nothing; they do not count.
Well, around the corner.
Well, down the road.
Climb back on, and all is well ♫

*Truth About Motorcycles: songs composed on-motorcycle don't have to be good.*

Musical talent is not required to ride, but what about being in decent physical shape?

Is riding like bowling—anyone can do it, even recovering decrepits? How often do you see bowlers at the gym pumping iron? Never. That's why they bowl.

NimRods (from *Scrape Your Lists*: "... people unable to comprehend motorcycles ...") believe that anyone dumb enough to want to kill themself can ride a motorbike. At the bowling alley, stumble, and it's a gutter ball. Wobble going into a corner on-motorcycle, and you may die.

*Truth About Motorcycles: it's hard to find J O Y if you're in poor shape.*

Fitness fanaticism is not required, but riding is safer (because it increases Ability) and more enjoyable when your body cooperates.

I know—do not take your body for granted!

Also remember the three As Awareness, Ability, and Accountability (from *Scraping Pegs*).

The way a wounded cowboy clings to a horse is how I approached climbing back on. Sheer determination. Do what you can and don't fall off. I knew I couldn't lie in a hospital bed with Bunny, scoot, stumble short distances, then close to a year later, climb back on and be in charge. My Ability would be below SQUID. On-motorcycle, a lot is going on. Arm strength to control the bars. Hands to grip and work the throttle, brake, and clutch. The heart and lungs pump blood to provide energy. Leg and feet strength to shift the center of balance. Flexible joints and spine to absorb bumps. Eyes are constantly processing information. Sharp reflexes. Tough ass. A well-balanced state of mind.

*You & Your Motorcycle: does your body need a tune-up?*

As part of Project Climb Back On, I prepared and chose a relaxed route home, an easy day's distance, on major highways, spread over two days. Little traffic thanks to the Essential Travel decree.

*You & Your Motorcycle: do you dial your ride (duration and difficulty) to your physical comfort zone?*

An hour out of Kelowna, I pulled over, stretched, and sent a text: Bringing baby home. [smiley face].

Getting a bike is like bringing a newborn home from the hospital (unless you're a dad, and mom does all the work, in which case, getting a bike requires more effort and dedication). As a responsible new Motorcycle Parent, necessities must be provided. Throttle lock went on my list, along with hard bags and a temperature gauge. Formula (oil type), must be sorted out. Like raising a baby or a pet, machines require attention. With each new bike, the process repeats. With babies, toys and clothes are donated and handed down. The new family sedan can remain as-is. Motorcycles are more complex.

*Truth About Motorcycles: being a Motorcycle Parent is a privilege and requires work.*

Dr. Peggy read my words aloud. When she got to the part about parenting, she stopped and scowled. “Really? You're going to compare a motorcycle to a child? Shame, shame on you!" She looked at Dori as if to say, you poor thing.

Russia appeared to be invading Scandinavia on Dr. Peggy's cheek.

I grinned like a nutter. *How many motorcycles or children have you brought home, Pissy? Zero!* Thanks to Pearly, Bunny, and my kids, I know a thing or two about bonding and care—don't be a sanctimonious, barren, electric car, witch. Pearl and Bunny have everything they need, and both my kids can change a tire!

Peggy means well, and I shouldn't allow her to get my goat. The world may end at any minute. Grendel Putin may push the nuclear button. Mother Nature may unleash gigantic natural disasters. The State of California may neglect to put a warning label on something risky. I'll shove an injector up my nose if God says, "Let's review your Dr. Peggy Test, shall we? Are you familiar with the saying, what goes around comes around?"

Never take forgiveness for granted!

I wondered if I could buy designer tweezers in Merit? They'd make a thoughtful gift. Surprise Pissy so she can yank the hairs from her witch's mole.

Other things to buy? How about a tall windscreen for CTX? CTX comes with a shorty. I held my left hand up to check for air blasts; in my shitty helmet, the noise problem was worse than the Ass Problem. Replacement windscreens are tricky. Naked bike owners may be right: windscreens belong on cars.

*You & Your Motorcycle: have you found a good custom windscreen?*

A new helmet would add to my JOY. Choosing one is tricky. Most retailers don't allow helmet road tests. Buyers must rely on YouTube, where there is no consensus. Once the helmet is on your charge card, pull it over your coconut, go for a rip, and find out if it sucks or not. Did your inexperienced YouTuber get it right? Shouldn't reviewers be compelled to disclose credentials and reach a fact-based consensus? Trust the Qualified Consensus Channel endorsed by motorcycle engineers. You bet I would.

Politicians don't have to be competent or truthful to run a nation or a town, but motorcycle design is serious business.

*You & Your Motorcycle: can you imagine a motorcycle designed and built by politicians?*

Besides wind noise, my helmet sported a major faux pas—pasted on the back was a large BMW label, a self-imposed styling miscue caused by a brand switch-up. A company rep gave me the sticker at a rally when I was a Beemer Boy. I also had a Harley screaming eagle on my bike; I like its look, and the diversity message proclaimed: Motorcycle Progressive on Board.

Now I'm a Honda Nice Guy, but the mismatch had me looking like a Chevy Silverado owner wearing a Ford F150 cap. There goes that mismatched dude on the weird bike. Sportbike or cruiser? Honda Nice Guy or Beemer Boy? t doesn't add up. Where's the State of California supposed to put its warning label?

Another issue to resolve, that, along with the temperature gauge debacle.

*Truth About Motorcycles: State of California warning labels should say:*

WARNING
Forget About It.
Just Ride!

Ride! Let everything Life, the Bully throws at you blow away.

**Ride until J O Y finds a way.**

Ride to forget all the bad things the State of California sticks its labels on.

*You & Your Motorcycle: does riding help you forget all the jabber?*

◆◆◆

Watching for deer on the Coquihalla is not like travelling on B.C. Ferries where captains make announcements: "watch for Orca whales on the port side." Except for navy tourists, passengers scratch their heads, "port?" There is an implied message on the Coquihalla Highway: watch for giant rats on both sides because the dirty buggers want to kill you!

A stag, in my eyes.

Despite their false narratives and Bambi disguises, deer are wicked. In farmers' fields, they wipe out our food supply. In league with COVID, deer want to take us down!

Turtles are nice. They cross highways but never target vehicles. Out of respect, motorcycles go around turtles. Cagers love to crush turtles and motorcycles. It's Vehicle Based Violence.

Why can't all animals be loving like Bunny, Pearl, turtles, and squirrels? Buddha, are you onboard? Pull your blissfulness out of the ABS sensor and explain this to me: how does compassion fit in a world where survival mandates one species must kill another to survive? And why are despicable creatures, like deer, thriving while peaceful motorcycle loving creatures, like the Oahu tree snail, are going extinct?

It's Mother Nature's way, is the excuse.

That is, pure horseshit! It's more complicated. I don't have a clue. Who knows what eternity has in mind?

"That is why we have bikes," Marta says.

I rode while in the forests that wall parts of the Coquihalla animals dined on one another. In another land, Mother Nature was encouraging boas to choke down cherished, adorable breathing pets. What a horrid, nasty cunt Mother can be!

Why didn't the Almighty make all animals vegan?

The answer, of course, is: because eventually humans would taste smokey brisket BBQ and the Vegan

Commandment would be shot to Hell.

Perplexing questions like these arise on-motorcycle. Then they're blown away in the wind. Plus, I was wearing my tee shirt that says:

**I Don't Care!**

◆ ◆ ◆

Unlike the two-lane secondary road where Horace crouched waiting for me, road crews do an excellent job keeping the sides of the Coquihalla clear. Still, I was part collision avoidance sensor, constantly scanning the area between the road and the forest. Ping. Ping. Blip. Ping. Ping. Go left! Looks like a turtle crossing.

Traffic noise warns intelligent animals, like elephants and owls, to stay off busy highways. Loud pipes help emphasize the point. Turtles are nice, but dumb plus hard of hearing.

*Truth About Motorcycles: riders don't worry about hitting elephants.*

Mostly giant mole rats.

Red Beauty passed small lakes. Little treasures. Does anyone stop to swim, catch trout, or look for turtles to make turtle soup on hot days? The lakes are not easily accessible, which makes them mysterious. You can't pull over on a two-wheeler and hike into one, clad in armor and wearing space boots. You can't launch a canoe or even an inflatable raft. There are many things you cannot do when you travel on two wheels. You must pass attractions automobiles and their passengers are free to enjoy.

*Truth About Motorcycles: riders must make sacrifices.*

"If you love your motorcycle, it's not a big deal," Conrad says.

The SUV I was tucked behind maintained a comfortable pace. To test acceleration, I twisted the throttle and pulled out to pass. I expected little, given the engine size. We flew by. No problemo! Well, not fly as in a 737 Max or Kawasaki Z H2, but faster than a Prius, TS-125, or a bi-plane.

I pulled to the right, out of the fast lane, ahead of the SUV.

Acceleration was adequate, given my newly adopted riding style. Not a rocket, but CTX gets the job done the way a motorcycle should. It has guts, genuine biker muscle—more than enough to give the SUV the finger.

Perhaps I won't need a large screen if I buy a better helmet, I contemplated? Large screens often disappoint; unless they're so humongous, they look like they belong on the Jetson's spaceship.

While I noodled, thinking about helmets, windscreens, and turtles, the grey over gray SUV passed me in a hurry to arrive somewhere. He looked at CTX and snickered. I wondered if the cager was irked by my out-of-place BMW sticker? Or noticed CTX is a standard, not the man-bun model? Probably not. Cagers don't see much. Too busy texting, eating, running over turtles, playing Halo, and running into motorbikes. Cager Based Violence.

I considered passing but stayed behind the safety. Brain Brian (right brain) warned, we're not up to doing that

Born to be Wild thing.

Passing, wind noise, Mother Nature, temperature, the Ass Problem, gadgetry; nothing bothered Mr. Pirsig, the *Zen and the Art of Motorcycle Maintenance* guy. He was old school, focused on investigating the meaning of quality and do-it-yourself maintenance. He wasn't concerned about physical comfort, dual-clutch transmissions, appearance, or boas swallowing monkeys alive. Mr. Pirsig turned his nose up at farkles; all you need is the included toolset, a coat hanger, duct tape, and a sewing kit. Facts like MPH, dB levels, and crash statistics did not factor into Robert's inquiry into values. *Listen to what your engine is telling you. It's better to Travel than to Arrive*—that sort of nonsense. Me, I like to know the temperature.

There's a segment of riders more eccentric than Mr. Pirsig. Let's call them Oddballs. They rarely have nice bikes, have worn the same gear for a decade, and are not helpful when choosing a quiet helmet. Most Oddballs pull modified trailers or have untrimmed beards. They say things like "go slow to reduce wind noise and buffeting. Enjoy the scenery. Travel and arrive." They're always smiling, haven't showered in days, and carry enormous paper maps. Oddballs have tire thread wear down to a science. They may offer a bite of their day-old roadkill sandwich or go ballistic at the mention of ethanol in gasoline. Engaging storytellers, but know this: Oddballs travel through black holes. Bob and I were experts at *please excuse us. We have something important to do, Mr. Oddball, sir.* Oddballs always look puzzled when their audience disbands but soon gather a new one——they're natural buskers.

I wondered if I'd meet an Oddball on my trip.

◆◆◆

Around suppertime, we pulled into the Quality Inn, Merritt. My Complainers were delighted. I stepped down, feeling like Sir Edmund standing on the top of Everest. "I made it!" Then he instructed Sherpa Tenzing Norgay to plant the Union Jack.

"But you're a New Zealander, and I'm not British. It'll be a branding screwup."

"The ensign sucks," Edmund replied. "I didn't climb all the way up here just to take my photo with an ugly flag. A picture that will make people ask, whose flag is that? Or who's that guy beside you?"

Tenzing anchored the Union Jack.

"Now, move out of the way." Tenzing snapped a photograph!

"I did it," Sir Edmund exclaimed!"

The two men hugged and rejoiced. Then Tenzing said, "If we're lucky, we won't be killed going down."

I sort of hugged CTX.

We've done it, Red Beauty!

Thank you, my friend!

Thank you, motorcycle engineers.

Thank you, Essential Travel.

Thank you, Buddha.

Like Sir Edmund and Tenzing, I'd conquered my fears, risked death, and felt the MAGIC on top of the world.

I parked CTX in a semi-sheltered spot, close to my room,

on the sidewalk, protected from reckless cagers. Thanks to COVID-19, there were few guests at the Quality Inn. "Don't cluster together," the war office decreed.

Motorcycles are not to park on walkways, but who cares when you're at war? *Yes, I realize they may wipe us out, but that's no excuse for parking your bike on our sidewalk, sir. Are you an Oddball?* Come on! No sensible hospitality professional would say that.

It's vital to display commitment when a rider accepts ownership of a new machine. Spending night one alone outside was bad enough—like bringing a child home from the hospital nursery and leaving it on the doorstep.

"Thanks for getting me here. It restored my faith," I told Red Beauty. *It's all I can do to keep from pushing you into my room.*

“I will be your rock,” Beauty promised.

*Is that heaven in your pegs?*

◆◆◆

I sent a photo of CTX to my WhatsApp family group: meet Therapy Bike. I'm on the mend, already feeling much better.

*Truth About Motorcycles: Motorcycle Therapy is impossible to explain to NimRods. They look at you as if you're an Oddball from the Osiris solar system.*

When I switched the light off, the left side of my body began its slow throbbing reminders. I swallowed one of my beautiful prescription pills.

# CHAPTER 13–ABOUT TRIBALISM

Size matters. Lying on my motel bed, I wondered what my friends would think when I drove up on my new bike. "It's more fun to ride a small bike fast," I'd say. It's what tiddler owners preach.

"Nonsense," large rally adventurer and cruiser owners scoff.

"Riding close to the ground is exhilarating... like driving a go-cart skimming over the surface."

"Riders on small bikes look up at big bikes and wish they were on one."

For penises, breasts, and motorcycle engines, size matters. Like the state of Palestine and glaciers, I was dwindling—down 100cc and 500cc from my last two machines. Shrink, and you become uneasy around the big boys.

Downsize, switch brands, change styles and you risk being cast out.

*Truth About Motorcycles: size matters.*
*Also brand and style.*

I'm made of flesh and blood and want acceptance in a like-minded community. Any group without "neo" or "UN" in their name will do. When I bought a therapy bike, I became the North Korea of two-wheel machines. A potential Oddball. Misunderstood. Not a team player. It's not a sportbike. Not a cruiser. Nope, not an adventure, dirt, bagger, custom, racer, trike, or mini. Is there a tribe for me, I worried as I lay on the motel bed wishing Bunny the Consoler was with me? A group willing to my odd machine?

I have Motorcycle Friends who wouldn't dream of betraying their brand, club, or style. They are as devoted as the Jehovah's Witnesses who remained steadfast after their prophecies fell short. *So what if the world didn't end in 1914 or 1994? We'll adjust the date. Pass the old prophecies off as calculation errors. We're not mathematicians, for Jehovah's sake. Nothing at all to do with our logic or the size and style of our bible. We're sticking with our brand no matter what! There's no need to join the Pentecostals.*

Perhaps the Pentecostals have something to offer and should be checked out? It couldn't hurt to kick their tires and sit in their pews. Followers of religions possess blind faith, which is why they refuse to swap doctrines. It's the same with many bikers.

Me, I'm not steadfast like Guzzi Marta or members of the Hells Angels. Bikers like to unite with similar machines. After long hours of solo riding, we pull over and come together in a union of brand or style. But what about me?

Here's another fact: motorcycling is tribal. The political science term is "multiculturalism" as opposed to "melting pot." Multiculturalism says, let's all be friends, but stay in your lane and preserve your identity. Don't blend in too much. Rarely do you see Harleys and BMWs side by side. That's practicing multiculturalism; it thrives in the motorcycle community and liberal societies.

Early on, I thought nothing of switching up. I was a naïve, open-minded motorcyclist. But, remaining a melting potter is tough. Motorcycle multiculturalism constantly pulls. *Now that you have some experience, you must choose a brand or style and join a tribe.*

*You & Your Motorcycle: have you belonged to different tribes?*

Four-wheelers went the melting pot route. Trucks mix easily with cars. Fords with Mazdas. Hybrids with diesels. SUVs with vans. Cager life is simplistic. *What's the big deal? It's just another stupid car. Don't care if it is electric; still a car, buddy.* Step out of a Chevy or a Ford, and cagers detach from their vehicle choice. On rare occasions, a branded ball cap, but that's it. Step off a big cruiser or a KTM, and it's like the occupants passed through two different wardrobe departments.

Historians suggest motorcycle tribalism has its roots in clubs and gangs. Today, liberals start those All-Welcome groups. A gracious gesture, but it's swimming upstream. At All-Welcomes, human nature prevails, baffling the well-intentioned organizers. Riders sneak out from under the equality umbrella. Soon they're clumped together in subgroups. Sportbikers over here. Cruisers here. Expensive machines in this corner, fixers over here. Scooter guy? Who the hell invited you? Get the fuck out of here or stand in the corner with the Trikes Matter Group.

"What the fuck?" wokes shout. "What's wrong with you typecasting assholes?"

Motorcycle Segregation, buddy.

Superficial declarations like "All-Welcome" cannot overcome human nature. Yes, there are interludes of mingling at mixed gatherings, but tribalism is a compulsion.

*You & Your Motorcycle: have you switched tribes and had to reorient?*

I'm part Loner-by-Choice. We're strong-willed. Confident. Seldom mistaken for Oddballs. Loners ride nice bikes and dress well. Loners-by-Choice prefer to maintain distance. We ride solo because "it's peaceful and enhances J O Y , like being a monk. You call all the shots." Loners appreciate encounters at gas stations, cafes, viewpoints, campsites, motels, and parking lots. Loners-By-Choice is a tribe, but like blue whales, they don't swim in pods.

I have a tire in the Loners' camp.

"We're all part of the biker community," Bob used to say.

*Truth About Motorcycles: on-motorcycle, riders are a family. When we climb off, not so much.*

Like families, bikers have differences.

Motorcycle's unique powers cannot circumvent human nature. The Almighty made us herd animals, but unlike cagers who must drive to meet their sports team, church group, gun club, or political party, riders climb on and become part of a brotherhood/sisterhood. Unlike divisive tribes like religion or politics, motorcycling has an honest unifier—MAGIC. On-motorcycle, it can transcend our differences. Then riders climb down and step back. *Isn't your bike a little too small? Somewhat of the wrong style? Have you considered my brand? A therapy bike, you say, hmmm.* That sort of thing.

I had to find my new lane; my identity as a proud Therapy Bike-Honda Nice Guy. It was a worry, but every biker climbs on alone. Differences disappear in the wind. I ride and let my tee shirt do the talking.

**I Really Don't Care!**

# CHAPTER 14 – RIDING THE COQUIHALLA I

On the Quality Inn TV, personalities worried we were close to Armageddon. The people-responsible-for-organization, were blasted for not being organized. We were "under resourced" and "too lenient" or "verging on totalitarian." It was a huge jabber fest. I hit OFF.

The following morning, the Quality Inn parking lot was like a motorcycle store lot in the dead of winter —desolate. No fellow travelers asking, how you do'in? Where you from? Where you been? No checking oil, cleaning metal, dislodging bugs, or packing panniers. No preparing to depart. Pandemics are quiet wars: no artillery bombardments, marching bands, or exploding fuel storage tanks.

"It's a funny war," I said, looking CTX over.

It was 9:30 AM when Red Beauty rolled off the motel's sidewalk. "Kickstands up, 7:30 AM," was the standard marshaling order when I rode in a group led by Marc and Judy. It didn't matter when I wanted to leave. In a pack, you must conform. Motorcycle gangs do not tolerate lone wolves.

"Builds character," Bob used to say.

"Bullshit," the loner half of me said.

As CTX rolled toward the motel exit, I read: Breakfast Included, on a sign above the office.

Except it wasn't.

The authorities had placed *Included Breakfast* on their *Pandemic Banned List.* No exceptions! If you're traveling on Essential Business, does it not follow that breakfast is an imperative? An indispensable necessity? Missing church okay, but breakfast? Political scientists smarten up! You ignored basic nutrition. Shame on you! We were at war. Try not to constantly fuck things up! At least get breakfast right! "The most important meal of the day," nutritionists insist. How are we supposed to win a damn war on empty stomachs?

No stale bagels to dunk in weak coffee. No tiny containers with runny yogurt, packets of instant oatmeal, waffle machines, or bruised bananas. I'm a frequent breakfast skipper, so it was only irritating due to the inn's sign—Breakfast Included. Bullshit!

Should I pull over, I debated? March into the office as Zatoichi Warhammer? Might the front desk staff flip the conversation—"did you park on the sidewalk, Mr. Warhammer?"

War makes a mess of things, even meals, but it's incumbent on citizens not to nitpick. Give our leaders the benefit of the doubt. Any leader can make a mistake like "I did not have sexual relations... or wait, maybe I did." Or, "Definitely weapons of mass destruction." That sort of thing.

Perhaps the misleading sign was a tactic? What strategists call a decoy meant to throw the enemy off?

While humanity sheltered at home, full of breakfast and fit as fiddles, the witless virus hung around motel dining rooms waiting for victims that would never arrive. Clever us. Stupid germs!

Really dumb germs: why target the elderly with pre-existing conditions? How foolish are you, Mother Nature? Aim your tiny germs at childbearing-aged females, Dumbass! That's the key to an effective human cleanse.

The COVID virus was asinine. Mother is not a good strategist. When the last human host suffocated, would the germs live?

Humanity was up against Dumb and Dumber. Still our leaders appeared to be over whelmed.

"It's our planet," I shouted into the wind, visor open, as CTX rolled through Merritt to get back on Highway 5. God gave it to us, along with free will, to do as we please. We'll damn well carry on doing whatever our top dogs tell us to do, like not eating breakfast at motels.

Do you think we're out to get you, Mother? Have you not heard of Earth Day (April 22)? Buzzard's Day (March 15)? European Day of Parks (May 24)? International E-Waste Day (October 14)? How many more days does the United Nations have to toss your way before you get the message? Are you dopey? We're the intelligent species with quite an edge on elephants. Why are you trying to cleanse yourself of us? Do you think ravens, chimpanzees, pigs, or dolphins will do a better job? Will they pass a climate accord (Paris, 2015)? What about a World Summit on Sustainable Development (2002, Johannesburg)? COP26 (2021 Glasgow)? COP28 (2023, United Arab Emirates). The list is long, but the point is, we're on the job passing agreement after agreement and tirelessly rolling out official days and holding conferences in your honor. We're doing one hell of a job, so back the fuck off, motherfucker!

Where's my bleach gun?

◆◆◆

A giant rat lay in its bloodbath in the eastbound fast lane outside the town of Merritt. The sight made me, rejoice!

No sign of what hit it, but, judging from the devastation, it had a lot more mass than a CTX. Maybe a Harley, Jeep, or Mack truck?

Given road safety experts are constantly warning vehicles to watch for deer, do you think they'd give me dispensation to carry a handlebar-mounted weapon? One with a mole rat deer sensor. I'd happily blow the vile creatures to smithereens, like in the movie Machete. I'd be Danny Trejo, payment enough to witness exploding deer and the warm feeling one gets from giving back. My proposal would state, "deer, and/or including any PETA members interfering with operations."

I know. I know. Even though the Committee on Innovation solicited proposals ("there is no such thing as a silly idea in the innovation business"), my submission will never see the light of day. Firearms are political kryptonite and "motorcycles are not on the table."

"Roads and traffic have been around for many decades, but deer have absorbed little knowledge," I would have pointed out to the committee in my twenty-minute oral presentation. "Deer have proven to be incapable of evolving and learning basic highway safety best practices. Despite Mr. Darwin's thesis, they remain too stupid to stay off our roadways. Sadly, the only answer is: blow them to smithereens." And then the kicker, to get their attention: "every year, deer damage thousands of automobiles."

◆◆◆

It was a beautiful morning, made even more delightful by the sight of one less stag. I wore a Cheshire cat grin.

A perfect 22C/72F when I left the motel. Onboard, I had to guess at the temperature. Showers were possible later in the day, closer to the coast. A high mountain pass lay ahead. Exactly where unpredictable weather likes to hang out. It's tough to choose motorcycle clothes in changeable conditions. In a car, flip on the AC, heater, or wipers. Sit back and relax. No worries.

My direction was southwest, toward the town of Hope, less than an hour and a half from the Quality Inn. Hope would be my brunch stop. Coffee, at the very least. Not that I needed caffeine, but breaks are necessary to guard against complaints, especially from Butt. Maybe I'd swallow an anti-anxiety pill to keep my agrizoophobia and monophobia at bay.

The COVID war office also fucked up motorcycle rest stops. Close cafés to cagers, fine. Reduced seating, okay. Defend against the cleanse, of course. But, for the love of God, accommodate Motorcycle Scouts on Essential Business! It's not safe to ride forever without relaxing breaks. Were they trying to kill us?

*Truth About Motorcycles: bikers need*

*places to sit and eat off-motorcycle.*

*You & Your Motorcycle: while riding, do you ever ask yourself, do the ideologues-in-charge have the slightest clue?*

"Don't write, 'the plan doesn't accommodate bikers down as a con," the chairperson instructed when drafting the committee's pandemic restrictions. "Motorcyclists are irrelevant. We're looking at the big picture."

Breathe. In. Out. In. Out. Let the wind blow uneasiness away.

All is well on the Road to Joy.

Moto-Skiveezes (padded riding shorts) helped defend against the Ass Problem. I wear underwear, so why not Moto-Skiveezes? I like to think they help. Today is better than yesterday, thanks to the Ass Problem team at Moto-Skiveezes.

"Moto-Skiveezes. Moto-Skiveezes." As a mantra, Moto-Skiveezes has motorcycle relevance and works much better than chanting something like Om pah, Om Mani Padme Hum, or Om Shanti.

I also wore a neck collar, a cheap medical brace. The Horace incident didn't affect Neck. I use the collar as a sound barrier; it stops wind noise from rushing up from the bottom of crap helmets. I've used it with different brain buckets. It's effective but makes me look like an Oddball.

I looked forward to resting in Hope before tackling the long freeway that delivers traffic to Vancouver. For my second stop, I'd picked a helmet shop in the suburbs. Traveling is more enjoyable when you insert waypoints, especially ones that involve motorcycles.

The divided highway leading to Hope twists over a high mountain pass that runs alongside canyons and snow-topped peaks. Waterfalls decorate rock cliffs. From rolling grassland to snow-topped mountains, then down to the coastal plain bordering the Fraser River on its way to the Pacific. It's dramatic: best viewed on a motorcycle. In a car, if you've been before, the grandeur is easily dismissed. Same old beauty. Sure, it's lovely, but so predictable, like watching *Machete* for the fifth time. Why bother paying attention? More exciting travel videos are on YouTube; nature spiced up with a human touch.

I followed a BMW SUV traveling at 84 MPH. The speed limit is 75 MPH (1 kph = 0.62137119223 mph). The SUV ran in the fast lane, even though the slow lanes were clear. I stayed put in the correct lane, following. CTX handled the speed well. On other bikes, I'd have zoomed by, driven by this loop: never, never, never miss an opportunity to overtake! Never follow, always lead.

*Truth About Motorcycles: broken bones change your perspective.*

Eventually, the BMW pulled into the correct lane, doing 130 km/hour (1 mph = 1.609344 km/h). Thank you, Mr. BMW SUV, for traveling in the correct God damn lane! Don't you know we're at war and discipline is mandatory? It's not the time to be fucking with sensible traffic rules. It's called doing your part to preserve our way of life. Did I make a scene over the Included Breakfast? No, I sucked it up for Team Humanity, as you should.

*You & Your Motorcycle: do you often think,*

*who issued that cager a driver's license?*

I felt safe in the appropriate lane with an advance car blocking, but then BMW turned right and disappeared at the next exit. A few cars flew by. I passed trucks and several slower cars. The traffic was going too fast or too slow to lock into CTX's sweet spot. There wasn't another ideal candidate, like Mr. BMW SUV to tail. I remained at smooth revs, traveling exposed, without a lead blocker, an open-field runner.

My radar scanned the sides of the road for wildlife as more signs warned: **Watch for Deer**. I did. I know from experience: workers don't plunk signs down just to have something to report on timesheets—there is solid research behind every **Watch for Deer** sign.

"I laugh at you, evil ones." *May an elephant stomp on Bambi's head and an orca snatch Horace's brother off the shore. May Mack trucks squish your babies*!

Wildlife is on Earth's side, even turtles. We're busy trying to save the Oahu tree snail, proclaiming UN Days like mad, and developing deer whistles, but to the animal kingdom, we're Nazis conducting a holocaust. "Go, Mother Go," they cheer! "Step up your game! Have your anacondas slither in at night and swallow their babies! We're with you, Mother Nature. Crush Team Humanity! Give us our planet back! Go COVID go!"

Always assume wildlife wants to eat you. Or eat your food.

CTX purred like Bunny, revving low and cruising easy. I disconnected. Nothing mattered. The wind blew my thoughts away. No temperature gauge - gone. Motorcycles don't rate an official UN hour - gone. Wildlife is against us - gone. No included breakfast - gone.

"Moto-Skiveezes. Moto-Skiveezes. Moto-Skiveezes."
I felt it. The JOY of Motorcycles.

# CHAPTER 15 - RIDING THE COQUIHALLA II

CTX climbed through thickening clouds and cooler air. The GT Horace took down would have displayed the temperature, but Honda engineers took the opposite approach. Use your noggins drivers. Don't rely on the machine. CTX has a soul but not a temperature gauge.

Perhaps a drop of 5C since leaving the motel because of higher elevation? Despite doing the math (F = [Celsius x 1.8] + 32), my temperature observations remained as reliable as a poorly installed tire plug. Maybe the temperature was holding steady, and my senses were dropping?

*You & Your Motorcycle: should meteorology training be added to the Parking Lot Cone School curriculum?*

Had I run into an Arctic blast, a nor'easter, or a monsoon, the call would have been straightforward, even for a SQUID. No judgment required: a solid, must pullover situation. Climb off, open bags, and fart around getting geared up. Climb back on and head off.

But what if you go through all that rigmarole and the weather doesn't turn nasty? You travel a short distance down the mountain to pleasant weather, only to pull over and fart around in the reverse order. What a monumental waste of time and effort! You played Motorcycle Roulette and lost.

Loser!

Dud!

Flop!

Pullover Judgement is a tricky business. Don't get down on yourself if you make the wrong call. Best bet: never take the weather for granted.

Spinning the wheel has no appeal without the risk of losing.

It was an easy call for Sir Edmund on his way up Mount Everest. He pulled over just before the Khumbu ice fall and said, "Gear me up, Tenzing. Don't fart around too long." Their schedule was tight, and the pair would perish if not bundled up. But, on June 24, 2020, on the Coquihalla, it was a dicey call. Not a mandatory, clearly required pullover. So I forged ahead, up the pass like Hannibal, headlong into sudden changes, giving risk mitigation the finger.

*Truth About Motorcycles: riders face challenges cagers are oblivious to.*

*You & Your Motorcycle: how's your Pullover Judgement? Are you cautious or do you like to spin the Motorcycle Roulette wheel?*

Gear up and be prepared is the smart choice (like eating three peanut M&M's instead of thirty-three, but my M&M judgment can also be shaky).

"If people understood risk management, there would be no motorcycles," Risk Management Guy says. "If folks were smart, they'd be in tanks where Pullover Judgment is seldom an issue." NimRods don't get it: making the call is part of the attraction. Pullover Judgment is a mental exercise. Try your hand at meteorological forecasting. Conduct a risk-benefit analysis. Make your best call, and then, for extra fun, play Motorcycle Roulette.

Cagers don't think. They plow on in a daze, listening to yacht rock, looking for turtles to crush and bikers to kill.

*Truth About Motorcycles: there's more to understand about riding than can be taught at Parking Lot Cone School.*

I often elect not to pull over.

Forward the Light Brigade!

Spin the Motorcycle Roulette wheel!

There are multiple overhead electronic signs on the Coquihalla Highway. Their primary purpose is to communicate winter driving conditions. During the COVID War, information officers had repurposed them. **Avoid Non-Essential Travel**. One hour into my ride, and I'd seen the same information four times! It was a bombardment! No wonder we were winning! One message followed another, like when Britannia ruled the seas. Dominance clearly established.

Was there no other important information to share? Did all other messaging fly out the window when the virus attacked? How about displaying the temperature? Information to help with Motorcycle Pullover Judgment. Or where motorcycle scouts might get a sit-down snack? Is the enemy grey or gray? Why do we need both imperial and those small gallons and what's involved in converting them to litres? Or is it liters? Should I ask the UN Committee on Standardization.

I pictured sign committee members and a Dr. Peggy type communication consultant huddled together through a series of long crisis meetings, complaining about their expense account meals while they hammered out the wording that ended up on the overhead signs. The heated debates before the group turned in its recommendation. The to and fro over word choices, like "avoid" and "non-essential." Both are ambiguous, but the committee concluded: "they strike the right balance." The outlaw who proposed "Stay the Fuck Home," right out of the gate, lost out. In modern warfare, civility matters. "Please Stay the Fuck Home" may have been acceptable?

Despite the committee's excellent work, travelers paid no attention. Not one cager wheeled around after reading the signs. Disgraceful! It didn't matter that repetition is the key to learning, travelers did not reconsider.

I had suffered from motorcycle abstinence, was dangerously uneasy and in need of therapy, and had sacrificed the included breakfast without making a fuss. My credibility was beyond reproach. Travel was fundamental to my existence. How do you get a therapy bike home without travailing? I was a highly developed social distancing practitioner with my head in a helmet and body in the wind. When will I receive my Outstanding Distancing by an Oddball Award, I wondered, even though mislabeled thanks to my neck collar?

RVs towing compact cars rolled under the **Avoid Non-Essential Travel** signs. Surely, they're not all suffering from Motorcycle-lessness or Tragic Accident Syndrome? Where could they be going that's essential?

I was grateful to the respectful, those who remained off the highways. Long stretches of traffic-less asphalt ensured a peaceful, healing journey filled with Pandemic Motorcycle JOY.

*Truth About Motorcycles: JOY loves sparse traffic.*

Have you seen those short ads that interrupt shows on streaming services? You're watching a nice movie like *The Sound of Music* with your kitty, and suddenly an advertisement for a new, improved turkey baster interrupts the musical. BOOM! Your mind flips to gobblers and the baster industry. Then back to the movie, where again, ♫the hills are alive with the sound of music♫ Turkeys-Alpine Meadows-Basters-The Sound of Music.

Flashbacks like that interrupted my ride. Except instead of basters I got Antlers. Pain. The Stephen King Soundtrack. Danny Trejo on a machete rampage. Sirens. Humongous Needles. Demolished GT. My old life dripping out of the oil drain plug, followed by the realization that a second crash would be akin to Tenzing Norgay tripping Sir Edmund on the summit. "Who's the famous one now, Eddie?"

Like an interrupted streaming movie, JOY always returned.

♫The hills filled my heart with the sound of music.

My heart wanted to sing every song it heard ♫

Until another Horace image played and interrupted.

I concentrated on a large sign before the summit. Very important information: **High Mountain Pass, Expect Sudden Changes.**

I did because it's locked into my Motorcycle State of Mind: always expect sudden changes. You never know when a cager or deer will try to kill you.

I had a lot to do. Avoid non-essential travel, watch for deer, guess temperature, and now, "Expect Sudden Changes." How much can a solo rider contend with? The Expect Sudden Changes advisory tipped the scale in favor of pulling over and gearing up.

Fuck it!

I didn't stop.

Once more I spun the Motorcycle Roulette wheel.

A renegade cloud descended, and unexpectedly, it began to drizzle. A bad omen, but my gear could withstand drizzle.

As Red Beauty continued its climb, I guessed, a further two-degree temperature drop on one of the two scales. Time to turn on the heated grips. WHOA! Honda engineers? No temperature gauge. No gear indicator. Now no heated grips! You went all-in on the, you're on your own buddy approach, didn't you?

As the outlaw Hannibal approached the Alps on his elephant, he ordered a slave girl to "cuddle up. I'm getting cold." The old ways should be cherished, but on CTX, I was on my own.

If the drizzle turned into a full-on mountain downpour before my descent, it'd be a JOY killer. I'd be shoved me into Motorcycle Misery and made to look like a Blockhead.

All because I made a poor Pullover Judgement Call. What was I to do? I'd passed the point of no return. The farther I traveled, the smaller the potential Gear-Up Payoff became —do the math. The rule of diminishing returns had kicked in. So you roll along with your fingers crossed begging: please don't unload on me, Mother Nature. I forged ahead like Hannibal, except Hannibal enjoyed pulling over to fart around with his slave girls.

*Truth About Motorcycles: hoping for the best and forging ahead is another skill not taught at Parking Lot Cone School.*

*You & Your Motorcycle: do you have a point of no return, where you forge ahead, overruling common sense?*

The math is complicated. Hoping for the best is a valid tactic when weighed against what could well be wasted time brushing up on probability theory. Why take the fun out of playing Motorcycle Roulette? JOY is complicated. It has many moving parts.

The highway began its descent toward Hope and sea level, resulting in a win! A successful pullover call. More JOY.

Motorcycle Roulette Winner! Beats slave girls, right Hannibal? No oppressive guilt or societal indignation. No answering to the UN Committee Against Sex Slaves. "Escort services are not the same," they informed an investigative reporter. "And yes, it's an eligible expense if you're away from home for over six days."

"We'll make Hope, stop and review adding rain protection," I assured My Complainers.

How much further to Hope? No GPS—I had to use my

judgment.

I was a Luddite concerning motorcycle GPS adoption. Most of my riding buddies had one before me. "Some of the best trips have no destination," I insisted. I was afraid of losing freedom but eventually, gaining directions won out. I've relied on my motorcycle GPS for years—not to find my way, but because touring conversation is GPS-based, and you're on the bench without one. Plus, having a GPS gives you something to do on boring rides, check GPS data, or guess how far you've gone since you last looked. I'll get one for CTX, along with a temperature gauge. Motorcycle brains are busy enough dealing with not getting killed.

If Mr. Pirsig had known about GPS units and their constant updates, would he have written: It's better to Travel than to Arrive unless you have a GPS Predicted Arrival Time, in which case it's fun to beat the Predicted Arrival Time? Or did Buddha constantly call out updates like: focus on the present, don't dwell on waypoints?

Incredible natural beauty surrounds travelers on the Coquihalla Highway. Snow covered the mountain tops near the summit, not far off the highway. A fine mist added mystery. On-motorcycle, in the wilderness, it was easy to think: peace on Earth,

And forget,

*Truth About Motorcycles: never trust Mother Nature. She can be a nasty bitch.*

CTX passed a parade of semi-trucks (hauling little packages of peanut M&M's and cheap motorcycle cleaning products to dollar stores across the land) on their descent.

Long-distance truck drivers deliver whatever is on their waybill. No questions asked; they don't wade into the debate about product usefulness and ecological ramifications. Truck drivers are solid transportation soldiers despised by the anti-fossil fuel, packaged snack eating lobby, and disrespected by Hollywood. Truck drivers get the short end of the persona stick. Motorcycles, cars, birds, everyone passes and thinks: child abductor? Wife beater? Fossil fuel abuser. Over-packaged product enabler. Addicted to porn? To compensate, truckers get dedicated lanes to crawl up steep hills, plus permission to turn their four-way blinkers on whenever they feel like it, so they'll have something to do when they get bored playing with their eighteen gears. Truckers also get brake check pullover spots where they can look for bits of deer flesh lodged in front bumpers.

They are deer-killing heroes, a band of brothers and sisters with brands, styles, and accessories. They don't lean into corners or wear humongous boots, but we travel the same roads. Why is there not a romantic, adventurous, philosophical mysticism surrounding long-haulers? Why no *Zen and the Art of Big Rig Maintenance*? Must our friends be depicted murdering hitchhikers, dealing with obesity issues, and being unwilling to hide their exposed butt cracks? Why do we hear about truckers losing themselves? Do they not find themselves on the open road? If you ride a motorcycle down the same stretch of highway, the world is your oyster. Trucker roads are paved with mandatory equipment checks, rest stops, and schedules. They can only sigh as bikers pass, giving heavy-handed regulation the finger. "There goes

JOY," they sigh. "Think I'll report him for speeding."

CTX rolled past Britton Rest Stop. I'd taken a break there with my dog, Pearly. Before the accident, we enjoyed hiking. It doesn't get more uncaged than being bitten by a rattlesnake or mauled by a big cat in the wilderness. But, like long-distance trucking, hiking doesn't have pizazz. The Hells Angels haven't spun off a hiking club. We have the South Surrey Strollers. No one notices them, except to wonder, why are those geezers using poles?

Pearl and I have never carried poles, bear spray, or a concealed weapon. It worries me now that I have first-hand knowledge of Mother's evil ways—it wouldn't surprise me one bit if Mother sent a deranged stag or starving grizzly to have a go at us. Terry once asked me, "What if you had hit a bear and didn't kill it... just pissed it off... made it thirsty for revenge, like a wounded Jihad combatant? What would you do?"

"What would you do, Terry?" I answered.

Pearl is oblivious to danger—willing to take on all threats. She's full of Mutt Joy, even when attacking delivery people, cats, and small wheels.

My Pearl would be snack food to a pissed off mother with cubs.

Mother Nature! Your Boss commanded, Thou Shall Not Kill! Keep your hands off of my Pearl! I'll carry my bleach gun, laced with pepper, if I ever return to hiking. Fuck you, Mom! Don't cross my line in the sand—stay the hell away from my dog, you two-faced murderess!

The highway leveled out in places as I descended, dropping toward the coastal river valley. In British Columbia, nothing stays flat or straight for long over most of its territory, which would cover the UK, Ireland, and Japan or Texas, with a large rugged uninhabitable chunk leftover.

A police officer had a car pulled over on the opposite side of the divided highway. What looked like a radar gun was in his hand. Except for some truckers, all the Essential Travelers were speeding—most by a wide margin. I wondered, how fast is too fast when you're at war? Travelers must arrive at their destination ASAP—it's critical when you're under attack. In wartime, should cops not make allowances, back off on, a rule's a rule? After all, there was a possibility Humanity would lose the war and life would end.

"Black and white, buddy. Don't care if there's a war on. Order must be maintained."

"But we haven't solved the metric - imperial question yet. So how is it possible apocalypse speed limits are sorted out? You're kidding… right?"

"Black and white, buddy."

"Even though my trip is essential?"

I'm old enough to remember when cops were encouraged to consider grey and gray, the way Mr. Pirsig inquired into values. Today, common sense and discretion are out the window in favor of numerical justice; "we don't want to be accused of playing favorites." Nabbing speeders is easy; a number proclaims guilt—color, sexual preference, firearm status, family history, and social standing are irrelevant. In the absence of a number, no one is sure who the bad guys are (unless you're on-motorcycle, in which case you're an identifiable outlaw). Is the stabber the bad guy, or is society guilty of mistreatment and responsible for the stabbing? Should we colonize Mars? What's happening with official UN hours? Who will protect the Defund the Police Movement? It's very complicated. No wonder the bar tab for Mayor Dumbass's conference in Mauritius was "through the roof," according to the Angry Taxpayers' FB post.

If there's a number involved in breaking a law, no problem. See? Here on my radar gun? Shows 121. That's 11 over the rule, buddy. Yeah. Yeah. Yeah. Explain why it doesn't matter to the judge when he's back from Mauritius, not me. I just enforce numbers, and you're an eleven-over violator, bucko!

The "no harm done officer, no one in danger" argument had a shot at success back in the day. It doesn't matter that it doesn't matter anymore. Numbers are golden. You're getting a ticket if you're 11 over. Even if it's just you and the justice department on the barren salt flats. If the stabber was 11 over when he plunged the knife in, he's getting a speeding ticket, otherwise "you're free to go, buddy. Our apologies for your tough childhood and society's failures. Here, take these free drugs. We use speeding ticket money to bring them in from Columbia."

Today, only trikes have a shot at no ticket. "What's with the extra wheel, buddy?"

*Truth About Motorcycles: speeding tickets are an assault on bikers.*

Performance-wise, two-wheels are far superior to four. Poor handling semis have reduced speed limits, so why aren't motorcycle speed limits higher? Of course, it's the work of cager regulators who dismiss the precedence of performance-based speed limits. But, beyond the injustice, unfair entrapment, and fines, radar and laser guns are murdering riders. Many bikers scan for speed traps over wildlife and other dangers. It's an unintended consequence of a regulation meant to mitigate risk but causes death and mayhem. "Bikers hit deer while watching for your speed traps."

Lawmakers shrug? "Don't speed."

"The speed limit is designed for cars, not bikes. We have no choice."

No one cares. "The few bikers who vote seldom mark their X inside the circle."

Rather than kill bikers, cops should patrol highways, stopping to shoot deer as often as possible. Maybe requisition a mobile Howitzer. A practical time saver; no more going to the shooting range or inner city to practice. Road crews could stop putting up, watch for deer signs. Flip the equation around: watch for Howitzers, evil rats!

A police car with its lights flashing and siren wailing headed toward me on the opposite side of the road. Did the pulled-over driver have an outstanding warrant? Or alcohol? Or guns for the apocalypse? Perhaps there was an argument over the definition of "Essential Travel?" Did the driver become irate when the no harm done, no one in danger, everyone is doing it, argument failed?

It looked serious, but flashing emergency lights always do, probably a case of a bored officer coming to assist. Viral wars aren't easy for law enforcement or the military. *What'd you mean we gotta arrest Kyrone for going to church? Why can't we fire our HK 433s at the virus?*

◆◆◆

I searched for a place to stop in the town of Hope. There's a major highway junction there, so Hope has plenty of roadside services. People used to say, "there's no hope in Hope," but it's no longer true. Except during pandemics, when there really is no hope in Hope, no hope of finding a sit-down cafe thanks to the war office. My Complainers grumbled. "What'd you mean there's nowhere to rest comfortably? You promised!"

"No hope in Hope. Is it my fault Mother's trying to wipe us out?"

NimRods assume sitting on a motorcycle is like watching TV.

No biggie.

Why do you need to stop?

Only been watching TV.

*Truth About Motorcycles: NimRods are stupid (about motorcycles).*

Turning every Hope diner into a takeout joint may have foiled COVID-19, but it pissed me off. Ever try takeout on a motorcycle?

"Riders will have nowhere to eat and take breaks?" a caring regulator said.

“No one cares."

“How about a Motorcyclists Only café?”

“A Biker-idiot Café?" The committee laughed. "They’d come out even more diseased, a danger to decent law-abiding voters.”

“How about requiring a few Motorcyclists Only chairs outside takeout joints?”

“How about you transfer to the roadkill cleanup crew? You're not cut out for policymaking.”

I spotted an Oddball sitting cross-legged on damp

Fraser River Park grass. He was eating a homemade sandwich beside an unidentifiable motorcycle (rattle can paint job) loaded with bags. Oddball waved. *Hello, friend!* Marta would have stopped.

I didn't.

*You & Your Motorcycle: do you know any Oddballs? Or are you one?*

I could have made an effort—stopped and picked up a few tips; Oddballs are adaptive. Lockdown? No problemo, if you're an Oddball. I returned the wave.

Sometimes there is no choice but to carry on. You want to land, like Amelia Earhart, but not a landing strip in sight.

◆◆◆

I wasn't far past Hope when raindrops fell. Soon it felt as if I'd veered into the Niagara Falls spray field. No option but to initiate a Mandatory Pullover.

CTX exited the freeway and stopped in front of a cement factory. After performing the Blind Yellow Duck Dance (to pull the bright yellow poncho my brother Ron gave me when he quit kayaking, over my head). I clapped hands together and rubbed fingers on my pants to speed circulation. After a few minutes of blood work, waterproof gloves went on.

*You & Your Motorcycle: if Parking Lot Cone School offered training in Advanced Rider Blood Circulation Techniques (focused on fingers and Ass), would you sign up?*

Geared up, I merged onto the freeway, thinking how lucky Hannibal was to have massage practitioners riding with him. Little wonder he conquered Italy, collecting new slave girls for his return trip to North Africa. Then, back in Carthage, he asked, "what do you think, boys?" the way bikers show off their new rides today. Hannibal wasn't hung up on tribalism. He collected different brands and styles. "Each has their strong points," he told his friends.

The rain was steady but light. The traffic threw fine water particles up. Despite the travel decree, the freeway was busy, dense like the drizzle—motorcycle visibility, pathetic. Road Vomit thick.

There was no escaping the fact—it was miserable. How miserable? No hope of finding JOY miserable. If you've ridden for long, you know what I mean. It didn't matter that I was on a new machine, wore Moto-Skiveezes, a neck collar, a bright yellow poncho, dry gloves, and had a new attitude; I was on Motorcycle Misery Highway. Nothing to do but hunker down and grind it out. I had to Be Stubborn in A Good Way (Rule #7).

*You & Your Motorcycle: have you found yourself on Motorcycle Misery Highway?*

Brian lost it. "What the fuck are we doing here? We're on a therapy bike, recovering from trauma, broken bones, and soft tissue damage. Why aren't we in a car like sensible people?"

Shut the fuck up, Brian!

A mile later I thought, Brain has a valid point.

We passed the exit where I thought I might scout for a place to stop. But the calculation didn't pan out: too far off the freeway. I didn't want to risk a detour, only to find no room at the cafe. Better to make a run for the certainty of the helmet shop. It's a common rider tactic: twist the throttle to make the misery end sooner.

*Truth About Motorcycles: sometimes, the only answer is—Hunker Down and Grind it Out. Or twist the throttle to get it over with.*

*You & Your Motorcycle: where were you the last time you hunkered down?*

Fifteen minutes from the motorcycle store in Langley (suburban greater Vancouver), I turned off the freeway. Cager-cunts waved, *can't take it anymore, biker-idiot? On your weird bike.*

I needed to check directions on my phone (Horace had turned my last GPS into electronic junk). *Surely, there will be a spot to eat and rest here in teeming multicultural civilization? A secret retreat hidden from the enemy?* I pulled into a strip mall off the freeway. In front of me, a Starbucks and two local cafes. A McDonalds nearby. None offered sit-down service. For the love of desperate bikers, who's running this war?

It was pure horseshit!

CTX wheeled into a nearby gas station with a roof covering four rows of pumps. I moved carefully, trying to keep My Complainers from shutting me down, "we can't take much more." For insurance, I swallowed a Tylenol 3.

Gas tank full, Red Beauty fired up. Despite being raised in showroom conditions, never a word of complaint from my machine.

*Truth About Motorcycles: motorcycles never whine.*

*You & Your Motorcycle: do you worry when your bike makes a strange sound? More or less than a child or friend who doesn't sound quite right or possibly has COVID?*

# CHAPTER 16 – AT THE HELMET STORE

Drop little Maggie, your pet Chihuahua off at the dog pound (along with an off-setting guilt donation). Pick out a new top dog and head home with bull mastiff, Rocky. It's off-putting, but you justify the change, "Newer, bigger, more power. All round, a superior mutt."

"Dog shit," say the Copley Park Small Dog Owners, who immediately ban Rocky from their group. "But he's smallish... for a mastiff," you plead.

"Get the fuck out of here," a dog mom orders!

You call the pound to reprieve Maggie, but yesterday was Small Dog Euthanization Day.

Another example: you return your foster kid to get a stronger, more talented, all round nicer one. Improved Kid is praised and you are congratulated, but old attachments linger. You were kinda fond of the original brat and its defects. Your new adopted son is flawless but not a fit with your loser parents' bunch—you become an outcast, alone and forsaken.

"It's the way you feel when trading a bike in," I had explained.

A crude, distorted world map became visible on Dr. Peggy's face. "Trade in a child... or a pet? Horrid!"

I watched as a blemish transformed into Iceland. It looked active, about to erupt—duck and cover! My trade-in comparison probably triggered painful memories of young Pissy's *Ode to a Daisy-less Creep* childhood. ♫Wish I was special, felt MAGIC, but I'm a creep ♫ *Poor, poor dear. Hug yourself, Peg... no one else will. There. There.*

"As usual, your metaphor is an insult to decent literature. Neanderthal crap!"

*What if I added some daisies*? I grinned like a nutter because Motorcycle Transition is unexplainable to NimRods. A switch from Mazda to GMC will not turn your social life upside down. With poems, readers flit from one verse to another, *just more words... who gives an allegory?* Switching motorcycles is an entirely different proposition. Move from a Harley to a MV Augusta and you may find yourself on an ice flow with little Maggie and a gang of unwanted foster kids.

For the love of God, Peg, put a tissue over Iceland before it explodes!

◆◆◆

Welcome to your new tribe, the sign said—**Honda Powersports**.

Another sign stated: **MASKS MANDATORY**.

I dangled my mask from a finger. Outlaws in biker stores frown on being told how to dress. *Wear this, asshole!*

It'd been years since I'd owned a Honda motorcycle, CTX being my third. The dealer was in a large, attractive modern building, not far off the freeway. Harley Davidson sat on the high side of the cul-de-sac, looking down, a proud, judgmental, screaming eagle.

The rain had stopped, and the sky brightened. Streaks of blue to the southwest, the direction I would head.

I did the reverse Blind Yellow Duck Dance, struggling to pull the poncho up and over my head, a tricky maneuver with a shoulder incapable of full rotation. Spectators were in the lot, so I was careful not to perform the Frantic Feeble. *Are you on drugs, Buddy? Injured? Homeless? Infected? Better come with us. We'll set you up at a safe injection site.*

The dry, comforting store delighted My Complainers, who nibbled on a fresh pill. Motorcycle stuff was on display at its best, like attending the Miss Universe Pageant with permission to touch. Lots to gawk at while I dripped. My riding jacket said, "BMW." *No, I didn't wander into your store by mistake. I belong here, as of yesterday. See my key, says Honda. Yes, I know it's on a BMW key chain, but heavily discounted bikes don't come with a free chain!*

Gear and parts on the main level. Bikes on level two. Service is all the way to the back. Use the outside entrance to hear Dr. Tire recite *Ode to a Tire Change.*

Like the dealership in Kelowna, the store was busy. Shoppers looked like they were on vacation—the power of community and the proximity to new gleaming steel horses unleashed J O Y . If I can muscle a CRF around, why worry about tiny germs? Motorcycles are COVID evaders.

Four different street helmet brands were on display, and many dual-sport models. I looked the lineup over and found one of the recommended brands. A Shoi Gt Air 2 full-face. No modulars for me; full-face helmets are quieter and offer better protection. There were no discontinued, discounted Gt Air 1s on the shelf. YouTube advised, "Air 1s are the smart choice." I checked the price of an Air 2. Yes, you'd have to be pretty dumb to shell out that kind of money to replace a "1" with a "2".

Helmets are not like the *Mission Impossible* or a superhero franchise, where each film is a unique work of art. How different can a brain bucket be?

Conrad would ask: think your coconut is worth that much? I checked the web—the dealer's price was less than a large online retailer. I expected the store price to be higher. *Maybe my coconut is worth their asking price?* Firing your head into asphalt greases your helmet purse strings.

I decided to try the Air 2 on to nail down size. A sign warned: **Don't touch unless you're buying! Ask for assistance**. Blunt, likely written by the Stay the Fuck Home highway sign guy. I didn't touch, but may have if the sign had read **Avoid Touching**.

I waved at a young blond, attractive, probably off-roader, accessories salesperson who looked like she could handle herself with gritty customers. Has she considered filing a complaint and moving upstairs to sell machines one day, I wondered? With the consultants and their fat commission cheques.

Shoppers must wear a head covering to try a helmet on. "Probably a medium," I said. "Maybe a large." The salesperson handed me a medium matte black Gt Air 2. Felt like my head was used to make the mold. I jiggled the helmet around the way eighteen-year-old YouTubers do.

The salesperson confirmed, "Looks like a perfect fit."

I thought so. Nice of you to acknowledge my ideal head.

Gt Air 2 felt way better than my old spare helmet with the BMW sticker. More comfortable than the Sena Inc that saved my life. I asked the salesperson if she'd ridden with the Air 2? No. But she'd ridden with other Shois. They're highly recommended. I'm aware of that; I arrived from Merritt, not Uranus. "You can't tell until you ride," I said, stating a fact. "Can I try the helmet? In the lot, at least?" *You can ride behind me.*

"Sorry."

The expected answer.

Check around, I reminded myself—don't rush. *Find a discontinued Air 1 for a lot less. Mustn't make a rash decision. Best to go with the smart choice.* I have sympathy for local stores. They struggle to compete with online retailers while dealing with annoying know-it-all YouTube-educated jackasses. "Any Air-I's?" *The smart choice?*

"None left."

"Can you discount the Air 2 price?" I'm a sucker for a discount.

I got the standard spiel. "It's a premium brand. Rarely on sale. The store must toe the line." It's the manufacturer's fault. She'd like to give me a deal but can't break marketing policy. *I'm pretty, like your friend Mary, so buy from me... even if you don't get a discount.*

I wasn't born yesterday and recognized the sales techniques. "I prefer white." I handed the flat black back. "Black will be too hot" when I ride through Death Valley. *Would you like to come to Death Valley with me, miss?*

"No whites in stock, but I can order one. Matte black is very popular."

"Big money to not get the color I prefer." The most popular color, white. That's why you have none.

"It'll take less than a week to get a white Shoi." *You'd love to come back... to see me, right?*

"From Victoria. Heading home." With my perfect-sized head. Just passing through on Essential Business. *Would you like to deliver it, Mary?*

It stumped her. Despite the growing sales professional-client attraction, Mary knew there was zero chance I would pay the ferry fare to pick up a helmet. And I was aware: after a sale is made, smiles are hard to come by. Buyers are directed to Parts and Service where employees seldom smile.

"Maybe if you discount the black one," I offered, thinking Mary would stick to her guns and say no, which would be fine. I didn't want black.

It wasn't, "No." Or, "I'll have to talk to my manager." Or screw off, I'm going to deal with a real prospect. The store was full of targets, but she returned promptly with an answer and another smile. "I can save you the tax." *We'd like to see your perfect head in one of our helmets.*

She really is impressed with my head and charm, I thought. Brain calculated: twelve percent on top of the bucks I'd save over the popular online store. Added up to one hundred dollars, a worthy farkle discount. Black can't be that much hotter, not with the ventilation system cranked wide open? Air is in the product name, after all. Add a white reflective decal for a few bucks, and it's no longer a black helmet. "Deal," I said, flashing the JOY of saving big bucks on accessories, smile. *I'll wear it to Death Valley. When shall we leave, Mary?*

*Truth About Motorcycles: finding a deal on an accessory is hitting the mother lode.*

◆◆◆

Clearing skies. Two helmets. A deep discount, head size admiration. In the parking lot, I was pumped up on Motorcycle Shopping JOY!

Life is beautiful!

Dropping Maggie at the pound or putting loser foster kid up for adoption takes guts, but it can be for the best.

Never take standing pat for granted. So long, Copley Park Small Dog Owners and loser parents' group!

*You & Your Motorcycle: have you regretted any trades or upgrades? Negotiated a terrific farkle deal?*

I had to unstrap the dry bag and repack to get my old helmet on board, which made me think: panniers and a top box next. There is always one more thing. *Does Mary sell luggage? We'll need it for our trip to Death Valley.*

No earplugs. No neck collar. I would conduct my Gt Air 2 test raw.

# CHAPTER 17 – ABOUT HELMET-LESS

Until my helmet rode the asphalt, I wondered about riding bareheaded, like the ultracool dudes in really old movies. Fortunately, modern helmet laws saved my coconut from being pulverized. Have I mentioned, some laws make sense?

Today, where permitted, helmet-less is more than giving the finger; it's a head butt. A refusal to kowtow to freedom crushing, we-know-what's-best-for-you autocrats. The buck stops here, at my exposed head.

Live free or die!

Two Wheels, Not Four!

Fuck you tyrants, despots, California warning labels, commies, zealous flag persons, and parking enforcement!

Helmet-less is pure biker; preserving a tradition that goes back to Harley and Davidson.

Or is riding helmet-less,

Horseshit?

Is it trying to kill yourself by doing something stupid (Motorcycle Riding Rule #2)?

Is it a principled stand taken too far?

I'm biased. Had my bare skull hit Highway 20, I'd be about a hot dog short of skull bone and squamous matter. A bug jackpot; those creepy ones who live in perpetual darkness, too disgusting to be seen, even by their mums. "Nice big entrance in the head, fellas. On the port side... wasn't wearing a helmet. Dinner's on this tasty Freedomite."

I did not legally have a choice, but wearing a helmet saved my life, so I bought another. For me, it's not a theoretical argument.

I know—taking your head for granted can kill you.

*You & Your Motorcycle: how much is your coconut worth to you?*

I wear a helmet but respect the right to choose. For example, Pearl and I often walk a trail with a sign that says, **No Dogs Allowed**, fully prepared to give anal bylaw officers the finger, along with a lecture on the value of personal responsibility and liberty. Perhaps fire a warning squirt of bleach. There is more than one way to be a Freedomite and skin a cat, right, Bunny?

Before her skull got squished like a tire coming off its rim, my childhood neighbor, sweet Mary McGregor, looked glorious. Mary was understandably vain. It's criminal to conceal beauty, and Mary loved to be on display. My neighbor was not making a statement about authoritarianism when she squashed her young, gorgeous head. Before being slingshoted off her bike, she sang:

♫ Look at me, I feel pretty

Oh, so pretty, I feel pretty and witty with,
Such a pretty face
Such a pretty smile
Such a pretty me ♫!

On the flip side, helmets conceal ugly. Heads like Alfred E. Neuman's and Pissy's were made for full-face helmets with dark visors.

"Looking mighty fine today, Pissy."

"Thanks. New dark tinted visor."

For a few, live-free or die is their raison d'être, They expose bare heads on principle alone, in defense of ever-decreasing highway freedoms as the know-it-alls determine what's best. Freedom riders have a noble cause, but society judges them harshly. "Dumbasses," we snicker without appreciating their virtuous stand. "Probably anti-vaccers who use inappropriate pronouns, too."

Like LGBTQs, Freedomites will lay down their lives to make the statement: it's my body, I'll do what I like with it. LGBTQs have their colorful, *I'm not a heterosexual like you assholes,* flag, but Freedomites are indistinguishable from Born to be Wild Dumbasses; they need a hi-vis emblem that screams, *conscientious helmet-less rider here*. It's the same issue differentiating doctors, Dr. Daisy or Doc Martens, from Dr. Phil. Perhaps the UN Subcommittee of Experts on the Globally Harmonized System of Classification and Labeling will take up the challenge at their next conference? Issue a badge to identify Freedomites and one for medical doctors. Perhaps a combo for doctors who are also Freedomites and another with a pride flag for LGBTQ-Freedomite-Doctors?

It's unfair to lump principled bare heads in with unhelmeted lame brains and the vain. Unlike Mormons and Hare Krishnas, Freedomites on-motorcycle cannot stand on sidewalks or go door-to-door handing out leaflets to advertise their cause.

It's hard to tip your helmet to a bare head when you can't be sure the head is fending off fascism.

*You & Your Motorcycle: can you tell a Freedomite from a Dumbass?*

Bareheaded highway riders would remain a rare sight if lawmakers did away with mandatory helmets. There's a reason automobiles have windshields. Wind in your hair may have been cathartic when the top speed of a cycle was thirty miles an hour; ever have a bug hit you at high speed? Or have your eyes blasted by sand or dirt?

I have.

It's not liberating.

Wear a helmet with a visor or goggles.

Motorcycle engineers agree—protect your head. "It's one of a handful of things political science hasn't fucked up."

Freedomites, with your fingers in the authoritarian dike, may you always keep the rubber side down. Pearl and I will continue to walk with you in solidarity on No Dogs Trail.

"Never take freedom for granted, but do it with your helmet on," Marta says.

BUCKETS FOR COCONUTS

The pull of gravity causes coconuts to fall from trees. Unfortunately, it results in harm or death to the nut farmers, all so we can enjoy curries and beverages with coconut.

The United Nations commissioned the study, Injuries Due to Falling Coconuts (1984), but coconut workers remain in peril to this day.

"Enough," Lab volunteers declared. Announcing the *Buckets for Coconuts Charity*.

Instead of trashing your old helmet after seven years (because of ultraviolet and environmental damage), donate it to the people who work under nut trees. In my garage, we conducted drop tests (large coconuts on old helmets) with impressive results.

Send MRR Labs your outdated helmet, and Marta will mail you a *Buckets for Coconuts* decal. Motorcycle Giving Back JOY! People will think you're a Beautiful Giver even if you're a Motorcycle Cunt, and Marta will call you a *Buckets for Coconuts Saint*, no matter what.

Hans will look into expanding *Buckets* to mobility noggins, and Den will research people who work under trees, other than palm trees. Terry and Dolores will help with operations. It'll keep the big guy's mind off of *Joy's* imminent release and asking, "What do I do now, about Brenda? The clock's running down."

Dolores suggested adding a charity plug on *Joy's* cover. "A sexy mama holding a helmet with a **Buckets For Coconuts, Please Help!** sign."

*Seduction of the Heart* is doing very well, she kept reminding me."

"Wanna walk No Dogs Trail, Pearl? Slowly."

# CHAPTER 18 – ABOUT WINTER RIDING

I missed my freeway exit.

It's what happens when you're GPS-less, conducting a helmet test, not riding in the middle, and wondering why politicians don't add curvy roads to their vote-buying list. I mistakenly crossed the Fraser River which had me heading toward the heart of the city. I would have to take the long way down to the ferry terminal, using roads traveled when I lived in Vancouver.

I screwed up, but Zen Jackasses make the best of circumstances and carry on.

But never assume you're going the right way!

*Is there a wrong way, on-motorcycle?*

My revised route took me through Lucky Intersection, named years ago after an unintended game of Motorcycle Roulette. It was winter: wet, west coast greyish-gray weather that makes cold and blue preferable. I was commuting to work on my second Honda, a CB500, not by choice, but because I'd lent my car to a relative who totaled it.

"Sorry," he said.

"That's life," I said. "You're, okay?"

"Could have been worse."

As CTX approached Lucky Intersection, it reminded me of all the reasons not to ride in winter, even when "roads are bare, and the weather is crisp," as Marta likes to say. Winter throws everything horrible about motorcycling at you, determined to turn even the stubborn and the foolhardy against riding. Winter shouts, cager superiority!

About winter riding, Marta says, "It can suck JOY out." She keeps Guzzi on the road year-round and when winter days are beautiful and "crisp," climbs on. "J O Y doesn't take winters off altogether. It's just harder to find."

I worry about Marta riding Guzzi in January and February and using "crisp" to support her dangerous obsession.

"The term 'crisp weather' has no meteorological credibility, Marta. It makes me think of bacon and potato chips."

It was a shitty, soggy winter day years ago when CB500 approached Lucky Intersection. I was grinding out commuter miles, Traveling from A to B miles, desperate to arrive on my Transport Bike as the evening rush hour wound down. A week of relentless rain had the four-lane roadway saturated. As I approached the busy intersection, the signal change caught me. Amber appeared at the worst possible moment. The roulette wheel spun; speed up or slow down? When you're dying to get home to be off-motorcycle, slowing down is not helpful.

"Fuck the light. Fucking weather! Fucking work! I want a car and crisper weather."

*Truth About Motorcycles: cages are far better at fending off winter.*

It's history now, but my showdown at Lucky Intersection remains etched in my brain. There was no option but to hit the brakes. No ABS, not that it would have helped; CB had no intention of stopping. Its should-have-been-replaced tires hydroplaned toward the intersection on a sheet of water. I pumped. Panic-ed. Prayed. A dim headlight signaled my intrusion. Here I come! Jackass on Motorbike! Clear the intersection!

*You & Your Motorcycle: do you have incidents etched in your memory?*

Like it or not, I was out of control and going into the danger zone between light changes. A damp, dimly lit space. Traffic will devour me, I knew. Car drivers wanted to arrive home almost as much as I did. No one likes to travel on miserable late work evenings, let alone dipsy doodle around a bike that should have been garaged for the winter. *Biker-idiot!*

I leaned the Honda over. CB slid into the middle of the intersection. Hello, end of days! The shattering of bone and crushing of organs. Execution, motorcycle style. Pray the cut is razor sharp, swift, and painless, not an off-centre, mangled crush leaving me spread out on a cold black bed. Dead, not in defense of a war-to-end-all-wars, or as a proud Freedomite, but because I'd missed my bus.

Momentum hurled me forward; you don't have to

be Sir Isaac to know winter demands extra diligence. I'd been a Blockhead, and motorcycle mistakes are unforgiving.

*Truth About Motorcycles: motorcycles do not always stop when you want them to.*

"Lord, if You could help me out this once?"

"Oh, it's you Mikey. So now I exist, do I? Wasn't it just last week you called Me, smoke and mirrors? Weren't you going to be dust in the wind, Mikey? Going horizontal is the end of the road? Finito. Suddenly you're a believer, begging for eternal life?"

"What I meant to say was, I don't believe in religion, but obviously, there's a higher power." I ride a motorcycle. I know it's true.

"I'll give you that, Mikey, but please watch your language. I'll be listening, son. Try to keep the rubber side down from now on. I'm up to my neck with universal issues."

Never take the judgment of a higher power for granted.

"Why not send your son back to Earth? To help out?"

"Concentrate on Awareness and ride smart, Mikey. I'll run the universe, thank-you."

Did Mr. Pirsig nail it? Faced with looming disaster, something miraculous happened, as if Buddha stepped up, reached out, and said, "not yet." An alert driver skidded to a stop and saved my CPU. Death denied! Not even ruffled to smarten me up. There would be no lying next to Mary McGregor, wishing someone would push us together. "Don't they make a cute couple?" people would ask. *Nice to see they finally got together.*

Was it divine intervention or dumb Motorcycle

Roulette luck? Close calls make you suspect, as people of faith know, there is more going on than is comprehensible.

I felt like a SQUID in one of those YouTube videos. SQUID is in the dealership parking lot on his new bike. He's never in control. His inaugural ride is an immediate crash. I got up, waved at the perplexed driver who had stopped a few feet from me. Our eyes locked. The driver's expression said, poor biker-idiot. Why must he drive a motorbike in winter?

Hi there, I'm fine. My fault. Just a Winter Blockhead. Thanks so much for being an excellent driver! A Cager Saint, but begone. Let's pretend this never happened.

Carry-on. All is well.

*Truth about Motorcycles: many cagers are Saints.*

Lab volunteers estimated 8% of cagers drive with Godliness while another 31% are lesser Saints but not cunts. I think their numbers are low. There are times car drivers swell my J O Y .

*You & Your Motorcycle: have you experienced cager saintliness as a rider?*

CB suffered a broken turn signal but carried on because that's what Hondas do. Shaken, nauseous, and thankful, I completed my last winter ride. The next day, I took the bus.

Some riders master winter, a skill I never developed. A few days after the accident, I bought a used car and, in the spring, sold CB. "Wrap duct tape on the signal light stem," I told the first-time buyer. "Throw in a new bulb. You're good to go."

Years ago, winter turned me against motorcycles at Lucky Intersection. Until I bought my next bike, one I swore would never be on the road in winter—unless the weather was extraordinarily crisp.

*Truth About Motorcycles: MAGIC may take winters off.*

Victoria enjoys mild winters. But I don't ride from November through March. Like everything, it's good to take vacations. My motorcycles enjoy winter teddy bear duty.

*You & Your Motorcycle: have you found JOY riding in the winter (in a land where global warming or geography hasn't eliminated winter)?*

# CHAPTER 19 – AT THE MALL

It was three o'clock, and I hadn't eaten thanks to the Pandemic Gestapo.

CTX turned toward Tsawwassen Mills, a modern, large shopping complex next to the ferry causeway. The government had locked down all the leased shops at the terminal, but many of the mall stores remained open. There's a Superstore and the usual assortment of takeout joints. I chose the quick option—a dollar store. Oatmeal cookies, banana chips, and a small bag of peanut M&M's. Breakfast of Champions. Easy to pack fruit, whole grains, and nut protein.

As I stuffed my meal into my dry bag, I noticed a senior rider on a step-through scooter. Eighties, I guessed, as one does, looking at his open-face helmet. The small bike maneuvered like Wayne Gretzky or Pele, with natural authority. An artist in charge, putting years of experience to work, allowing muscle memory and instinct to guide him. What's his story, I wondered? What bikes has he owned? Where has he traveled? *If Marta were here, she'd be on it.* No hesitation—"let's get this guy's story. For sure, he's experienced J O Y ."

I dillydallied; no Marta or Conrad to give me a jump

start. I guessed Senior Rider had a Spyder at home for road trips? "Best bike I've owned, and I've owned them all," he'd say.

*You & Your Motorcycle: do you travel on three wheels? Was adding a wheel weird?*

"But is a trike a motorcycle or a motorcycle-trike?" I'd say.

My phone beeped: a Marta text. "Shelly stopped by the lab, looking for Terry. Luckily, he wasn't here. Shell was on a mission, full Warhammer mode. Lent her *Seduction of the Heart* and talked about *Buckets*. Explosion averted!"

"So you had a nice visit?" I replied with a smiley face. Marta said she had a plan that might fix the Terry situation.

A sign behind the scooter said: **No Parking, Loading Zone**. Senior Rider gave the mall's regulations the middle finger as he walked toward the entrance. The back of his tee-shirt read, "Old Enough to Know Better, but Doing it Anyway."

I wanted to mask up and hobble after him.

He moved at a good clip for an old guy.

I did the math. There was no way I was going to gain on senior rider.

# CHAPTER 20 – ABOUT DREAMERS

Senior Rider would be about the age of my Uncle Arthur. Tish's father was a Motorcycle Dreamer. He loved to talk about the Zen book, quote Goldwing specs, and ask, "where you been riding, Mike?" He's dead now. Died dreaming.

Take that trip!

Buy your dream machine!

Install a tall windscreen, if that's your pleasure.

JOY waits for no man or woman.

Arthur planned to retire at age sixty, buy a Goldwing and drive across North America with his pal, Stu. It was his *something to live for*.

*You & Your Motorcycle: have you experienced Motorcycle Road Trip Anticipation JOY?*

Perhaps if Arthur had put a plug in a cylinder, as they say? Bought a starter, perhaps a Vespa? Did something to gain momentum? From nothing to 3,800 miles on a large touring machine is a giant leap, especially when your comfort zone is nuts and bolts. "Fasteners," my uncle would correct me. "Non-threaded, corrugated, rivets, brads, metal snaps... not just screws. The business of helping folks join things together."

"Dad could spin a tale and screw on a nut," Theresa says.

Motorcycle dreams spun in Arthur's head, but at heart, he was a fastener guy and a storyteller. One of Art's stories supported his decision to put off buying a motorcycle until he retired. He'd tap his Wing bucket list fund box and declare, "There'll be plenty of time to ride once I stop working. Take Stu's Uncle Henry, he's seen eighty, and he's still rid'in. There's plenty of time for me."

There wasn't.

*You & Your Motorcycle: do you have a Motorcycle Dream? Better get on with it.*

I've had plenty of impromptu chats with Dreamers. Mostly late middle-aged men who "always wanted a bike" but never got around to it. Too late? They never speak those words, but they know too late came and went.

"Maybe I'll buy a Harley like my neighbor Pete's and ride to Sturgis with him," they say in an offhand way that trivializes the commitment required. Or "think an off-road bike would be okay... at my age?" "Which bikes are easiest to learn on?"

Sometimes I mention my uncle, who spoke about buying his Goldwing for as long as I can remember. "Don't wait too long... as my uncle did, and his friend Stu."

Stu worked for the city in Permits and planned to join the cross-continent retirement odyssey, "if my bursitis isn't acting up." Stu never also owned a motorcycle, but his Uncle Henry rode with the British Biker Boys. "It's in my blood," he assured Arthur.

Art, Stu, and Henry met regularly at Cherished Waters Retirement Living where they enjoyed complimentary afternoon tea and cakes. Henry liked to spin stories which fueled Art's Motorcycle Dream. Arthur's favorite tale rationalized why there was no need to rush. "I'll still be riding at eighty-five," Henry promised.

Horseshit, I thought when I heard the prediction, but looking at Senior Rider, I thought, may be possible.

"It'd be stupid to wait too long," Tish had told her dad.

I'm not a gifted storyteller like my uncle, but I've heard the Biker Boys story so often; if you get a beer or two in me, and the conversation turns to Dreamers, you're going to hear my version of Art's Henry Biker Boy Story.

◆◆◆

"A racket, somewhere between the death scream of a bunny and the smoky grind of a low-speed dentist drill, violated the serenity of nature's annual extravaganza, spring's first perfect day of the year." Uncle's stories were like that. Flowery. Grandiose. Over the top.

"The buzzing and vibrating befuddled eighty-four-year-old Henry Foster... as my uncle Arthur told the story."

Henry struggled to find the source of the noise, and when he could not, turned the key of his nineteen fifty-eight Norton Dominator and silenced it. He suspected it had to do with the electric starter. It had irritated him since being installed nine years earlier.

Even when annoyed, Henry did not look like a man

used to giving society the finger.

*Truth About Motorcycles: not all riders look like outlaws.*

"What a bloody racket," Henry told his friend Clayton. Despite wearing his old leather British Biker Boys club jacket, Henry didn't look like a man who would own a machine that acted like a misbehaving child, especially on a beautiful day.

He brought his shoulders back, straightening his five-foot-ten, well-portioned frame, and stepped back to inspect the Norton. His father had purchased the bike brand new and passed it down to his only son. Henry knew every inch of the motorbike except for the retrofit starter mechanism, which he believed to be the source of all problems and "a bloody abomination." The starter "upsets the balance."

The Norton was Henry's child, and he teased Clayton about being buried "with my iron horse."

At eighty-three, Henry declared he would ride seven times a year, twice in spring and fall and three times in the summer, for no longer than an hour on each occasion. He was throwing in the polishing rag, but not the towel. On fine days, if he felt as bright as the weather, he cheated, proud to be the last of the British Biker Boys on two wheels.

Bouncing around on the old motorcycle was invigorating, but Henry wondered about getting one of those modern three-wheelers. Or a mobility scooter faster than Clayton's. "Perhaps when I turn ninety-three," he told friends. "The old girl and I still get along."

The first spring ride of the Norton Dominator was a

highlight at Cherished Waters. Henry felt it more than fulfilled his obligation to pitch in. When asked if he'd like to volunteer with the garden club or decorating committee, Henry answered, "Busy getting the old girl ready for the ride," which wasn't true, but folks respected his devotion. "History is important, Henry," they'd answer. The residents thought their Biker Boy was quite the renegade. Suspected he was a badass back in his gang member days.

The day before, to prepare for the event, Henry and Clayton had reconnected the battery, and Henry rode to the filling station to add petrol.

The residents expected their biker boy to be at the front entrance at 10:30 AM. The electric starter turned the engine over just before ten, and the machine sprung to life without a fuss. When the bike was halfway up the underground parking ramp, it grumbled. Henry pulled up beside Clayton on the grass next to the exit. Getting out of the garage was the test: "I'm good to go if I make it up the bloody ramp in one piece." Henry made it sound risky and dangerous, but thought nothing of it.

Clayton held a cleaning rag, ready to give the metal a final wipe-down before its spring performance.

*You & Your Motorcycle: got an old motorcycle? Do you nurse it?*

Henry was sure the noise originated from the electric starter doodad. "Confounded contraption."

“Everything around the Norton had a swagger about it. The warm air, the vivid greens, the light breeze, the fresh scent, the thin wispy clouds against the blue sky,” Uncle

Tarter would say. “A chorus of birds welcomed spring.”

Henry took a deep breath.

"Damn contraption," Clayton said, wiping a smudge away.

Another deep breath.

A car with a rusted muffler careened past the lawn where Henry, Clayton, and the Norton stood.

"Bloody cager," Clayton said, an expression learned from his friend.

Henry concentrated, deep breaths in, out, in, out, eyes closed, breathing in, out, in, out. Then, slowly, he opened his eyes to the warm day and kicked the starter. "That ought to do it," he told Clayton.

Across the street, a man sat, or slumped, on a bench in front of the Cherished South Residence building. "Owned a motorcycle, I hear," Clayton said, pointing his glasses toward the man.

As if he had urgent business to attend to, Henry marched across the street. Clayton followed.

The stranger sat alone, taking in the glorious day, perhaps expecting a Dominator to roll by.

Henry felt he should apologize and explain the situation. How he was very familiar with his motorcycle, but the electric starter was not meant to be a part of it. "Hello there. Beautiful day, isn't it? Sorry about the racket." When the stranger glanced up, Henry noticed he looked like a chubby-cheeked Jesus.

"Good morning," Clayton added.

"Used to ride with the British Biker Boys," Henry announced proudly, as if a member of an elite sports or physics research team. "Mind if I sit? Join you?" *Jesus?* Henry didn't wait for an answer. Instead, he plopped himself down and swung one arm over the back of the bench.

Clayton also sat. He checked his wristwatch and showed the time to his friend.

Jesus straightened up, raised his right foot, and said, "Wasp."

"Dead," Clayton asked?

"Dead."

"Lived here long? Looks like a Triumph on your tee shirt?"

"Bonneville," Jesus answered. You could almost hear the silent, are you stupid or something? He returned to twisting one foot, grinding the dead bug into the cement. "Hate stingers."

"We'd best be going," Clayton said, checking his wristwatch. "Don't want to keep the troops waiting."

Henry turned his head and pointed at the main entrance across the street. "They're gathering, waiting for my Norton. To see an old fool ride. The bike's there." Both Henry and Clayton pointed in the Dominator's direction. "They love to see me, on the bike, giving age the finger." He paused. "Of course, there's the possibility of a crash. I'm not exactly Steady Eddie these days." Both Henry and Clayton laughed.

Jesus smiled. "Me too." He stood, kicked the dead wasp away, pointed toward the Norton. "Dominator? Fifties or sixties."

Henry scratched his forehead. He stood, looked at Clayton, and then back at Jesus. "Know anything about electric starters," he asked?

"Fully restored, R60." Jesus looked toward the car park. "In the garage. Did the work myself."

A CBer, Clayton thought. "Maybe you could do the ride? Is it an old bike... like Henry's?"

Henry frowned.

"Worked on a couple of Nortons."

At this point in the story, I always pause because that's what my uncle did. No doubt he was thinking: if Henry Foster can find a riding buddy at his age and be re-energized, what's the rush? The break gave me time to marvel at the enduring power Motorcycle Joy can have.

Henry and Jesus became known as the Cherish Biker Boys. Coffee rides in good weather—slow cruises down country roads. A few overnighters, close to home, but they traveled. "Both men much older than I'll be when I retire, buy my Wing, and drive across the continent. Stick a toe in the Atlantic. Enjoy fresh east coast fish and chips," Arthur would say. "Me and Stu. Way younger than the Cherish Biker Boys... and on modern, comfortable machines."

“As long as my bursitis isn’t acting up,” Stu would add.

My uncle never lathered tartar sauce on Atlantic fried fish; he waited too long.

Sad.

J O Y waited as long as it could.

◆◆◆

Time doesn't have to run out on motorcycling. "There they go. Our two biker boys," Cherished Waters residents said proudly when Henry and Jesus rode. "Both boys look so young on their bikes."

It's true. J O Y is a fountain of youth.

Art and Stu mostly talked lawn tractors. Every once in a while, they plotted: do we buy identical smaller bikes? Less expensive? Second hand? Ride over to Stony Creek for coffee? Don't have to go all the way to the Atlantic.

"Hope would be far enough."

"No hope in Hope."

"As long as there's fish and chips."

The friends never made it but did taste JOY. It can happen while eating fish and chips, daydreaming about motorcycle possibilities.

*Truth about Motorcycles: motorcycle dreams can go on forever.*

The Cherish Biker Boys rode into their nineties. "If Henry and Jesus can ride to Hope, we can make it to the drugstore," residents said.

Live your Motorcycle Dreams.

Like Henry Foster.

Chubby cheek Jesus.

Senior Rider.

Tish's dad passed away a month after retiring from the fastener business. Sad. “Why didn't dad put down the book and buy a bike?”

Because, Tish, your dad was a Motorcycle Dreamer.

# CHAPTER 21 – AT THE FERRY TERMINAL

2:20 PM. Tsawwassen Ferry Terminal.

CTX passed long lines of cars and trucks waiting to catch the ferry to Vancouver Island. I stopped at the front of the queue, joining a Harley and a Triumph scrambler. "Go 'round the cars to the front of the line, friends," ferry operators direct bikers.

Hundreds of drivers curse as motorcycles slip by. "Fuck'in idiot-bikers!" A few bang their heads against steering wheels. To them, we're despised receivers. Catching hail Marys to steal games from the home team.

Motorcycles board first, at a much lower fare, without reservations.

Like motorbikes, ferries are outsiders, never represented at Global Transport Conferences and not acknowledged on World Maritime Day (September 22). "Banks have their day—International Day of Banks (Dec

4th). They're not lumped in with World Finance Day. It's horseshit," ferry operators complain. Our friends are pissed and raise their middle fingers in solidarity with bikers.

In non-pandemic times, it's common for cars without reservations to wait for two, three, or four hours to board due to lack of capacity at either of the two large B.C. Ferries terminals. Not if you're on a motorcycle! Feel the J O Y as you roll past waiting cars.

Welcome bikers!

Go to the front of the line.

From your friends, the ferry operators.

It's the same if you take the state or private ferry to Washington state. It's an international protest and a J O Y shot in the arm.

A man riding a new Triumph scrambler had also bought his bike on Wednesday. "Two thousand bucks cheaper in Kelowna."

He radiated Motorcycle Discount Joy.

Although not as severe as my case, Scrambler Guy had also endured motorcycleless-ness. We compared notes.

"An occasional rider now. On the lookout for deer more than twisties." I spat—vile giant rats.

Harley dude said his friend hit a deer a year earlier.

"What happened?" Hope he killed the fucker?

Despite his leathers, bandanna, and goatee, dude's laughter slayed the stereotypical Hells Angel biker image. His grin said: "What happened is a silly question. He was on a Harley dude... nothing happened." The deer went up and over his friend's big bike, leaving his buddy uninjured. No bouncing off asphalt. A blip. Dude's friend may have had time to react, but he was doing the same speed as my smaller GT when it slammed into Horace.

The deer flew up and over the big Harley. The bike never went down.

It put a smile on my face: one more dead deer. A slow, crippling death. A punch to Mother Nature's gut, the way Jorge Jorgensen like to slam Feeble on International Day of Persons with Disabilities (December 3rd) day.

I have a friend who hit a doe on a decked-out RT and came through it with only minor bruises. Smaller than Horace, but the physics worried me; did I have the deer-motorcycle equation wrong? Buying a small bike, driving in a tamer fashion may not be the best approach? Colliding with a deer on a small machine is the equivalent of a home run. You're the ball flying full force toward the pavement. Hit a deer on a tractor-sized motorcycle, and it's a walk. The reaction is the opposite—the bike jettisons the deer; the rider is safe on base.

My deceased friend, Bob, owned a Ducati and a Japanese cruiser. He liked to say about his big cruiser: "This motorcycle is heavy but able to glide like a feather in a beautiful world." It was an absurdism that made us laugh—at the ferry terminal, it had me thinking about motorcycle mass and how little of it CTX has.

More bikes arrived at the head of the queue. Two VFRs and a Husqvarna. Another Harley. A BMW bagger. A custom-painted Ducati stood spotlessly beside a dirty African Twin. One carbon black Ninja. A girl on an older well used Transport Bike parked away from the gang. She wasn't interested in joining our motorbike chat circle. Didn't care to take in the Baja trip story or how the Harley's air cleaner sucked in rainwater around Hope.

A Girlie Rider lifted a small spaniel cross off of her bike. *WOW! The dog is three-legged.* Weird, like a trike. Motorcycle accident, I wanted to ask?

The pet had no clue it was down a leg; joy flows constantly for dogs with caring owners. Add a motorbike into the mix and it's J O Y unlimited.

*You & Your Motorcycle: have you had a pet onboard? Does it boost JOY?*

I ate my meal and gave Biker Dog an oat treat. Others also snacked. Fancier food than mine, but not Breakfast of Champions. Everyone had something to say —Camaraderie JOY. It spilled onto the asphalt, engulfing our troop with MAGIC. Cagers fumed. Must they enjoy waiting so goddamn much?

Motorcycle chit chat is easy. There is no searching for an appropriate topic; the subject is bikes. No commitments are made; soon, we'd all climb on and bugger off.

Lineups, where motorcycles muster, are natural melting pots. Multiculturalism is overridden. There is no hesitation; nothing is odd about striking up a conversation with another rider.

Behind us, where the cars clustered, it was the opposite. Drivers do not step out, stroll up to their neighbor's vehicle and start a conversation because they're both driving cars. They don't compare trunk space or inquire about the brand of wax used. They remain in their vehicles, sealed off, texting and playing *Call of Duty*. Even enthusiasts with muscle cars or classic cars remain caged, scattered around the vast parking lot. "Don't care if you're a car club member, Buster," our friends, the ferry operators tell them. "You're in a cage, and you're staying put with the rest of the cunts."

Except for commuter gal, the ferry motorbike group was connected and at ease. Bet Transport Bike Gal wishes she was in a car, I thought.

*Truth About Motorcycles: some riders discover they're meant to be in cars.*

None of bikers wore masks. Cagers watched in disgust as we flaunted COVID regulations, gambling with humanity's longevity. It was not a conscious protocol kick in the crotch. The power of the herd fuels a collective societal snub. Banded together, we would not be threatened by directives or pushed around by a puny virus.

The B.C. Ferries lot attendants kept a wide berth. "They're friends," supervisors said. "It's okay. Leave them be"

Statistic were very popular during the pandemic. This many people in these categories died of COVID today and this many will die next week. That sort of thing. "Had the number crunchers report on bikers killed by COVID," Conrad speculated, "I suspect they may have found that the virus was afraid of bikers."

"Ride. Balance your state of mind. Immunity is boosted," Marta added. "Could be valid."

Is there no end to the J O Y ?

◆◆◆

The MV Spirit of British Columbia has cafes, a gift shop, and a video game room, but all were closed. Citing COVID regulations, the ferry operators ordered car passengers to remain below deck and inside their cages. "Riders, come on up, away from the cunts. Relax in peace."

We nodded; thank you, friends.

It takes an hour and a half to sail between the Gulf Islands to Swartz Bay, north of Victoria. A pod of Orca whales may swim by on the port side. They're always on the port side, probably have a Pod Captain "everyone to the port side, staggered formation."

Motorcycles don't have port, starboard, captains, crews, or lifesaving equipment. If you get into trouble on a ferry, no problem: throw on a life jacket, lower the lifeboats, and ring the coast guard—nothing to worry about. Motorcycles are always on their own.

*Truth About Motorcycles: unlike ships,*
*motorcycles do not have life rafts.*

The crossing can be spectacular, but I don't take notice. Seen it many times. It's not like being on-motorcycle where you must pay attention. On a ship, you can sleep, read, play with your phone, or scratch your ass. A whale? Port or starboard side? Don't care. Seen whales before. They'll be in the water on the port side. Rising and falling, searching for seals to eat chunks of. I prefer elephants; let me know if you see one. Or if you spot a killer whale dragging a deer.

Mr. Pirsig got it dead wrong if you apply his thinking to ferries. On a ship, it's far better to Arrive than to Travel. The only reason you're Travelling is to Arrive at your destination. Onboard passengers become impatient —when will this tub Arrive so I can Depart on my motorbike? Mr. Pirsig should have tossed a few facts into his book, like: it is always better to Travel On A Motorcycle than to Travel By Ferry. Truths like that.

There is zero chance of having a mystical experience Traveling by ship. It doesn't matter what body of water you're floating on. Cruise lines don't advertise: join us to get in touch with your inner self or to move on from a horrific life experience. Cruisers prefer to come onboard, overindulge, get pissed up, watch corny entertainment and occasionally line up to get off and then back on their floating mall. Suppose you're unlucky enough to be on board when a pandemic breaks out, welcome to no-man's-land. You really, really, really want to Arrive, but the authorities insist virus-laden ships continue to Travel. "Sail around looking for whales on the port side until the viral war is over," the coronavirus gestapo dictates. "Maybe launch a couple of lifeboats and invade Guadalcanal."

For example, The Grand Princess departed San Francisco on February 2020. Three thousand vacationers soon found themselves stuck in quarantine hell. No more self-serve buffets. The ship wasn't allowed to return to port in California. Princess passengers were stuck at sea. Motorcycles cannot be locked down.

The ferry inched me ever closer to the end of my inaugural climb back on mini-ride. It wasn't a test of secondary roads where Deadeye Dick and Warhammer deer thrive, but it was therapeutic. It was progress, one click of the torque wrench at a time.

I was an islander again when we unloaded, detached from the mass. Vancouver Island extends 285 miles (460 km) north to south, with an area slightly larger than Belgium. It's home to musician Nelly Furtado who wrote the motorcycle traveling song, *I'm Like a Bird*, I'll only fly away, and the sorrowful motorcycle-less lament, *Why Do All Good Things Come to an End?* Come to an end? Come to an end? Nelly knows how to bring a tear to the eye of this curmudgeon.

Vehicles form a ferry parade, heading south down Highway 17 toward Victoria, a city of 250,000 on the southern tip of the island. Twenty minutes from home for me. When I turned off the highway, Triumph scrambler honked and waved. I waved back. We had just met, but a Motorcycle Connection formed. Then Biker Dog went by in his basket enclosure. His chauffeur waved.

None of the cagers honked or waved as they broke off from the pack.

Back at the terminal, ferry operators directed more two-wheelers to drive past the cars to the front of the line. "Welcome, friends!"

At home, in my garage, I parked Red Beauty in the #1 spot (after pushing Softy farther back). "Motorcycle-less no more," I told Pearl and Bunny. "What do you think? Project Climb Back-On was a success!"

Pets know how to suck up to get a treat. Still Pearl, Bunny and I, along with Red Beauty, shared a moment of JOY.

Bunny brushed my leg. He understands. Days and months of life can happen in minutes and hours on-motorcycle. Riding is a quest, like life condensed in time. The perfect ride doesn't last long. Life is like that, right, Bunny?

Bunny purred; so this is my new seat?

*Truth About Motorcycles: riding is a journey.*

We went upstairs to see Dori. "Sometimes hugs work best," I heard Bunny purr.

*You & Your Motorcycle: do you carry hugs in your tool kit?*

The route home, via Hwy 5, the Coquihalla.

# CHAPTER 22 – ABOUT NEUROTRANSMITTERS

A schoolmate, Cam Marshall, owned a Ducati scrambler, similar to the Triumph I met at the ferry terminal. Cam can tinkle the ivories, as they say. When we talk JOY, he says: "Riding is like playing the piano. Players, like riders, must become technically proficient, but MAGIC is in the soul."

*Truth About Motorcycles: there is MAGIC in the soul of the machine.*

"Riding is playing *Great Balls of Fire,* Jerry Lee Lewis revved up," Cam says.

When Bob and I dropped by a few years ago, Megan, Cam's teenage daughter, said, "Zooming around, bent over, Dad looks like Daffy Duck, riding that thing."

Is a scrambler a quirky choice for a middle-aged Emergency Medical Technician? Are there age appropriate motorcycles?

"My Daffy Dad."

Cam used to sign off, "Mr. Duck."

When I was recovering on the eleventh floor of Royal Jubilee Hospital, Cam rode down the island to wish me well. He brought coffee from the hospital bistro and grapes from his backyard. We talked about school days and Cam's dad, Frank. I remembered when we were boys, Cam said something I thought was odd, "Even my dad cries sometimes. Only when he can't ride."

Frank was broad-shouldered, an indestructible looking man. He was a down-to-earth superhero, capable of just about anything, we thought. When Cam was fourteen, Frank's number came up in the Death Lottery. He was waiting to pick up a DQ ice cream cake. The server was writing "Happy Birthday, Cammy Boy!" when Frank keeled over. He wasn't dead, but would be soon. Tumor: brain and spinal cord. Welcome to Life Part II.

"Probably working too hard," Cam's mother had said when her husband complained of headaches and dizziness. Cam and I were in grade seven.

Birthdays still aren't a happy time for my pal—Cam once fired a banana loaf into the garbage, insisting, "it's cake."

Frank owned a motorcycle. His riding buddies told Cam, "Your dad went to the great salvage yard in the sky."

Never take parents for granted!

Old people die, and everyone over twenty is old when you're a kid. Kids can't conceive of getting as old as Frank. They understand you get old, then you die, but can't comprehend aging. What bothered Cam was the unfairness; many people older than his dad were alive.

Cam's dad was forty-four when "the good Lord took

him." His wife always added, "to a better place."

Cam had his doubts. Despite requests, he received no sign "Dad is in a better place. Why doesn't dad tell me about it if it's so great? He used to tell me everything. Is he in a concentration camp? Like being in detention, no talking, ever? Why the gag order?"

Frank's treasure was a Harley Panhead. "There's something magical about it," he told Cam and I. At the time, we couldn't put our finger on what it was.

Whenever Frank announced, "I'll be taking her out tomorrow," a spark of excitement lit us up. Cam's dad would roll down the driveway and disappear for hours. Other days, father and son rode slowly around the neighborhood. Everyone looked. Cam waved. Frank took me as well. My first motorcycle picture, sitting on Frank's Panhead.

Pure Childhood Motorcycle JOY!

Cam's older sister, Arlene, also died of a neurological disease. Her signals went haywire, like a CPU malfunction. There was talk Arlene had inherited bad genes when she passed at age fifty-one. Medical science gave her seven more years than her father, who seldom saw a doctor. Cam's mother said, "Arlene's gone to join Dad in a better place."

"Horseshit," Cam told me. "If my saint-like father didn't get in, my sister sure as hell wouldn't." Arlene's nose was in stuff other than the grindstone.

The Marshals are "ticking time bombs," folks said when Arlene kicked the bucket. To Cam, that meant: I'm next. "I have a death sentence."

When Bob and I visited Cam, we were all older than his dad was when he passed. Not that Cam felt old. "Young enough to bomb around on that silly little bike like Daffy

Duck," Megan said.

Cam never talked to Megan about "riding away from my death sentence." Medical science is unlocking DNA secrets, but the message remains: you can't escape bad genes. Cam lived in a minefield and was not confident he'd end up in a better place. "The scrambler unburdens me," he told Bob and I. "It's the best medicine on the market. Beats playing piano. You can't travel on a piano or scrape the keys."

Cam follows the research. It's encouraging. Genetics and neurology may soon discover how to manipulate the genome and train neurons to, for example, avoid genetic quirks handed down, slow the aging process and increase healthy lifespans. Cam adopts hacks he thinks "may get me off of death row. While I wait, the scrambler acts like a relief valve. Wipes thoughts of Dad, Arlene, and I'm next away. It works like a hot damn."

"More evidence," Marta says, "Supporting motorcycles as therapeutic devices."

*Truth About Motorcycles: measurable neurological and physiological responses are objective evidence of JOY.*

It's not pie in the sky. Marta speculated: "Perhaps one day they'll find the molecular pathway that regulates JOY."

"Make a pill that targets damaged cells to cure Boneheads and NimRods," Conrad said.

"Can you imagine?"

"A world full of Motorcycle JOY?"

*Always, always, always, nurture your neurotransmitters.*

*Tune your Motorcycle State of Mind.*

Multiple studies have reported significant changes in hormone levels and nervous system activity during wind therapy sessions. The brain is a map of experiences; under the right conditions, it will learn to associate motorcycle riding with pleasure, throwing the door wide open to JOY. *Come on in! This is your cuddle place. Disconnect. Forget the horseshit. Be happy!* With a tuned up state of mind, a motorcycle is like visiting friends—it will naturally make you feel good. Nothing like eating junk food, which is manufactured to light up brains chemically and then make you crave more junk. It's a downward spiral cluttering your systems like dirty oil. Motorcycle JOY is clean and remains uplifting.

*Truth About Motorcycles: chemically induced pleasure cannot put you on the Road to JOY.*

Riding produces rapid information flows. Stimulus and change are high octane fuel tickling sensory neurons. Add in abundant fresh air and perhaps sunshine—spirits naturally rise.

Perception is under human control. Riders choose to be aware of the weather, road conditions, traffic, machine operations, wildlife, everything Mother Nature and humanity can throw at us. Our neurons are constantly stimulated.

In a well-balanced state of mind, natural neuromodulation occurs. Riders are bombarded with stimuli which produce electrical pulses that act on target areas (just as pharmaceutical agents manufacture chemical neuromodulation). Receptive riders experience dopamine, serotonin, epinephrine, cortisol, and other chemical changes. These neurotransmitters stir emotions that build the sense of well-being we know as JOY.

Motorcycle JOY doesn't rely on false agents. No concoctions are ingested like dark chocolate or crystal meth to whip up dopamine or serotonin surges. Drugs require increasingly larger dosages to be effective while destroying baseline hormone levels. Easier than riding? More fun and joyful? Surges manufactured by swallowing chemicals are short-lived. Subjects soon become numb and find themselves on Deadend Road devoid of MAGIC.

*Truth About Motorcycles: unlike chemical addiction, Motorcycle JOY must be nurtured, not swallowed or mainlined.*

Developing a Motorcycle State of Mind is complex; sticking a needle in your arm is simple and immediate. Experienced addicts may look around, smile for a moment, and say, "all is well," but they know it's not. Drugs are part of Life, the Bully. Motorcycle JOY is part of Life, the Beautiful. Yin and yang.

Based on short rides, researchers have measured decreases in the levels of the stress hormone cortisol (up to 28 percent), significant increases in the happy hormones, and elevated heart rates (equivalent to light exercise).

"Medical science proves," Marta said, "that Cam is not

daffy."

*You & Your Motorcycle: does your motorcycle clear your head and ease your mind?*

◆◆◆

Marta admits, "I'd probably be fat as a whale or a workaholic, if not for Guzzi."

Everyone agrees. Marta can be obsessive.

Megan, Cam's daughter, had no sympathy for "Dad's bad gene delusion," nor did she buy into Motorcycle Therapy. I don't know Megan well, but she can come across like Warhammer Shelly. "What's wrong with my dad?" she asked when Bob and I dropped by? "Is Dad losing his marbles?"

I stared back nervously, grinning like a nutter.

Fortunately, Megan added, "just kidding."

Bob described Cam as "a prince of a man," noting how he cared for both his bike and his daughter (Cam's a single parent).

"I like the stripped-down, wind in my face, nothing but bike approach," Cam told us. "The scrambler reminds me of sitting behind Dad on his Panhead, except way smoother and quieter. When the engine starts, it clears my mind. 'Go fuck yourself world, the engine says when it revs. It never fails to plant a grin on my face. I can hear Dad encouraging me. Go for it, Cammy Boy!"

"A bit daffy," Bob said later.

◆◆◆

The day it happened, Megan, "Had a bee in her bonnet. Some days, everything upsets her." Cam and I were chatting by phone. "Should have kept my mouth shut. Walked away. Instead, I fanned the flames. Raised my voice. Became defensive when she lashed out; about her mom." Megan blames her father for "Mom not being able to live with Daffy Dad." Unfair, but that's life being a bully.

Cam heard his daughter sobbing in her room. It's a stab to the heart of a wounded parent. Don't pound on my child, Life! Cam had retreated. As a parent, it's tough not being able to snap your fingers to fix your child's problem.

In the garage, Cam put his riding gear on, following a ritual, an ordered routine, as if breaking the steps would change the outcome. He pushed the scrambler outside. The garage door closed. *When I return, I'll hug my daughter.*

There was no choice but to ride. "Things build up in me. Megan's right, I am daffy."

*You & Your Motorcycle: do you feel, sometimes there is no answer but to ride? And then, sometimes there are no answers? Do you keep riding until it no longer matters?*

Cam swung his right leg over the seat and started the Ducati. "The rumble of the engine immediately calms me."

Twenty-five minutes later, the scrambler was on a rural road surrounded by farmland and thin forest. They didn't build roads straight for long back in the day. Cam knew every curve, every dip, every patch where there might be loose gravel. He confessed: "It's my unofficial race track. Riding hard stomps on my obsessions."

The scrambler screamed through the first s-curve, accelerated out onto a straightaway, and then slowed for a tight corner, fast but under control.

A car approached. The bike slowed. A father and child were in the front seat, the girl a bit younger than Megan. Talking and smiling on their way to town, enjoying one another's company, as fathers and daughters who travel together in automobiles do.

The bike entered the next corner, high revs and accelerating, not well dialed in. "I knew it was wrong, but didn't care. I can cheat physics, I thought. And if I don't..." The left footpeg scraped. The bike drifted wide.

"Felt the tires slip. I was in a Zombie-like state. It was like I wanted to crash to punish myself. For not being a better father... to kill my obsessions. I knew I was going down and didn't give a shit."

*Truth About Motorcycles: you must always give a shit.*

The scrambler was on its side. Rider and machine separated. Cam lay in the gravel, ego bruised, shoulder aching, heart rate peaking. "I thought, what would Dad think? Didn't raise you to lie in dirt. "Cam paused. "Both my bike and I were broken."

"A beautiful wreck. I've seen a few." Cam had crossed the line. Dismissed his riding rules. Rode numb and dumb. "Always give a shit, Cam. Always."

Cam nodded. "When I looked over at what I'd done to my bike, I imagined Dad, sitting on his Panhead, shaking his head. Then I heard him say, go Cammy boy. He always used to say that to encourage me."

A few months after the accident, Cam bought a new

MICHAEL STEWART

motorcycle.

# PART THREE: HOME

*I know why Pearl sticks her head*
*out of our car window.*

# CHAPTER 23 – ABOUT NARCISSISM

Marta pointed to Rule #11 on the lab's whiteboard. "Dolores changed her tune about the number of items in a list. No longer insisting on ten. Sixteen. Thirty-seven. Any number, she says."

"She's becoming an outlaw? A rebel? She is considering buying a bike, right?"

"Likes red ones." Marta paused. "Going with eleven Motorcycle Riding Rules, Dolores says, is perfect for a promotion. Buy *The Joy of Motorcycles* and get a free rule."

"People want free rules?"

"That's what I said."

I pictured the book cover. A hunk and a babe, one with *Buckets for Coconuts*, the other *Get Your Free Rule*.

"Want to take in some therapy with us? Tony needs to ride." The pandemic was mincing Tony's deli business.

"Maybe Tony could sell helmets while pastrami's outlawed?"

"A free battered pickle with every purchase?"

I showed Marta my new matte black Gt Air 2. "Got a nice discount."

Marta patted CTX. "Let's see what your baby will do. Is it a cruiser or a sports bike?"

"Motorcycle."

Bunny recognized the signs of an imminent hullabaloo. He doesn't appreciate the combustion or motion aspects of motorcycles; why not use bikes as permanent teddies? Peaceful JOY instead of unholy noise generators?

◆◆◆

When Tony revs his Indian, I hum loudly or sing, ♫ Every time I hear that oom-pa-pa. Everybody feels so tra-la-la ♫. Tony's a polka music freak—my interpretation of his loud pipes is a distraction technique. Like closing your eyes when something terrible is about to happen, except *oom-pa-pa* works.

Imagine Dr. Peggy hollering, "Oh, bellis perennis" over and over. Well, not that annoying, but loud pipes are worse than listening to "we're experiencing higher than normal call volumes" when you know it's business as usual, and the agents all got hammered in the bar the previous night.

Tony's pipes are not as obnoxious as the twin Harleys with third party pipes that shook the ferry car deck. But his custom tubes fire a warning shot: beware Ears! Secure plugs, prepare for bombardment. Or if you're Bunny, get the hell out of Dodge.

"The racket turns me against motorcycles," Dolores said. "Worse than kids hammering on pots and pans." Pipes are like words. "Cager-cunt," "political science," and "speeding ticket" drill into your brain while others like "automobile driver," "scientist" and "no harm done" barely register.

"There are no cars with noisy mufflers?" Marta

challenged Dolores, feeling compelled to defend her comrades. "How about diesel trucks?"

"Sophisticated," Tony calls the sound of his boisterous machine. He works the Indian's throttle like a volume control. The engine revs. Pipes blast a few *oom-pa-pas's* and Tony smiles. Loud pipes are part of the deli owner's JOY; Tony believes everybody feels a polka coming on when they hear *tra-la-las*. "A throaty orchestra. Come on; you love it. Admit it, my pipes make you want to dance."

Pipes are one of motorcycling's dividing walls. Do you love Insane Clown Posse but detest Celine Dion (or vice versa)? Pipes are like musical taste. Some love polka—others punk rock or gospel.

*You & Your Motorcycle: do you have a loudness threshold?*

Do loud pipes save lives? Boast horsepower? Reduce weight? Enhance appearance? Blast a beautiful noise? Are pipes a personal prerogative, like going helmet-less?

Or are they obnoxious infringements?

There is no holy book of motorcycling. No Ten Commandments to separate right from wrong. Ride this way to go directly to Heaven. Fall into the arms of seventy-two virgins. Poke an unwed virgin on Earth and end up on a sore-ass motorcycle seat for eternity. Unlike religious doctrines, motorcycle culture is a black box.

God respects list structure and stopped at ten rules. "That's it. After ten, they're on their own. Tell Humanity to use free will, Moses." God chuckled. In Eternity, there's no hurry which explains why He didn't intervene when Moses wandered around lost in the desert for forty years.

"Let's see what riders get up to. Remain stock? Go with slip-ons? Full replacement? Maybe drill a few holes?"

"Works for me, Your Lordship," Moses had answered, knowing not to argue with The Boss. The Commandments were written in stone, not on a modern tablet, making them a bitch to revise and a challenge to lug around on Commandment Tours. "Free will it is."

Governments have gone the opposite direction trying to pin every detail down. In their quest, bureaucrats turn to numbers. "We'll use decibels to resolve the Loud Pipe Issue. If your meter reading exceeds this number, ticket," lawmakers instruct enforcement. "You know? Works exactly like speeding tickets. Simple right?"

"What if I stop seven hogs and each one is slightly below the number, but together they're obscenely over the number?"

Numbers cannot paint a picture the way 72 virgins or spending eternity in a blast furnace does. *Who are you to dictate musical taste, styling, and deny the safety of loud pipes? Who made you, God, politicians?*

Individual perception determines which side of the sound wall listeners fall on. "Loud pipes save lives," advocates lecture. "Better deaf than dead." The louder the bike, the more you're noticed, the safer you are, is the theory. Get loud pipes! Motorcycle Lives Matter! Fuck laws and norms!

Ferry Dude might have told me, "If you'd had loud pipes, Horace wouldn't have jumped onto the highway in front of your quiet, barely noticeable bike!"

I'd rather have been pounded by sound waves than asphalt, that's for sure. Loud pipe logic makes sense: noise can scare killers away. The louder your pipes, the stronger your defense. Get loud pipes! Sure, the racket triggers massive migraines and infringes on librarians and cats, but isn't safety a little more important than a few throbbing, overly sensitive heads? Down a couple of aspirin. Chant Om-Aum. Buy better earplugs! Consider the big picture, selfish, inconsiderate quiet bike pussies!

"A steady, loud sound is way more effective than beeping a horn at the last minute," Tony says. "Rule #11 should be: Don't Kill Yourself by Not Having Loud Pipes."

The other side of the Loud Pipe Debate offers the Doppler Effect. It states loud pipes are at their best when a bike has passed the listener. In other words, when it's too late, noisy pipes do their best work. "We want the killers to know before we meet up, not after we've gone by," Marta tells Tony.

"Doppler-smoppler. What kind of BS is that? Can't you hear me coming? That Doppler BS doesn't fool anyone."

Tony is right. Science can be twisted. Never assume science-based media reports are scientific. Despite the Doppler Effect, I always hear the Indian long before it arrives at my house, and Tony's pipes aren't super loud.

"Don't Kill Yourself by Not Having Loud Pipes can't be a Motorcycle Riding Rule because it contravenes the law," engineer Marta insisted. "Besides, riders with loud pipes risk being punched out by enraged peace and quiet types, like Dolores and Dr. Peggy, driven mad by your racket."

The truth is, listeners are unlikely to confront dudes driving obnoxious street bikes. Instead, they curse when assaulted, choosing to cover their ears while they grin and bear it. Better than getting pounded by scary-looking outlaws living on the fringe of society.

Loud pipes turn people against motorcycles," Dolores insists.

*Truth about Motorcycles: loud pipes piss off more people than cagers cutting bikers off.*

*You & Your Motorcycle: has pipe noise upset your neighbours?*

"My pipes are a musical instrument," Tony says. "Throaty, not loud. Ever hear a bad trumpet player? That's what noise sounds like, but the authorities don't ban trumpet playing. No loud pipes! Close delis during pandemics. But murder a musical instrument on the street outside a business or camp on the sidewalk... Mayor Dumbass doesn't give a shit."

In the hands of a master, pipes can impart a rising and falling sense of power. Like a well-orchestrated symphony, volume reaches a crescendo before easing as the driver backs the throttle off.

Tubes are tuned in search of the perfect exhaust note. There is tolerance, even respect, for throaty pipes. Raise the level a few decibels or sustain peak volume too long, and throaty becomes a hullabaloo.

In the hands of a skilled operator, loud bikes can run incognito, gliding by the noise meter equipped police. Then, maestros open up, blasting sound waves, rattling dishes, and tickling neurotransmitters.

"Loud pipes are very effective at drawing attention," Dr. Phil wrote in *Life Code: The New Motorcycle Rules*. "Which is their real purpose. Let's call loud pipes what they are, agents of Motorcycle Narcissism. Safety and performance are red herrings." Dr. Phil's dual sport had throaty pipes.

There is nothing subtle about assaulting people with

dangerous amounts of noise. Exceeding ninety decibels for any length of time can cause hearing damage. Riders who wouldn't dream of beating a stranger's ears with a claw hammer have no qualms about hitting people with invisible sound waves. The driver isn't thinking; excuse me for being a safety nut! No! It's all about look at me and my big, powerful, loud machine. That's pure MAGIC between my legs, baby. All eyes on me and my beauty.

It's pure Motorcycle Narcissism.

Exhaust noise is not enough for some. Loud Pipe-Loud Music Lovers (LPLMs) play selections using speakers mounted on fairings for an extra dose of narcissism. To drown out exhaust noise, they crank their volume controls. What's the point of music if it's not heard? Turn it loud!

"I don't have speakers," Tony points out. Thank God!

Polka Man likes to team up with a Harley to play the occasional duet. ♫ *Every time they hear that oom-pa-pa. Potato. Everybody feels so tra-la-la. Potato-potato* ♫.

You don't hear Lady Gaga coming from motorcycle speakers. Heavy metal, classic rock, and rap are popular. Often full of words you'd prefer junior didn't hear. "What does motherfucker mean, Mommy? Is it as bad as cager?"

Never take silence for granted.

"Outrageous," my musician-audiophile friend Denis says. "Music is meant to be enjoyed in its purest form, sheltered from interference. Why not enjoy your song, the one with "motherfucker" you like to play, on an excellent sound system in an acoustically correct environment? Let the artistry shine. Make the lyrics comprehend-able. We'd hear how the artist uses 'motherfucker' to drive a point." Den shakes his head at the technical folly of motorcycle-based sound systems.

Put loud pipes and fairing music together, and you'll piss everyone off except yourself. If you're an LPLM, get help! Call Dr. Peggy, Dr. Seuss, Dr. Who, Dr. Pepper, or Doc Martens. These doctors all understand: loud pipes are a failure of free will.

"If You don't add an Eleventh Commandment, there's bound to be hearing loss issues," Moses told his Boss. "May lead to problems communicating the ten big rules. Then what?"

"Humanity can evolve," God assured Moses. "I've got an idea about a guy I call Darwin II."

An expert on motorcycle exhausts, Moses speculated?

"I like where they're going with the new touring exhausts," God told Mother Nature.

"We need to talk," Mom replied, "About "the Greta Thunberg thing." Greta was getting noticed as an up and comer in the environmental crusader business.

"Greta's getting loud pipes," God asked?

"I'd like to see her on a mobility scooter," Mother suggested.

"Darwin II will help with that. He'll be a biker," God said. "Time to shake things up."

Mom smiled. *That's why He's the Boss and swells me with JOY.*

◆ ◆ ◆

All riders are narcissistic.

Thanks to free will, the sound of a perfect ride will remain undefined for eternity. Art can't be reduced to a meter reading.

Polka Man admits, "If I could start over, I'd pay more

attention to protection. Tinnitus is way worse than catching COVID." Ringing in the ears isn't contagious. Riders do it to themselves. Narcissistic riders become quiet riders or throaty riders. Still renegades at heart, but deaf later in life, with a presence, like Clint Eastwood.

*You & Your Motorcycle: is it all about*
*you and your steel horse?*

# CHAPTER 24 – A RIDE WITH MARTA AND TONY

A yellow banner said Respect All Protocols! It was intended to discourage loitering at the rest stop. Brave soldiers had draped it around our picnic table, a potential ambush platform. Tony pulled the ribbon away before putting a towel down.

"Locked," Marta reported. "Gotta pee in the bush."

In the summer of 2020, the people-who-know-best were keen on locking doors and taping public facilities off.

Polka Man placed three Cosmic Specials on the table in an exaggerated professional manner.

I sat facing our machines. Parked bikes are like flowers in a florist shop. The big Indian in the middle, flanked by CTX and Guzzi. It's a fun aspect of traveling together, Bike Arrangement JOY. A little harmless bit of group narcissism. Not for all, but many appreciate parking artistry. Our arrangement may have appeared haphazard, but it included a subconscious calculation—an instinctive jockeying for position. Beautiful steel.

It begins on arrival. Does the lead swing around to

guide its back tire toward the curb for a front-facing display? Do the others follow, or will one alternate to stand out? An inch this way or that can make a difference to a bike being featured or fading into the collection. Leave your helmet with the bike for an added touch? Wipe off that speck of dust before walking away?

Rest stoppers checked our three stallions out. Dad dreamed: when I retire, I'll buy a bike like the big loud one in the middle and drive to a far-off land (or at least as far as Hope). Finally, I'll find myself. The Indian is always the kid's favorite. Youngsters aren't into therapy or classic bikes. "They're for pussies." Little boys are all gonna get hogs when they grow up—a bike like Tony's. Tony loves the attention. Wait till you hear my polka pipes, boys!

When I unwrapped my special, I saw Tony; always the joker, had garnished it with a vile Brussels sprout, the Freddy Krueger of small vegetables. I picked the round pale green turd up and lobbed it at him. "Hilarious, Tony." It's nice that the pandemic never quashed his sense of humor the way it killed his business.

Tony batted the round turd away. "They're tasty done right. I'll convince you one of these days."

"Not possible."

"Smothered in a rich sauce, with bacon bits, maybe deep-fried? Served with stout."

I'm not fond of stout.

"Sprouts aren't popular like peas and carrots, but nutritionally they're rock stars," Marta said. "Who'd have thought the Flemish, a gentle, inconspicuous folk, would be behind the bad boy of the vegetable world? What drove them to adopt the obnoxious sprout? Why didn't they go with something marketable, like peas or beans?"

"Or lettuce? No one hates lettuce."

Tony faked a biker dude expression. "A misunderstood vegetable in a delicious sauce. On sourdough. I'll call it the Outlaw Biker Special. Hot peppers optional." He looked at me. "Bet I could sell a ton of them... if I had a deli."

"Bikes have a rebellious pizzazz," Marta said. "But not sprouts. Despite being on the fringe of the vegetable world, there's no bad veggie attraction."

"A vegan option would sell... anything new without meat."

"Perhaps if a few diners crashed, trying to cough up sprouts... there'd be respect for Brussels as the outlaw of veggies?"

Lunch with Marta and Tony. "Battered pickle?" I offered Marta's The World's Getting Battered and in a Pickle, pickles around to change the topic.

"Hey!" Tony yelled at a kid twisting the Indian's volume control.

"Would you like a battered pickle, little boy?" Marta called to the startled future biker.

A horrified mother grabbed her son's arm and marched him away from the bike display. "When I grow up, I'm gonna get a big one, mommy. Like the loud one in the middle."

Not a bloody chance!

*Truth About Motorcycles: just about every little boy starts out wanting a big bike with lots of chrome and loud pipes.*

"Girls too," Marta says.

Babies pop out of the womb full of wonder, filled with Childhood JOY. Life the Bully hogties them. Kids are caged. Some will escape by discovering Motorcycle JOY. On-motorcycle, they'll remain kids at heart.

# CHAPTER 25 – ABOUT THE WAVE

Three bikes pulled out. Noise from the Indian assailed the rest stop, causing marauding COVID germs to take refuge in a Porta Potty. "Damn pipes. We'll attack once the racket dies down. Pipes are worse than their bleach guns."

A boy watched the Indian leave. WOW!

Tony smiled.

A small, sensible bike approached on the Island Highway. Tony twisted his volume control to say hello, and I sang ♫ Every time I hear that oom-pa-pa. Everybody feels so tra-la-la ♫.

The advancing rider's arm raised. The finger? Shove this down your polka tubes, loud pipe cunt. Instead, hello, nice to see ya. *On-motorcycle, we're all friends.*

"Part of the evolution of things," Darwin II told Moses. "Motorcyclists are way ahead of the United Nations."

COVID-19 ended the handshake, but it couldn't kill the biker wave. We returned the gesture. Hello there, camouflage green Kawasaki Sherpa.

Marta did her exuberant cheerleader wave, making my minimal response acceptable. One well-executed, or two token gestures, suffices to represent a group of riders.

Marta is a Wave Power advocate. "An express of J O Y ," she says.

◆◆◆

North American riders, more likely to hurl foul language and a derogatory salute if they met off-motorcycle, often wave as they pass. "It's a sprinkle of pixie dust," Marta says.

In other parts of the world, riders may nod or stick their foot out (where they drive on the opposite side of the road) to say, WOW, another two-wheeler! A comrade. Good to see you, buddy! Ride safe!

The wave is a curious melting pot phenomenon rooted in a time when motorcycle outlaws were a true breed apart. A symbol of fellowship and a wink; yes, we know about MAGIC and J O Y .

Mazda drivers don't honk to acknowledge other Mazda drivers, let alone worry about extending a greeting to Peugeots or any other vehicle. A renegade group of Jeep owners may wave, but there is no historical foundation for their gesture. Don't demean motorcycle culture, Jeep-cunts! You're not fooling anyone.

Would automobile engineers develop self-driving cars if operating four-wheelers produced J O Y ? No! The product direction is: more time to text, watch videos, play Call of Duty, concentrate on getting to Mars, and eat junk food. They strive to reduce the monotony of automobile travel. Their goal? Enabling people to sleep while driving is a worthy therapeutic advancement, but napping cannot compete with Motorcycle Therapy. Motorcycles focus on the opposite experience.

Travel.

Engage.
Scrape Pegs.
Neuromodulation.
Disconnect.
JOY!

*You & Your Motorcycle: your motorcycle social interactions are far more interesting than your automobile-based relationships, right?*

It's not just drivers stuck in cars that lack fellowship. Rather than tip their rods to say hello, trout fishers glare: don't go near my secret fishin' hole! To them, people carrying poles are like the Gestapo with detention lists.

Poetry lovers keep their books hidden in backpacks because theirs' is a reflective pastime—no tossing out couplets or free verse on the streets. Absolutely no waving. No loud sonnets. No, wink—yes, I know about the secret sauce of poems.

Gobbler hunters are the worst: bitter, petty, deceitful, small-minded, bird rivals. They have no qualms about spinning lies. "No, didn't see or hear shit this week. A couple of crap jakes, no toms. Not a hen in sight. Nothing. This is a shithole. A complete waste of time." They drop all moral pretense and screw over their hunting comrades for a chance to shoot a foul-tasting bird often served with Brussel sprouts. *All gobblers in this area belong to me, and you're gettin' shit.* "Fuck off to Kentucky and get some fried chicken."

Take warring turkey hunters, place them on bikes, and suddenly it's a banjo-playing Juggalos love fest. On-motorcycle, even hunters, rejoice. They wave to fellow turkey hunters. Hope you nail a big fat tom today!

Step off and they're back to being Hatfield and McCoy petty gobbler rivals.

Unlike poems, turkey hunting, trout fishing, or driving a Jeep, Motorcycle JOY is transformative.

Groups like NATO portray solidarity when their officials meet, standing shoulder to shoulder (thanks to COVID, for a time, assistants had to distance their bosses), with unified smiles, for their annual photo op. Tiny nations rub up against powerful ones, but there is derision aplenty behind the scenes.

"Why must I always stand next to Luxembourg?"

"Who voted to let Albania in?"

"What'd you mean it's Belgium's turn to host lunch? Eat your sprouts or there'll be diplomatic repercussions?"

That sort of thing.

NATO flags don't wave when their bulletproof limos pass. "The world would be a better place if nations waved," Marta suggests.

When bikers wave, differences blow away—let's try for peace on earth—goodwill through motorcycling. Forget about forming alliances. We'll all just get along. Blessed be your ride.

It puzzles the hell out of both the Institute for Interreligious Dialogue and Diplomats for Peace. *How do they do it? These bikers. Is magic involved?*

Folklore attributes the origin of the etiquette ritual to Arthur Davidson and William Harley, who, in 1904, passed each other and waved. Not all riders respect the tradition. There is the Motorcycle Wave Dilemma.

*Truth About Motorcycles: riders face unique predicaments.*

Being socially lazy, I'm not a good initiator, not a Marta. Return a wave given? Yes, of course. I'm lazy and blunt, not rude.

Is it acceptable to ignore a biker unlikely to reciprocate? Extreme chopper dude, for example, who is on a different trajectory? Or an Oddball pulling a homemade trailer through the cosmos? Or the dirt bikers trying to maintain a low profile, hoping to make their turn before the cops nail them? Are trikes and electric scooters included? Must a two-thousand-dollar bike acknowledge a one percenter? What about motorcycle cops? These questions weigh on the community of wavers.

The Hesitant Wave is the most challenging situation. A bike approaches. It feels like a clear, no-wave situation; both riders are reluctant. Tired. Not in the mood to waste an unnecessary gesture and be diminished by an unreturned wave. Both riders relax, confident it's a mutual scenario. We're outlaws, not compliant soldiers—two progressives on motorbikes, free to give our ritual the finger. Scrape our pegs.

But at the last minute, one rider breaks rank, executes a graceful left-handed peace, two wheels down sign pointing to the asphalt. Entangled in The Hesitant Wave trap, the other rider scrambles, curses for being caught in the Wave Dilemma by an expert deployment of the Hesitant Wave. With no time to attempt a full-extension, an unnoticed lame wrist wiggle is the only response possible. Neither person is content with the outcome. One gave but did not receive. The other, a violator of a sacred trust going all the way back to Harley and Davidson, is uncaring and joyless. If only there were rules to address the Hesitant Wave.

Unique to our community, the wave expresses JOY in the hands of willing participants and seems worthwhile. Everyone returns Marta's wave. *I have plenty to share. Here, have some of my JOY!*

A former Curmudgeonly Jackass, I'm not a talented wave executioner and, susceptible types, such as myself, feel uneasy when a wave given is not returned. It's the Wave Dilemma—a gesture meant to be joyful can be problematic. I'm going to see if the lab can work up a solution. Maybe have Dr. Tire attach (like a mirror on a handlebar) one of those perpetually waving hands, so all bikes, everywhere, all the time, will always be wave compliant.

The perpetual wave.

# CHAPTER 26 – ABOUT GROUP RIDES

Tony led. CTX middle. Marta was sweeper.

In a trio, Sandwich Bike is always two wheels from moving to the lead or the tail. Lean forward. Punch Go. Goodbye middle! In a crowd of many middles, boxed in, escape can be impossible. Not only is there physical confinement, but packs also quash individualism. Gangs are about the strength of numbers, like soldiers in an army platoon or a battalion. Hemmed-in bikes are not in charge, but are never alone.

As we approached a bend, I moved closer to Tony. *Are you worried about your pickled eggs going bad, Deli Man?* The big Indian often brakes for corners. CTX is agile and stealthy. Not as quick as my teal R1100 RS, the bike that introduced me to Bob and riding in formation, but up to waving goodbye to Tony.

Tony saw Red Beauty make its move and twisted his volume control. He came out of the turn, blasting. ♫ every time they hear that oom-pa-pa. Everybody feels so tra-la-la ♫

Too late, deli owner!

I waved. Tony braked for the next corner.

Marta remained at the rear to monitor my agrizoophobia (fear of wild animals leaping in front of my bike). I've never told her about my cleithrophobia (fear of being trapped in the middle).

My Complainers whined. I thought about past relationships. Bikes like Teal Beauty.

◆◆◆

Teal Beauty sat, majestic, proud of itself, like a European garden statue, content to be on display, with its color-matched panniers and leather tank bra, on a neighbor's front lawn. Dressed to kill, it waited for a new home. For me—I had been pressured into being motorcycle-less and felt uneasy. A voice, from a distance, called: "I'm beautiful. Look at my curves. The softness of my leather. The glow of my metal. I'm gorgeous, everything you desire."

"Trying to quit," I said. "Switching to a tent trailer or a used RV."

The BMW was one block over from our house on Mission Avenue, a for sale sign taped to its windscreen. The asking price: $5,900 OBO.

"OBO implies a reasonable offer," I imagined Bob saying. "Don't be Mr. Lowball Jackass."

"Doesn't say, best reasonable offer. If that's the intent, state it. Take twenty-five bucks, hand over the keys, or I call my lawyer."

"You don't have a lawyer," Bob would say.

"Will you lend me twenty-five bucks? I'll tell the seller, hand over the keys, or I'll send a demand letter from Self Serve Legal Forms.com. Same as a lawyer, but ninety percent cheaper."

*Five large for a beautiful teal racer?* WOW! The bike was eleven years old, older than any motorcycle I'd owned. Would it be fatigued? Failing electrics? Leaky gaskets? Leave me stranded with my helmet down, hoping a friendly CBer pulling a ramp-equipped truck would stop?

"Six years old in bike years," Conrad would say, because motorcycles are used part time. "As long as it was respected."

"Old Beemers run forever," I'd heard, but took with a click of a cheap torque wrench. "If you look after them." What does that mean? Look after them? Like those rebuilt old cars you see pulled over on the side of roads, hood up, and a classic car buff scratching his head? *Spent two decades and huge bucks, and this piece of shit strands me after just twelve miles?*

RS sure didn't look like it required CBer attention. It was beautiful and knew it. It sang:

♫ I feel pretty,
Oh, so pretty
Yes, I'm teal and quick and bright,
And I pity you,
If you don't drive me into your garage tonight ♫

"Have you ever seen such well-sculptured lines? Take me to your place, straddle me, ride me, grab my bars! You cannot remain bike-less with me around, don't kid yourself. I see you're uneasy; I can fix that. Wait too long, and I'll be gone; you'll end up with a tent trailer. Think you'll find another magnificent creature like me hanging around these parts? Not a hope in hell."

The best thing about buying a bike privately is that it can be conducted incognito. The alternative is to have your buddy drop you at the dealership, then drive your boisterous new machine home following two loud pipe escorts. An oompah band springs to life in your front yard. ♫Every time you hear that tra la...♫ Neighbors snicker; shouldn't he be buying braces for his bucktoothed kid? If he's killed, we ain't taking care of Bucky. What an irresponsible son-of-a-bitch. It's like re-enacting the Charge of the Light Brigade:

Cannon to right,
Cannon to left,
Cannon in front,
Volleyed and thundered;
Stormed at with shot and shell,
Boldly rode and well the new machine,
Into the garage... theirs not to reason why.

"Nice," Dori agreed, admiring RS's curves and color as we walked by.

How many miles, I wondered? Suki, a sheltie-spaniel mix and the best dog ever, wanted to pee on the wheel (sorry, Pearl—you are the sweetest dog ever). I tugged on her leash while my neck twisted to look back. "See you soon," RS called. "Won't be here long. So many have eyes for me. I'm coveted, like young Mary McGregor. Don't kid yourself; I know your type. There's no way you'll pull bike-less off."

Teal Beauty was right: my uneasiness was growing out of control. Eventually, I'd become unglued—like in the movie *Pulp Fiction*. $5,100 would be a small price to pay to avoid a calamity. Counseling appointments and drugs would cost way more. Maybe offer $5,250?

It'd be great to take off on Teal Beauty to rediscover JOY.

*You & Your Motorcycle: have you suffered*

*from Motorcycleless-ness?*

I'd been motorcycle-less since selling my Kawasaki Concurs the previous fall ($7,949 OBO). A couple bought it to ride cross-country two-up. They were nowhere near retirement age, but unlike Uncle Arthur, they were not Dreamers. What the fuck? I swore when the couple rode off. Come back with my bike! I've changed my mind!

I gave the couple $50 off after they made a stink about "OBO."

Why am I stalling, pretending to be a tent trailer guy, I thought as Suki and I passed RS? Owning an eleven-year-old bike is a sensible way to ease out of riding.

*Truth About Motorcycles: bikes are addictive.*

*You & Your Motorcycle: do you have a motorcycle teddy? If yes, you may be an addict.*

Dori knew what was going on. "Not another one, hon. Not now. Done riding. We have kids. Camping time."

Tent trailer. Two killer words.

"One like Feeble has."

*Truth About Motorcycles: life wants to put you in a tent trailer.*

Years ago, Dori and I did weekends on a Suzuki V-Strom, but now, one wants a tent trailer, the other a Teal Beauty.

"Affordable. I'm sure the owner will come down. Says best offer." I pointed toward the sign. I'd have to clean up a bit and rearrange a few things, but it wasn't too late to reclaim my motorcycle spot in the garage.

"Who would you ride with," Dori asked? "My motorcycle days are done."

I shrugged. Why must I ride with anyone? Heard of Loners by Choice?

Suki and I walked by RS every day. Each time I worried it would be gone, an opportunity lost while I dithered. Suki always wanted to pee on the tires, mark our property in advance—dogs know the score. I approached the bike from different angles, discretely checking the oilhead out. Definitely a racer. "I'm in perfect condition," RS assured me. "New battery. I take care of myself. Better hurry. I'm very desirable."

*Truth About Motorcycles: motorcycles are like a song you can't stop humming.*

*You & Your Motorcycle: do melodies play in your head more often when you're on-motorcycle?*

Larry was in the driveway on the fifth day when we approached. "Nice bike," I called, pointing to the RS as if we were in a showroom full of bikes. "You don't see many for sale."

Larry nodded. He hated to let her go, but explained, "There are circumstances."

I told him about the V-Strom—how Dori preferred traveling slowly on country gravel roads. "The perfect bike for exploring." I tapped the RS. "Not meant for gravel."

"Not an adventure bike," Larry agreed. "Made for twisties."

"My wife likes the back-country," I said in a way that diminished RS's suitability. "Hiking." *In the great outdoors. That's why we're looking for a tent trailer.* I bent to inspect the rear tire. "Tent trailer. You know how it is?"

Silence.

Larry rode with a Most Bikes Welcome Group and offered to introduce me. The unspoken words—no tent trailers.

We chatted about the rides he'd enjoyed. "Up to a dozen in a group. Usually two or three groups." Larry had been all over with his buddies. "We'd ride a hundred miles on a Saturday for coffee," he laughed. A couple of Oddballs and Blockheads, but he made it sound like riding with a large pack was tons of fun. Larry had owned five bikes, the RS being his favorite.

"Comes with a top case. For her stuff. Or for an overnighter with the gang. It's in the garage."

I smiled and depressed the brake lever. Bonus, the bike comes with riders and a case.

"ABS. New tires last year. New battery. Always kept her in tip-top shape."

I didn't doubt it; Teal Beauty was in showroom condition. I had a best offer number in mind. If Larry didn't bite, I'd walk, condemned to a bike-less future, hitching a tent trailer to our shit-box. Not a dollar more, I promised myself. *At least I'll have swung.*

"How is it on gas?" Stupid question. A SQUID question.

Larry answered, and I wondered, should I go a little higher on price? Based on fuel savings, riding RS to work a few times a week.

"Try her," Larry suggested? "Haven't forgotten how to ride, have you?"

I laughed, but it was a fair question: I hadn't been on a motorcycle for ten months and was a nervous. Fearful I'd look like a tent trailer guy, unworthy of Larry's racer.

◆◆◆

"Made for each other," RS whispered as we circled back through the neighborhood, avoiding Mission Avenue.

It overjoyed Suki to see I'd returned. Larry held two beers. I took his riding jacket and gloves off. Does it get better? Yes! Larry would, "Throw in the Schuberth helmet. Has three or four years left on it."

I recalculated and spat a number out; better get this over with.

Larry kicked the ground as if lashing out at my best offer.

"I know it's low, but I won't have much time to ride. Dori wants to get a tent trailer. I'm sure you'll get your asking price if you're patient."

"Tell you what. That, plus Suki, and it's a deal. Or how 'bout another hundred and it's yours? Hell of a deal. I can't let her go for less. Love to keep her in the neighborhood, in good hands."

I gave myself a silent attaboy. Way to go! Would have gone two hundred higher.

Winner!

Rejoice!

New Motorcycle JOY!

My uneasiness faded.

I stuck my hand out. "Sold." I was both ecstatic and nervous about pulling Teal Beauty into our driveway.

Addict? What are you talking about? I've never owned more than three motorcycles at any one time! And now, just one old neighborhood bike.

"So much for, done with bikes!" Dori wasn't happy. I wasn't moving on.

I made up for my indiscretion by cleaning the gutters. Most importantly, I reclaimed my spot in the garage. *You'll be on teddy bear duty for a while, Teal Beauty. Until the dust settles.*

◆◆◆

Larry escorted me to the coffee shop on the third Saturday after the sale. I jokingly told Dori, "Off to raise hell with Larry's old gang." Actually, Larry left and I rode with the pack to Maple Bay for coffee. RS and fourteen other bikes parked in front of the cafe. An impossible-to-miss, large Bike Arrangement. RS cemented in the middle.

I rode in an organized group, not racing around like Daffy Duck Cam. It was a Most Bikes Welcome group (favoring sport touring bikes and their friends). They met every second weekend, year-round. Groups are ideal for the socially lazy. Just show up. Everything is arranged, no farting around required, no making a call or waiting for a text. Don't feel like attending?

Don't.

Stay home and watch *Itchy Boots* on YouTube; no questions asked and no apologies necessary. I had instant motorcycle acquaintances and one new friend, Bob. RS was back with its buddies. It was easy going and going easy.

Motorcycle Club JOY.

In our second year, Bob and I rode with the pack to a

couple of events. Management verged on Oddballism, a desirable biker leadership trait. "Great job," I'd say, even though the organizers did next to nothing, but they always did enough.

I grew to love the camaraderie more than the knee pain RS occasionally delivered. We were a solid band of mostly like-minded brothers and a few sisters. We split into riding groups, ten or fewer—fast, moderate, and slow. Teal Beauty was always in the lead group and never stayed cemented in the middle. We exchanged positions, practicing free form riding; J O Y was our leader.

In year three, Marc and Judy Petersen joined our group, well, not so much joined as raped, plundered, and pillaged. They brought their friends and together throttled the old dynamic. Most Bikers Welcome fragmented.

To Marc and Judy, every cup of life is half-empty due to a lack of order. They like their affairs and clubs buttoned-down and signed off. They weren't Motorcycle Cunts but were damn annoying.

Overwhelmed by forceful personalities, the old leadership shrugged. Most Bikes Welcome fell out of kilter, and Marc and Judy became undisputed pack leaders. Riders scattered. Bob and I should have bailed, but the socially lazy don't like to make a fuss. Instead, we rolled along like chicken strips on new tires.

Marc and Judy are terrific organizers, which is fine if you're Boy Scouts or members of a marching band. It's irritating if you're a badass motorcycle gang. Some of the old crowd didn't give a contaminated spark plug, as they say, but it rubbed Bob and me the wrong way. Must there be written club rules? Formal committees? Project plans? We took great pleasure in grumbling about the new state of affairs.

The riding pace was too slow, cautious, consistent, and predictable. The newly assigned Ride Captains made horrendous pullover decisions. Bob would say to me, as if I was a captain, "Just passed a magnificent spot, and you pull over in this shit hole? My ass isn't sore yet. Don't need to gear up. What the hell is wrong with you, jackass?"

"All about smoke breaks." I'd glare at Bob. What are we doing here? Waiting for Jerkwad to finish puffing.

What we were doing was complaining.

Never complain about complaining; it can be a lot of fun for a short while.

◆ ◆ ◆

It was early summer. Dori had a master gardening class with Dr. Daisy and their flower friends; take dandelions out of your lawn, chop them up, and put them in a salad—that sort of thing.

Marc and Judy had the group riding in staggered formation. Initially, it was fun. Formation riding made up for flunking Boy Scouts. The Ride Captains always stuck Bob and me in the middle. Before long, it felt as if we'd been conscripted into a parade.

Formation Riding works in areas where there is no choice but to be in close quarters. I prefer free-form on open roads where it's possible to spread out. For me, formations can wall J O Y out. There was no arguing with M&J. They'd attended National Advanced Rider Safety Training and had all the answers.

*You & Your Motorcycle: do you often ride in formation? How do you feel about being in the middle?*

*Truth About Motorcycles: for some, large groups can suffocate J O Y .*

◆◆◆

I sat eight inches off the ground on a collapsible chair. We'd spent the day riding to a private campground in our designated groups, often in formation, with plenty of smoke breaks at mundane stops. Now we relaxed. Alcohol was permitted the evening before a ride, but there was a zero-tolerance drug policy.

Food committee members offered snacks. Finance kept the receipts. We would break camp by 7:00 AM. Kickstands up at 7:30 precisely, arriving at our next stop, a motel at 3:30 PM. The route planners were rigid. "More about the schedule than the ride," Bob said.

"Like Pearly," I said. Pearl is aware of schedules and the order of things—when to eat, where to sleep, what time the letter carrier arrives. Suki was a Dog Loner-By-Choice, but welded to me.

We sat around a small campfire. The Ride Captains went over the itinerary for the next day. "Good idea to do an oil change when you get back," the chair of the Maintenance Committee suggested. He proposed setting up a Bulk Oil Procurement Team. I don't have an in-depth knowledge of fluid dynamics and often buy the OEM recommended oil. It costs a few extra bucks but doesn't involve committee meetings.

Judy poked me with a motorcycle magazine bought from the Membership Incidentals Fund. The cover showed a photo of a solo adventure rider in Argentina heading north. I flipped to the story. The guy, about my age, quit his job, flew his bike to Buenos Aires, and had five thousand dream miles ahead of him. Alone. No formation riding or dumb pullovers. No Rules of the Road Guide book.

How great for him, I thought, to be the master of his destiny on a bike that can go anywhere. A Loner-By-Choice. Never in the middle. Total responsibility, without compromise, both the good and the bad. Riding as it should be, on dirt tracks, through dry river beds, and down lonely highways. No parades, imposed discipline, or forced socialization.

I passed the magazine to Bob. The following morning, we rode off, platoon deserters. AWOL? No, I sent a text to our Ride Captain: "something came up. Must hurry home." We didn't want to invoke a Missing Rider Investigation.

Over coffee, Bob and I agreed that four is the perfect number, with no one stuck perpetually in the middle. Plus, one or minus three. "You can't go wrong with solo, as long as problems don't crop up," Bob said.

Bob and I weren't in South America, but we rode home full of Liberation Motorcycle JOY.

Larry laughed when I told him I'd quit Most Bikes Welcome. He's thinking about getting a new bike. Said he didn't feel at ease being motorcycle-less and agreed, "Small numbers are great."

Larry said he came close to making an offer on a used RV ($64,999 OBO). "But a guy can get a great bike for far less than half that."

"Especially if it's OBO," I said.

◆ ◆ ◆

I don't miss riding in formation in an organized pack. However, I regret losing the camaraderie of Most Bikes Welcome. It brought J O Y .

# CHAPTER 27 – A SAFE HARBOR

I relinquished lead to Marta as we headed home. Middle again. We're a solid trio, knit together without a Marc and Judy-like desire to impose order. A Trinity of Bikes where the middle constantly ebbs and flows. Three is sufficient mass to draw attention; cager-killers prefer to pick off solo riders.

"Hey, Marta," I yelled. "Still pissed about Rule #8?" Another good thing about motorcycles is that you are uncensored; say whatever you like. No audience means there are no wrong words. Unleash a rant in a car, and, at a minimum, there will be hurt feelings and regrets for mile after uneasy mile. Motorcycle Therapy encourages letting it all out.

*Truth About Motorcycles: motorcycles can be safe harbors.*

*You & Your Motorcycle: do you say what is otherwise left unsaid, on-motorcycle?*

It's good to ride with one, two, or a few solid people. Something happens; it's a blessing to with a capable companion, not a Blockhead. Someone able to sort things out—fix a flat or step into the breach, like Conrad did when I went down on Highway 20. It explains why Sir Ed brought Tenzing along on his Everest adventure. Solo, the buck stops with you, and you may be stopped dead in your tracks by an evil mole rat.

In harmony and rolling along, Marta, Tony, and I were *Stayin' Alive* and *Jive Talkin'*. We were the Polka Bee Gees.

"Yeah right," My Complainers said. "Time for a rest."

◆◆◆

*I try to be the person Pearl thinks I am.*

I've noticed, dog social groups don't have middles. So when Pearly goes to Copley Park to visit her buddies, there is no jockeying for position or imposing order, no canine Marcs or Judys. Observe social off-leash mongrels, and you'll agree: dogs possess natural Mutt Joy.

*Truth About Motorcycles: on-motorcycle,*
*you may become dog-like.*

I'm a member of the Copley Park Dog Moms. I like that they only have one rule. Unfortunately, it reeks of segregation and sexism: I cannot be a mom. They are not woke. *Honorary Dog Mom, take it or leave it. Are you in or out? What'll it be, Mike?*

The Dog Moms haven't progressed, so I filed a complaint with the Human Rights Commission.

Kidding!

I didn't want to invite ridicule—*you're a Mom, Mr. Tough Biker Dude?* Besides, the Moms are supportive and kind, and the commission files all biker complaints under No One Gives a Shit. *Yes, the Moms give a shit, assholes! And so does the rover pack!* The dogs always welcome me—I think they smell my mongrel gene.

The Moms are not natural-progressives like their pets; like bikers, dogs have always been free-spirited.

Even though I'm a diminished member, the Tenzing Norgay of the group, I try to be understanding, like Andy Gibb, the brother left out of the Bee Gees. For Pearl's sake, I soldier on with a brave face. "Don't worry, Pearl. Honorary means special." Honestly, Pearly doesn't give a shit because dogs exist in a state of permanent Mutt Disconnectedness.

When I was a rookie Constant Walker, I heard Mom Gail had begun chemotherapy. Gail is angelic and the only Mom who lobbied for "full and equal acceptance." So the news of her cancer knocked the faith out of me. Why does Life stomp on angels? Perhaps there's an argument for infecting humanity with COVID-19, but must you attack Saint Gail?

It's troubling when Life picks on someone indisputably known to be a good person, like Frank (Cam Marshall's dad), Hans, Nelson Mandela, Gail, or Jesus. Why did you shoot John Lennon and Martin Luther King? The attack on Gail pissed me off—I wanted to round up the biker gang and kick Life's butt, like in the movie *V for Vendetta.* Push Life the Bully off a bridge. Why Gail, I'll ask before the fall? Why not pick on Marc, Judy, pedophiles, or politicians? How about a person with a motorcycle dilemma and no solution? Or amuse yourself by blasting giant mole rats with cancer. What the fuck is wrong with you, Life? Dogs are nicer than you!

After listening to the news, I tell Bunny and Pearl, “Thank God we’re atheists.” It’s an old Woody Allen joke. To be safe, I always add, “Open-minded though, for Heaven's sake,” just in case there is a God, and He doesn’t appreciate Woody’s sense of humor.

I admire people who have faith despite shaky concrete evidence. I suppose it provides religions joy. *Zen and the Art of Motorcycle Maintenance* established Buddha as a biker, which explains His J O Y . The next time Siddhārtha pokes His head out of the oxygen sensor, I'll suggest He update how karma works. Is it fair to hold Gail, Hans, Feeble, or anyone accountable for misdeeds that occurred Before Motorcycle rather than After Motorcycle. Start fresh Gautama! You’ve done a lot of riding, are enlightened, and understand:

*Motorcycles are game-changers.*

Wipe the BM karma slate clean!

When I asked Mom Karen: "Think Gail is up to going for a nice ride on my new bike?" It's good to climb on and disconnect?

"Gail's doing well," I was told.

Recovery is a reason to believe. Like Motorcycle JOY.

◆◆◆

Red Beauty pulled away from Guzzi, making Marta middle. The chase was on. I knew I could hold the pair off if I kept CTX's revs up. I wondered how it worked on the DCT (automatic) model? Hit sports mode and hope the lead engineer was a racer?

*Truth About Motorcycles: Valentino Rossi never raced an automatic, but J O Y is OK with that.*

*You & Your Motorcycle: have you ridden an automatic? Ever meet a rider with one leg, like my cousin Stumpy?*

# PART FOUR: ANNIVERSARY RIDE

*"Sometimes it takes a whole tankful of fuel before you can think straight or disconnect." – Anonymous*

# CHAPTER 28 – PREPARING TO DEPART

"May a pod of killer whales snatch his children off the shore," Conrad said on the anniversary of Horace's death and raised his glass.

"May mutilated Bambis be dragged past ferries on the port side," I said. Our glasses tapped, then I symbolically spat on Horace's grave, missing Pearl by a spark plug length. My Complainers cheered.

Marta took down the lab's dartboard with its mole rat picture. She tapped a print of a reindeer taped to the whiteboard. "Reindeer work with Santa. They're all about delivering good cheer."

"Reindeer fly. Horace couldn't even walk across two lanes."

"Fly or not, they're still deer—time you changed your attitude, Mike. Deer are cute and usually peaceful."

"Murderers are peaceful until they draw blood."

Marta drew a smiley face beside the reindeer. "Look at the picture. Do that om ohm... Moto-Skiveezies chant thing if it helps." She picked up her helmet. "Tomorrow, we'll go to Oak Bay for exposure therapy. Deer all over the place there." Marta moved toward the door. "Sharon and Anita are expecting me." Something was up. "And Hans."

I didn't ask.

Manny was the last to leave. He's Catholic and likes to play Biker Confessions.

"I was late changing the oil, Father."

"Used a cheap wax."

"Coveted biker chick's new bike."

That sort of thing.

Before leaving, Manny wished me a happy anniversary. "Because," he said, "Years cannot be taken for granted."

"Would you like to come to Oak Bay and chase deer, Pearl?" I dropped kibble on a COVID protocol pamphlet, *How to Wash Your Hands*.

"It's like putting Feeble up against Jorge Jorgensen," I told Marta when she handed me the *Hand Washing* instructions.

Marta had answered, "You'd think... with all her pestilence experience... Mother would have a killer offense—like one of the old powerhouses: Patriots, Canadiens, Celtics, Manchester United, Yankees, All Blacks. But, like Feeble, Mom is not a home run hitter."

I nodded because it's true—the pandemic was bogged down, like the Nazis when they invaded Russia. Our technologists were dialing in. Soon it would be vaccine bombs away! With luck, some would land on deer. That would make me,

Rejoice!

And fill me with,

JOY.

Humans died, but statistically, the pandemic was a blip, not a cleanse-to-end-all-cleanses, like WWI, the war to end all wars, until WWII erupted.

We had gained defensive muscle. Physiotherapy clinics reopen with strict protocols. My Complainers were delighted. *More soft massages!* But Chris, my new therapist, stabbed needles into them to reclaim every smidgen of normal possible. Sometimes he'd jab, then electrocute. My Complainers spasmed and screamed, "We promise not to whine. Stop! For the love of God, Chris, stop!"

Chris didn't stop. My Complainers enjoy the kid-glove treatment, but you have to lean hard if you aim to recover.

I'll always have accident souvenirs, but it's neat how injured bodies learn to absorb wonkiness. Parts that don't work the way they used to become habituated, requiring little attention. Eventually, a new normal is developed. "Look at us! Wobbly? No, it's our new style. It's who we are now."

*You & Your Motorcycle: has motorcycle damage shaped who you are? Is there a point at which you stop riding or ride much less?*

I rest more now and avoid specific movements. When My Complainers act up, I warn, "Smarten up, or we're going to see Chris!"

By the summer of 2020, the people calling the shots had allowed more businesses to reopen, including Tony's Deli, for takeout only. "No tra la la's," Polka Man called their plan. "It's horseshit." People, including bikers, were divided on the subject of quarantine and strict controls versus building natural immunity. Me, I clung to Just Ride. J O Y can be found on the pandemic highway.

Testing had expanded. Many intensive care units were

at their breaking points as the infection rate rose. Mother Nature worked on improving her variants while the WHO pointed fingers and made dire statistical projections. Leaders enjoyed printing money and pissing off Freedomites. The media folks were in heaven (first the Donald, now COVID. Does it get better?).

"Wash your hands," Marta reminded. "It's not a big deal."

I disinfected myself.

"Don't assume hands won't kill you."

"Wear your mask." Dori made me one with motorcycles.

I wore it where required.

"Don't assume air won't kill you."

"Unless you're on-motorcycle," I said.

I understood Mother Nature's position. What is Earth supposed to do? Twiddle its poles while political science makes a mess of one civilization after another? Mom has been patient, reviewed our Green Deals, and analyzed projections, but "despite their rhetoric and official days, human shit keeps piling up."

Wars never end well. Despite hashing it out in WWII, the Jewish community still irritates the hell out of some groups. Jews must constantly keep an eye on nations wanting to eradicate them. Palestinians must make way for settlers.

That's life on Earth.

"Ride toward the silver lining."

"Toward Life the Beautiful."

"Where there are no wars."

"Where everyone rides."

"Two Wheels, Not Four!"

"Two Wheels, Not Four."

"Two Wheels, Not Four."

Many would say our chant is simplistic. They are NimRods.

◆◆◆

Friends offered to escort me on my Anniversary Ride, but I declined. It wasn't their anniversary (well, sort of Conrad's). Incognito is the way to go when Public Health orders Essential Travel Only. Riding solo, accepting total responsibility, is the way to go when tuning a Motorcycle State of Mind.

"The pandemic's great," I'd say. "Perfect for a therapy ride. Less Road Vomit"

Even Dr. Peggy stepped up.

<u>Ode to Agrizoophobia</u>

Go forward, half a league,
All in the valley of the virus,
You will ride.
Forward, Red Beauty!
Lean into the curve!
Past the giant mole rats.
You will fear no more.

Peg flipped that verse out after several glasses of wine. She's a better person when tipsy.

# CHAPTER 29 - DAY ONE, AUGUST 26TH

After the ferry crossing, I rode east for six hours in perfect weather, to the Travelers Motel, in Princeton, B.C. Had I continued another three thousand miles, I would have arrived in Princeton, NJ.

A family of immigrants had purchased the old motel, a block off the main drag, in the picturesque town of five thousand. When I checked in, the owners were attempting to spruce the building up. I chose not to deliver a National Geographic-like expose on western wood rot.

"Sometimes Truth is best left under the covers," Marta says. "Unless it has to do with motorcycles."

I agree—Direct Honesty often is not appreciated. "You're ugly, Pissy" for example, would be factual but rude. "Have you considered a bulldozer or an insurance claim?" would discourage. "Have you considered jumping?" would be frowned upon. I'm not always discrete, which can be problematic, off-motorcycle.

I wondered what it was like for the immigrant family? Moving. Threatened by COVID. Imagining they'd be living close to Carnegie Lake in a metropolitan university town. Instead, they ended up fighting a losing battle against wood rot and sagging foundations. An adventure? Like Christopher Columbus, but with Asians instead of Italians, and COVID instead of smallpox?

*You & Your Motorcycle: does riding make you feel like an explorer?*

*Truth About Motorcycles: cultural norms can make discovering Motorcycle JOY impossible for some.*

The family member who assisted me spoke broken English. Our chat involved making assumptions about what was heard and what was said. The family was from Taiwan, or maybe Tai'an, China? I told her my dentist was from Taiwan, which formed an instant geographic bond. My expression conveyed I understood. They had immigrated due to the possibility of China invading Taiwan the way their escaped germs had invaded humanity.

The owner rewarded me with a newly renovated room featuring cheap laminate flooring. Gone was the old stained carpet which had forced lodgers to tiptoe, fearful of the dangers lurking underfoot.

My spray gun came out and fired a few random warning blasts. Armed and ready for action. *Go ahead, make my day, little viral buggers!*

While my disinfectant bomb settled, I went outside and put CTX's cover on. Sun had confused Princeton with Death Valley. Whose side is Sun on anyway, Earth or Humanity? It probably doesn't give a basal cell carcinoma. When you're a star, all you have to do is twinkle.

After a rest, having forgotten to pack sandals, I pulled my motorcycle boots back on—basically Gestapo boots without swastikas. "We're here to kick ass," motorcycle boots say, "We don't guarantee ankles won't break."

*Truth About Motorcycles: protective gear is like a knight's armor—both limbs and armor may be lobbed off.*

I marched down the main drag wearing shorts and my tall black Gestapo boots, searching for microwaveable food in the agreeable town. I noticed a few signs of order and control, like protocol posters taped to shop windows. Pandemics are more impactful than world wars because viruses are everywhere. During WWII, there were no Nazis in Princeton, B.C. (a few sympathizers lived in Princeton, NJ). There were no Jews either, even though the town would have made a great hideout. Princeton, B.C. wasn't on Hitler's radar. But, thanks to Emperor Hirohito, the lone Japanese family residing in the area was deported to a containment camp. It's hard to imagine the shenanigans our NimRod leaders were up to, not that long ago.

The locals didn't care that my Gestapo boots made me look like an SS invader. Walkers stepped to the side and smiled. Have a nice day, stranger! It wasn't like Victoria where the timid risked being run over or falling into a ditch trying to avoid me. You're walking funny, mister. Are you infected? Shouldn't you be in a containment camp?

In Princeton, B.C., it was going-easy and easy-going, all friendly dog-people or bikers, like me.

Meanwhile, in Princeton, New Jersey, JOY struggled. COVID had "unmasked and amplified existing racial inequities. Rampant fear and misinformation provoked a wave of discrimination, harassment, and hate, targeting those of Chinese and Asian descent," according to the media.

In west coast Princeton, people had pragmatic thoughts like, Asians don't understand wood rot. So, perhaps the virus escaped from Heilongjiang Province through decaying wood walls? Stuff like that.

# CHAPTER 30 - DAY TWO, FORWARD TO DEER COUNTRY

CTX crept over gravel, a road meant for TS-125, Thumper, V-Strom, or Conrad's 310. A fifteen-mile unpaved shortcut through the backcountry to reach my test track, a twisty connector to Highway 33. The connector is a not-so-secret-out-of-the-way glorious 40-mile stretch of nonstop twisting asphalt.

Never assume secret motorcycle roads will remain secrets! Ride them before they are overwhelmed and bulldozers are dispatched to straighten them. Secret motorcycle roads are J O Y unlockers.

My test track offered motorcycle ambush opportunities galore. I was a willing participant, nervous but calling the shots in the land of evil mole rats.

CTX moved at the pace of a bike trying to stretch its last drops of gas, careful not to be pulled by ruts or throw up gravel. A pleasant way to kickoff my exposure therapy. The scenery encouraged plodding; the gravel insisted on it; wildlife is not a threat at crawling speed. The local COVID life-forms were lackadaisical. What, we're at war? We're always the last to know here at Out-Of-The-Way shortcut where life is always beautiful. Still, we could have taken that Oddball out had we known. We'd like to do our part.

My GPS provided location updates, predicting when the gravel would end. A newly installed temperature gauge read 25C (77F).

I leaned against the only motorcycle backrest I'd owned, actually against the backrest pad I added to the optional Corbin backrest (Corbin Upholstery having used gorilla arms to design the placement of their backrest). The modification worked well. Leaning back was a pleasure. Backrest, Slow Speed Motorcycle JOY—perfect for rolling through some of Mother Nature's best work.

*Truth About Motorcycles: backrests act like engine governors, slowing bikes down, which is why you never see them at racetracks.*

For years you frown on certain things, then suddenly find—I'm a Backrest Guy. Or just getting old?

I was fortunate to find a used Corbin seat with the backrest included. It filled me with Used Accessory Big Savings Motorcycle JOY while diminishing the Ass Problem.

Of course it made me,

Rejoice.

The countryside was calming. I almost regretted reaching pavement. Gravel to a street bike is like an overcooked Brussels sprout to a plate of decent food. Get the hell out of here, sprout!

I pulled over, not to fart around and gear up but to prepare mentally. Unlike Hannibal, I did not have slave girls whispering sweet encouragements. Or Tenzing poking Sir Edmond—*we'll go down after we summit, Eddie.*

I was committed to a drug-free test which left only: In. Out. In. Out. *Om Mani Padme Hum.* Do generals order soldiers not to practice mindfulness? I wondered. "Moto-Skiveez. Moto-Skiveez. Moto-Skiveez." I pulled my Moto-Skiveezies up. Practicing mindfulness had been a complete waste of time; I tried not to let it irritate me and climbed on.

"A pills work," Brain said.

*Truth About Motorcycles: motorcycles are about escape, even if you don't need to escape.*

The key turned. I pushed start. Red Beauty said, "Let's go." So I pulled onto the paved connector where one curve followed another, and then thirty more. Eerily similar to Horace's Highway 20, except with far better curvature and no traffic.

CTX accelerated toward the second sweeper. It was like riding a roller coaster on its inaugural run—one with wildlife hiding beside the track, threatening derailment. Terrifying. My adrenaline spiked. All senses were on high alert. *Fuck you deer! I'm going for the cure!*

I imagined reindeer, my guardian angels, in the forest, smiling. *Lovely to see you back on-motorcycle. We're not all like Horace. Go in peace, friend.*

I leaned, caught the apex, twisted the throttle, and then slowed to watch for danger. "Don't push your luck," Brain said.

I didn't, because I know,

*Truth About Motorcycles: riders are always in season.*

Driving is better when your motorcycle requires attention. GT couldn't detect deer but it otherwise it may have been too clever—it knew what to do much of the time. *Point me in the right direction. I'll take it from there, buddy*. CTX demanded I drive. I had to use my noggin and adjust my balance.

*Truth About Motorcycles: unlike driver-less cars, bikes are meant to engage and shouldn't be over engineered.*

*You & Your Motorcycle: is your bike over-engineered? Does it make you complacent?*

Hannibal loved to ride elephants because "they have just the right balance and a lot of low end torque."

Marta rides an aging Guzzi, "because I like to be involved, not be driven."

"We make a good team," I told Red Beauty. "A perfect mix of technology and involvement." A YouTuber said about CTX, "This is the 5th bike I've owned since I started riding. Overall, by far my best motorcycle (what other bikes did he own?). It doesn't take much to get the CTX going, and it will cruise at interstate speeds with no trouble at all at low RPMs. At 50 HP, it's not a powerhouse, but don't let it deceive you. It will walk away from anything but exotic supercars at the traffic light effortlessly." YouTubers are opinionated, but I agree with five-bike YouTuber more than man-bun YouTuber. If cost, comfort, reliability, and therapeutic value are factors, CTX tops the list of road bikes I've owned. At least at this point in time, because bike preference changes with circumstances. Are you headed for the track or dealing with agrizoophobia? For me, there is no best bike. Unless it's an It'll Do Bike, fixer, or Killer Bike; the best bike is the one you own.

*You & Your Motorcycle: are you in a motorcycle rut? There are many excellent bikes on the market (including some with three wheels).*

"Find a Guzzi and stick with it," Marta suggests.

Like any bike, CTX isn't perfect: the rear monoshock must be upgraded. Also, no temperature gauge, heated grips, or gear indicator.

A stop sign, where the connector joins the main highway, marked the finish line. I throttled down and rolled to a stop. Not a single deer; the odds are always in the rider's favour. No mistakes. Not like when the Secret Bunker rookie reported: "atomic warheads in the air." On investigation, it was determined to be a bug on his radar screen.

When I stopped I was full of Gigantic Accomplishment JOY!

Breathing easy.

Proud. I'd come a long way since lying on Highway 20.

It felt like my first ascent of Impossible Hill on TS 125. Or Sir Ed when he returned to Base Camp. "I'm off to meet the press now—time for you to skedaddle, Tenzing. No need to go on and on about leading the way and carrying most of the weight." Ed proudly addressed the world. "I did it!" Or Hannibal when he pulled into Carthage. "You're one hell of a ride," he told his elephant and slave girls.

In the past, I may have swung around to admire the beautiful curvature, but at the stop sign, I had smelly stuff in my shorts.

Kidding!

Breathe: In. Out. In. Out. Deer pull Santa.

"Moto-Skiveez. Moto-Skiveez. Moto-Skiveez."

It was a short PTSD (Post Traumatic Stress caused by Deer) test. Just as COVID necessitated multiple boosters, I would need to repeat, but the proof-of-concept ride was a success.

Be aware.

Be cautious.

Have fun.

Recover and **J O Y will find a way.**

◆◆◆

I sat on a patio facing the main street of a small town southeast of Kelowna. I was full of Motorcycle Travel Stop JOY. Always take time to savor the experience.

The building was a bank before transitioning to coffee roasting. Back in the day (before the UN declared December 4, International Day of Banks), far-sighted engineers, architects, and craftspersons constructed sturdy works of art. They would become boutiques of the future.

The owner was chatty, delighted to be open, and not the least bit concerned I had traveled to make a purchase. As she filled my cup, I watched JOY flow.

The coffee was dark and bold, the way I like it. Relaxing

on a patio, facing a peaceful, scenic street, in fine weather, outside a re-purposed building, sipping excellent coffee, after a successful therapeutic ride followed by a warm barista welcome is magical; JOY for the price of a cup of coffee and a bit of gas.

*You & Your Motorcycle: have you spent large sums of money on fancy dining, five-star hotel rooms, or any extravagance trying to find JOY, only to discover it on an inexpensive motorcycle ride?*

Does it get better? Yes—there was entertainment on the street. Not an Elton John impromptu concert, but a city worker watering hanging flower baskets. A store window getting washed. Yamaha rider spotted my helmet and waved. Locals stopped to greet one another on the sidewalk, happy the worst of the war was behind them (they believed, unaware Mother was about to unleash a new variant offensive).

I sat outside at a small table. People said hello as they passed. Some shared their Motorcycle Dreams. "Plan to buy a bike when I retire. Drive across the continent." *Or at least as far as Hope.*

Did you hear? I passed my road test today! A mini-exam. No pills. Aced it!

WOW! Congratulations. Elton may sing a few celebratory bars. Believe that's him, over there, the chubby one with the mask, shopping for cherries.

It's good to chat with strangers when you're Bob-less, especially when it requires little effort. Locals approached me, said hello, spoke, and drifted away. The exchanges were easy and transient.

Mr. Pirsig ignored the Motorcycle Reward Stop. Travel. Travel. Travel. A philosopher, he hadn't a clue about neuroplasticity. Feed your brain. Exercise your pathways. Create new connections. Change things up. Arrive. Stop. Prep for Departure by drinking coffee to bind to adenosine receptors.

"Which bike do you think I should get?" a Motorcycle Dreamer asked. “Are loud ones the safest?”

*Truth About Motorcycles: J O Y is contagious.*

# CHAPTER 31 - DAY THREE

There's a connection, a transference that occurs, in something as simple as pulling the cover off a machine to reveal superb engineering and graceful design. It's the exact opposite of what welcomes UN staffers. Employees open the door of the Secretariat Building in New York City and think—we had such high hopes, but where is the magic? Despite World Toilet Day (November 19), human shit piles up.

In the parking lot, two-wheel machines whisper, we are MAGIC Carpets. In the Secretariat Building, policymakers shake their heads; official days, conferences, declarations, peacekeeping, but we cannot conjure magic.

*Truth About Motorcycles: bikes do what the United Nations cannot.*

As ritual preparation begins, the anticipation of climbing on nudges and pokes while bug carcasses get wiped away and gear is packed. Red Beauty waited patiently. I caught shy glimpses of the machine that would soon take me down the road toward the coast. The grandeur of a rolling landscape. The seductive rush of asphalt and sweeping curves that lay ahead.

Climb on, and the world is your oyster.

*You & Your Motorcycle: have you been seduced by a motorcycle?*

*Truth About Motorcycles: bikes can be impish.*

An SUV stopped as CTX waited to turn left out of the lot. *Proceed, biker-friend.* Beyond the Secretarial Building, some of the nicest people drive automobiles. When they perform a courtesy, I swell with J O Y .

I was heading home; my mini-test completed.

Category: backrest rider.

Uneasiness: diminished.

Grade: pass.

When I began to write, I wondered if I'd end up frustrated and go on a vendetta, like in the movies *Kill Bill* and *True Grit.*

I persevered and MAGIC stepped up.

**J O Y found a way.**

Life is complex; motorcycles can help to sort it out. They allow you to shout: I Don't Care! *Come here, Life the Beautiful. Give me a hug.*

Or maybe I simply needed to be somewhere?

*You & Your Motorcycle: do you need to be somewhere?*

Bob used to say. "The way to heaven is heaven."

# PART FIVE: THE ENDING

*"Never ride faster than your guardian angel can fly." – Anonymous*

# CHAPTER 32 – RULE #11

Some people lose faith and turn away from religion, while others go through life unattached. Passion can be fickle.

*Truth About Motorcycles: Never take JOY for granted.*

Here is the list rebel—Motorcycle Riding Rule #11 (for the first ten, read *Scraping Pegs* or, for an overview *Scrape Your Lists*):

Rule #11: No Motorcycle JOY? Do not ride!

The unwritten part? Because riding joyless may kill you. You are under no obligation to climb on.

Words can send Dr. Peggy to another place. For me, it's two wheels. *Ode to a Daisy* falls flat. It isn't easy to comprehend, but the same phenomena can happen with motorcycling—it can fail to lift spirits.

A person may have Awareness, Ability, and be Accountable, but never, or seldom, experience JOY. It explains why universal happiness evades Humanity.

*Truth About Motorcycles: the MAGIC of motorcycles does not work for all and may lose its effectiveness for others.*

As Cam says, "you can learn the piano keys but never tickle the ivories."

If you knew J O Y but lost it and can't recover, park your bike. Or try balancing your Motorcycle State of Mind.

*Truth About Motorcycles: it's better to be a cager than to ride like a joyless Blockhead.*

Joyless riders are doomed. Their radars are switched off. Unable to settle for Transport Bikes, they work throttles with their egos, pumping adrenaline spikes, desperate to feel J O Y , but tragedy is more likely.

*You & Your Motorcycle: If J O Y does not come, will you apply Rule #11?*

Those who suffer from Motorcycle Anhedonia (the inability to feel Motorcycle JOY) should take a break, nap, walk a dog, swim with sharks, watch the Dr. Phil show, and balance a wheel with Dr. Tire, and proceed cautiously.

# CHAPTER 33 – THE TERRY DILEMMA

I asked Dolores, "What is the exact launch date for The Magical Joy of Motorcycles?"

"No Magical," Dolores said. "Beaten Stick rejected the title... too long, and magic is not on-trend at the moment."

I shrugged. "They're the experts."

"Terrible time to release a book about joy, Pete, in marketing thinks. Readers aren't in a good mood. They want escape ... from the pandemic ... not truth."

Ride, I thought.

"By the way, did you ever finish *Seduction of the Heart*? It's selling like eggs at Easter."

"Shelly borrowed *Seduction* and never returned it," I said. "So I couldn't read it." According to Marta, she's racked up quite an overdue fine.

"Shall I book you on the local cable show? To push your book. Talk about recovery."

*Truth About Motorcycles: riders who haven't gone down hard cannot grasp the uneasiness of those who have.*

*You & Your Motorcycle: have you had a severe accident?*
*When you climbed back on, were you a different rider?*

*Truth About Motorcycles: J O Y 's ebbs and flows*
*are more dramatic for those who go down hard.*

"NimRods wouldn't understand," I answered, thinking about the Terry dilemma. I would soon need something more than, what would you do, Terry?

# CHAPTER 34 – GUZZI LOVE

Guzzi and big Indian make a cute couple," Big Terry said, grinning like a nutter. Yes, Marta and Tony are getting hitched! Can you believe it? What's more, Marta told me, "We're doing it because we love one another."

"What's that, Marta?"

"We're in love."

"You what?"

"L.O.V.E., Jackass!"

"Oh?" Hit me over the head with a loud pipe, but I believe they really are in love. They ride together, communicate in code, adore battered pickles, and are both clever and outgoing. Holy F'ing Cow! Love blossomed right here in my garage! What do you think about that, Bunny? No more worrying about Marta.

"See Dolores. I didn't have to read *Seduction of the Heart*. Life the Beautiful stepped up. Give it a chance ... JOY happens."

"Makes a nice ending," Dolores admitted.

It is more than nice; it's J O Y overflowing. Dolores will be Marta's maid-of-honor.

Bunny's unmoved, but the announcement left a lump in this curmudgeon's throat. "Will they be like penguins," I asked Earl and Cam? "Swans? Gibbons? Will they mate for life? An American Indian and an Italian Guzzi, will that work?" Earl and Cam are both daft when it comes to relationships; they should binge-watch Dr. Phil. Bunny rubbed the side of his face against my arm. Bunny knows the score.

Marta and Tony set a date for "after the pandemic, assuming we're not all viral zombies." Following the wedding, the newlyweds will ride the endless highway. The Indian will be outfitted with Tony's engagement present from Marta, quieter pipes (get used to big changes, Polka Man)!

The couple hopes to start a battered pickle production and distribution business when they return. Manny and Cam will put up some of the seed money. Their forgivable loan application and diversity checklist are in the queue (no mention of bikes).

Guess who will walk Marta down the aisle, formed by a Guzzi, Indian, Softy, and CTX? I'll try not to look like Mr. Jackass. I'm walking pretty well these days.

Pearl will be the ring-bearer.

I've asked Dr. Peggy to write something nice that sounds intelligent to read at the reception. Otherwise, it'll mainly be biker gibberish. "It should include the words joy, magic, and motorcycle," I explained, because the doctor is a little thick about some things. "Guzzi and Indian, as well."

Peg loves to perform with words and is "on it."

"Do not slip in *Ode to a Daisy*! I'll have my finger on

Mute."

I cheated and looked at her notes—*Ode to a Motorcycle Couple*—very, very nice. I think a touch of J O Y has rubbed off on Peg.

There will be a group ride to send the newlyweds on their way. Having an exact date to work to is critical for planning purposes, something I picked up from Marc and Judy. I've made my date concerns known in no uncertain terms. "Let's nail the day down." Screw the protocol police. Bikers can mass together. MAGIC will be our shield.

More Big News: Terry will ride Brenda in the lead position with Dolores on the passenger seat. "Changed my oil," the big guy announced in the lab a few weeks ago, grinning like a boy with his first motorbike. "Warhammer's out!"

Dolores confided to Marta, "Terry's a hunk." The pair giggles and acts like starry-eyed fourteen-year-olds when they're together. It's annoying, but I'm happy my Dr. Phil viewings paid off. Terry went from looking like he needed a push off the Pul-e Sukhta bridge to a Dolores makeover. "A hunk fit for the cover of *Riders and Lovers*," Dolores said proudly.

His new look is embarrassing, but Marta assured us, "It's a phase. It'll wear off soon." She's included riding gear in Dolores' biker education. "Guess we'll be kissing Terry's monthly storage income goodbye."

Conrad accepted the position of Wedding Ride Captain. He's good at sorting things out. As a joke, I gave him a doctored version of Marc and Judy's Ride Captain job description from Most Bikes Welcome and pointed to, "a clear, cool head is essential."

"Don't get too emotional." Conrad has control, like

a motorcycle engineer, so no worries. "If you have questions, phone Marc or Judy." He'll ride one of his three bikes and bring his dog Axle over to help Pearly with tire inspections.

Tish will catch the ferry from Vancouver. She rides an RT now and may link up with the newlyweds to "spread some of Dad's ashes in the wind." Uncle Arthur's motorcycle dream may yet come true. Deceased Motorcycle JOY. Do motorcycles ever stop giving?

Cam will drive down the Island on his Yamaha Ténéré, and his daughter, Megan, will perform the motorcycle song, Imagine, at the reception.

♫ Imagine a world of motorcycles,

It's easy if you try ♫

She has a beautiful voice and a scooter.

Dori will climb on, "if I go slow."

There will be thirty to forty bikes, including one Oddball (Barry) towing a trailer as decorated by Dr. Peggy, Dori, and Anita and Sharon. "Peg," Barry says without being corrected with, "it's Doctor Peggy."

A medical doctor removed Peg's witch's mole. "Has to do with Barry and J O Y ," I explained to Dori.

A member of Scooter Crowd is an avid photographer and has offered to put a wedding video together. DJ, I-won't-play-the-*Beer-Barrel-Polka*-more-than-three-times, Den will perform at the reception. Hans will assist "where ever needed." His new cat is "just like Bunny" and loves to Travel on EV Rider.

Feeble adopted a wiener dog and will attend with the Copley Park Dog Moms (as an Honorary Mom). Saint Gail completed chemotherapy and is down for carrot cupcakes (with extra cream cheese icing on mine. YUM!).

Motorcycles and tons of J O Y. There will be an

anniversary ride. Will you come? Don't worry about making a ferry reservation.

# CHAPTER 35 - FINAL THOUGHTS

*"One may as well try to ride two motorcycles going in opposite directions as try to explain Motorcycle JOY" - Marta.*

Is that the truth about motorcycles? That each rider has their own definition of Truth, MAGIC, and JOY? So there is no point in trying to package an explanation and fit it into a tank bag?

"It's about the experience," Bob would say, or perhaps something sketchy like, "Sheep spend their entire lives fearing the wolf, only to be eaten by the shepherd."

"So, never take the shepherd for granted?"

"Or the wolf."

Take nothing for granted, I guess.

All you can do is,

Climb on.

Ride.

Trust that **JOY will find a way.**

That's the Truth about motorcycles.

# THANKS & CONTACTS

NONFICTION BEATEN

WITH A STICK

**Thanks for reading!**

*Enjoyed the book?*
*Please consider leaving a review.*

Contact the author:

Messenger: Scraping Pegs on Facebook

Email: beatenstickpress@gmail.com

Say hello. Thoughts. Questions?

# BOOKS BY THIS AUTHOR

## Scraping Pegs, The Truth About Motorcycles

Book one, an investigation into Truth and GT meets Horace the Horrible.

## Scrape Your Lists

The motorcycle experience expressed in point form.

## Motorcycle State Of Mind

Why ride a motorcycle? Every revolution of the wheel is an opportunity if you read between the lines.

Printed in Great Britain
by Amazon

34598138R00169

# CONTENTS

## Introducing the Speaker

Rev Joel Edwards is the General Director of the Evangelical Alliance UK. The Evangelical Alliance represents over 1 million Christians, with membership spanning a broad range of evangelical churches across the United Kingdom.

Joel was born in Jamaica and came to Britain at the age of eight. He is married to Carol and has two children. He was a Probation Officer for ten years and former General Secretary of the African & Caribbean Evangelical Alliance. Joel is also an Associate Pastor of an East London New Testament Church of God and serves on the NTCG National Executive.

His first book, "Lord Make Us One - But Not All The Same!" was published in February 1999 and is a semi auto-biographical work which presents his own pilgrimage as an object lesson in contemporary evangelical diversity in the UK.

The sub title of the conference, "God's Policy on Social Exclusion", reflects the emphasis that the Government has given to the work of the Social Exclusion Unit. Joel Edwards is well placed to speak on the subject with his perspectives as an immigrant black man, with experience as a Probation Officer and from his position as the Director of an alliance of many evangelical churches in UK.

*The material presented in this publication is based on transcripts of the talks given at the Conference. The spoken style has been retained and should be read as if hearing the speaker talk in the conference setting.*

# 1. THE LAST SHALL BE FIRST

## Introduction

I am always glad for any opportunity to escape from the enclosure of what is described as full-time ministry, to meet with those on the front end of the contemporary missionary enterprise in our culture and society. I have a great deal of admiration for those who, day after day in difficult circumstances, find ways to make the principles of scripture come alive for those people who I may not bump into in every day life.

I have a certain empathy with your theme - the first shall be last - primarily because it happens to me quite a lot. I have a rare gift that enables me to calculate which queue, in a supermarket or bank, is likely to take me to the counter first and I always get it wrong! But there is obviously a broader challenge than our ability to get in the right queue when considering this subject. I want to approach our first session from the wider backdrop of the text that introduces us to the theme.

## The workers in the vineyard

The story of the vineyard is in Matthew chapter 20 and it is probably fairly familiar to you.

> *"For the kingdom of heaven is like a land owner who went out early in the morning to hire men to work in his vineyard. He agreed to pay them a denarius for the day and sent them into his vineyard. About the third hour he went out and saw others standing in the market-place doing nothing. He told them, 'You also go and work in my vineyard, and I will pay you whatever is right.' He went out again about the sixth hour and the ninth hour and did the same thing. About the eleventh hour he went out and found still others standing around. He asked them, 'Why have you been standing here all day doing nothing? "Because no-one has hired us,' they answered. He said to them, 'You also go and work in my vineyard.'*
>
> *When evening came, the owner of the vineyard said to his foreman, 'Call the workers and pay them their wages, beginning with the last ones hired and going on to the first.' The workers who were hired about the eleventh hour came and*

*each received a denarius. So when those who came who were hired first, they expected to receive more. But each one of them also received a denarius. When they received it, they began to grumble against the landowner. 'These men who were hired last worked only one hour,' they said, 'and you have made them equal to us who have borne the burden of the work and the heat of the day.'*

*But he answered one of them, 'Friend, I am not being unfair to you. Didn't you agree to work for a denarius? Take your pay and go. I want to give the man who was hired last the same as I gave you. Don't I have the right to do what I want with my own money? Or are you envious because I am generous?' So the last will be last and the first will be last."*

The story is actually quite true to its cultural context, even though it is a parable. The scenario we have in this passage would not be unusual for the Middle East at that time. It may have been grape harvest when there was very little time between the harvesting and the rains that would follow. It would be important for the grapes to be picked and processed as quickly as possible so they wouldn't be spoiled. The owner of the vineyard would need to replenish the workforce from time to time to ensure a good work rate as the day wore on. So the kind of situation here is true to reality. The people hearing Jesus' story would have recognised immediately the accuracy of the events he was describing.

**Topsy Turvy Values**

The implications are important for us as well. You will be relieved to know that the parable is not an outline of a pay policy but is a story about grace. It is a story about the grace of God applied generously irrespective of effort. The landowner decides to pay the last the same as the first. It is his choice. He made a bargain with the first man he employed, but he decided to be more generous with the later employees. It is also a story about radical topsy-turvy values. That's the heart of the thing. It is about a kingdom value that runs counter to what would have been normal practice. In order to make sense of this story, we have to go one step back to the previous chapter.

In Matthew chapter 19 there is an encounter with a rich young man. We will try to unearth some principles to build on as we unpack the theme. The young man is rich. The fact that he is rich immediately puts my back up. It is easy to react negatively to those who have a lot of money. Our own situation may be more like the comedian who said, "If money talks all it ever seems to say to me is 'Goodbye'".

**Riches**

You may know that the Sunday Times compiles a "rich list". I read it some years ago and it suggested that if you were worth less that £50 million you were not seriously rich. It mentioned Paul Getty II worth £135 million, the late Robert Maxwell worth £1,100 million, Richard Branson, the man of the train and balloons, worth £488 million and Paul McCartney worth £350 million. The richest, the Duke of Westminster had a mouth-watering £4,200 million. This was quite depressing reading on a Sunday afternoon. This young man in Matthew 19 may well have invoked certain kinds of feelings from the disciples. How did he get his riches? Were they earned or inherited? It may have been a bit of both. He may have had a very entrepreneurial streak to him. I'll explain why I think so. It's the way he goes about things. He's got the right motive, but his line of questioning is rather intriguing. What do I do to get eternal life? What's the output that I have to make to get the input of eternal life? Jesus pointed him to the commandments and told him to obey the law. The young man's response was a version of, "I've done that, got the T-shirt, bought the video." Jesus says, "I know your problem son, you need to sell up and follow me." Well, it was quite a crippling statement. The young fellow couldn't quite get his head or heart or motivation around that. I believe his enquiry was very genuine. He wanted to know how to get some of what Jesus was talking about. He was offered a way to do it but he couldn't quite make it.

**Is Jesus opposed to riches?**

It is easy to assume, especially in the context of social exclusion, that somebody like this with so much money, deserved what he got. It served him right. The interesting thing is that there was quite a strong feeling between Jesus and this young man. The Bible says that as the young man disappeared beyond the outer rims of the crowd, Jesus looked on him and loved him. There is a powerful encounter between this rich, possibly spoiled, young man who couldn't quite make that extra journey and Jesus' passion and desire for him. There is a temptation for us to marginalise him because he was rich and to conclude that Jesus is anti-wealth. But that is not in the text.

It was Martin Luther King Junior, who could not be accused of being pampered by wealth in his life and ministry, who said, “Jesus never made a universal indictment against all wealth. It is true that on one occasion he told the rich young ruler to sell all, but on that occasion he was prescribing individual surgery rather than setting forth a universal diagnosis.” Jesus knew exactly what the problem was - that wealth had got hold of the young man to such an extent that it was stopping him getting what he really wanted and needed. It was not an anti-wealth message of itself and we need to be cautious, as we try to stand with those who are poor and excluded, that we don’t have a simple anti-wealth attitude.

Jesus told the disciples later on that anyone who left everything to follow him would get a hundredfold in this life and eternal life in the next world. This is quite a down payment and quite a promise! The Bible tells us in Isaiah 53, that Jesus was with the poor in his death and with the rich in his grave. I love that. There is something so entirely inclusive about the death of Jesus that it spans the whole spectrum of humanity. His title on the cross was written in three different cultural languages of his day and his death was an absorption of all human pain and suffering. He profoundly identified himself with the poor, being crucified on a cross of all places between two thieves, and yet he is identified in his burial with those who are wealthy.

No, this isn’t simply a teaching against rich people. It is easy for us, who are not so well off, to distance ourselves from the principles being extended to us here simply because we can’t identify with this rich young ruler. There is a tendency for us to engage in inverted snobbery towards those who are wealthy. But that is not the kind of cosmic generosity which Jesus expressed and displayed in his ministry. It is not what you have, so much as what you do with what you have, that matters. Or to put it another way it is what wealth does to you that is the issue. Whatever we have has to be handled lightly so that when God wants to use us we remain accessible to him.

**Holding things lightly**

I remember some advice from Tim Buckley who taught music at the London Bible College. He said that the way to get the best sound from a violin is to hold the bow so lightly that someone could come along and take it out of your hand without a struggle.

awareness of future things and eternity. However, I find this very difficult for a number of reasons.

**Escapism**

I find this difficult because I fear a theology of escapism. My own theological background, Pentecostalism, is tainted with a strong holiness theology. "Come out from among them" and "Be ye separated" may be in the Bible, but such texts can raise some difficulties. Huge sections of the Christian community at the earliest stages of this century, and possibly into the 1970s and 1980s, abandoned the real world. We subscribed to a dualism that promoted a huge divide between the sacred and the secular. We considered that we belonged to the sacred realm into which we retreated having earned our money in the harsh secular world.

This involved a separatist theology that was reluctant to engage with "the world" any more than was necessary. The abandonment of the "real world" was the result of a spiritual escapism. There is a part of the church's life and experience which is sometimes guilty of being so heavenly minded that it is of very little earthly use. So now when we are caught in the sharp end of social engagement with people with real needs, up against the odds, the last thing that is likely to occupy our minds is any notion of tomorrow, another world, another kind of reality. We want to get on with justice now, we want it to happen yesterday preferably last week, and we are not really too much interested in talk about eternity. So it becomes very difficult for us if we are committed to people. If we are activists we don't want to be too theologically theoretical.

**Confusion**

There is another reason why I think it becomes very hard for us to engage with this big picture. We don't understand it. There are divisions into pre-millenialists, post-millenialists or a-millenialists. Some churches require you to be one of them even if you don't quite understand them! In that kind of theological confusion we do not want to preoccupy ourselves with those huge discussions as to when this thousand year reign of Christ will actually happen. The easiest thing is to retreat from that sort of preoccupation.

**Immediate gratification**

There is another reason why we don't engage with eternal things very often, and that is because we are bathed in existentialism. The immediacy of experience that meets the perceived needs in the here and now becomes very overwhelming. In a competitive environment where the battle is played out in front of you, nobody wants to be preoccupied with any other kind of reality. We are people of experience. We are trying to survive... so who wants to think about any other kind of context in which to work.

I remember when I was doing my social work training in 1976, having completed three years in London Bible College, I went to the probation service in Tottenham to take up work as an ancillary for 18 months. In the interview they said, " Mr Edwards, you've done three years in theology, why do you want to do social work?" My answer suggested that since the Bible is a book about communities and a God who is totally committed to people, what better training could I have for social work than the Bible. They must have liked it - or they were very desperate for black people in the service at that time. But I got the job.

From the secure family environment of the London Bible College I was catapulted into the polytechnic where they taught me about immediate gratification. I always remember that expression because we Pentecostals are into tomorrow and so immediate gratification was a funny sort of phrase. However, it described the motivation behind many of the people with whom I was going to work. There was very little point in telling the teenagers I met about the future. They wanted their needs met now; they wanted to feel enfranchised now; they wanted to redress the injustices that society had perpetrated upon them and they wanted to be somebody now.

As I worked alongside them however, I wondered just what separated them from some of my colleagues. Many of us were getting a lot of immediate gratification from satisfying the apparent needs of our clients and there were very few of us who had any kind of notion about anything beyond what we were doing. We were totally engulfed in the intensity, the immediacy and all the political paraphernalia of the present moment.

**An eternal perspective**

The office was at times a very claustrophobic place with an atmosphere where you watched your back if you wanted to get on. I hope I was able to bring another perspective to my work. Obviously I wanted to be relevant and helpful to my clients but I wondered if there was something else that I was able to bring into that environment - which was about another time slot, another reality, and spirituality which did not ignore the now but actually was able to go beyond it. I hope so because eternity is the reality.

Eternity is the kingdom context in which we work. Eternity is the kingdom context in which values are challenged.

The church is only able to be prophetic in the realm of social exclusion if it maintains a commitment to a kingdom context which operates on a different value system from the market place of political choices. It doesn't want to be politically naive, but it does aim to critique society from a different context.

I wasn't sure I was always able to do that in my late twenties, as I didn't have the tools to draw an intellectual line between my theology and social policy. But I believe that the context of eternity, the context of the kingdom, is the final context for all accountability. Social exclusion in the bigger picture is not just about social engineering. It is not just about sloganising on justice issues. It is about kingdom accountability. The average politician is unlikely to accept this but I believe human history is moving to the accountability that is found in Revelation.

> *"The kingdom of the world has become the kingdom of our Lord and of his Christ and he will reign for ever and ever."* (Revelation 11 v 15)

That is either a myth, in which case there is no point of reference beyond this world, or it's a reality. If it is a myth then any attempt to transform communities must be worked out from no bigger platform than the social theories to which we are exposed in our practice. However, if there is a higher accountability then there is a bigger backdrop and something else we are working towards. It seems to me that this bigger back drop is the only way to really understand ultimately how the first can be last and last can be first.

**A higher accountability**

The kingdom context and kingdom values suggest that at the end of the day God will call us all to account. Therefore we do our work not just because we are doing it to earn a crust, not just because we like working with people, but because we are totally committed to an accountability beyond this planet. It is an accountability that comes from God himself. I believe it is the proper context for work. Do you notice how easily Paul writes about accountability to God? He moves comfortably from philosophical debates about the nature of Jesus to talking about marriage, work relationships, slaves and masters. Employers are not to abuse their servants, and servants are not to take liberties with their masters because their accountability is not to the working contractual relationship but to a higher accountability (Ephesians 5:22-6:9). Now that is very challenging.

Unless we have this bigger perspective we may be good social workers but we may not be kingdom people bringing transformation. It's the difference between good work and the optimism of the cross. This is the proper context for work. In estimating the value of work, we must take into consideration not only the time we have spent on it or what we have achieved but also the motivation behind it. That's a piercing one for preachers who love to be loved. That's a piercing one for social workers who love to be needed. What's the motive? What drives me to see this client yet again? What keeps me going in all the political challenges in the local office, the character assassinations, and the lack of resources and closures? It is the sense of optimism and accountability that goes beyond the here and the now. I don't think that's just political and theological theory nor do I believe that this kind of eschatology, properly understood, takes you away from reality.

**Hope**

Lord Shaftesbury, one of the greatest philanthropists of the church world in the last two centuries, signed at the bottom of all his letters "Even so, Lord come quickly." When I first heard about that I found it astounding. He was a man who was totally committed to the poor, totally committed to the excluded, totally committed to fight the political machinery on behalf of those who were dispossessed and disenfranchised, but he never lost sight of the other accountability. The extent to which we bring optimism and transformational hope into some of the desperate situations we encounter, may well depend on our ability to be focused on the sense of the bigger picture. This rescues social work from being caught up with practical limitations and frustrations. Hope belongs to people who draw the values of the kingdom into the present. We work with and for those in the back of the queue because we know that, in the greater scheme of things, the last can be first and poor people can still make it when rich rulers have failed the test.

**Commitment**
So Jesus seems to be irrelevant doesn't he? "What's in it for us?" the disciples asked. And Jesus replied, "Think about the future." I think their minds have made a quantum leap. Can I challenge you in the same way to consider the work you are doing in a wider context? I am not suggesting that you should be politically naive but that you may be reinforced and invigorated in working on behalf of those who are disadvantaged. Jesus not only presented the bigger picture but he also presented the disciples with the need to be decisive. Jesus said anyone who has left everything to follow me would be rewarded. The language indicates a final determined act – a clear choice. It implies a non-prevaricating moment, a sense of being radically sold out to God's enterprise, a sense of conviction that this is the place to be. We may not have all the questions answered, we may not have all the details available to us, but this is the place to be. We have left everything. He said it twice, in Matthew 19 verses 27 and 29. Those who have left everything will be rewarded. I wonder if we need to rediscover a clear commitment to where we feel God has called us to be.

Jesus had said to this rich young man, "Sell everything you have and come and follow me." He couldn't do it. Peter, however, had done exactly that to all intents and purposes. He had made a clear decision to follow and his life would never be the same again. Jesus underlined that this is the kingdom principle. There is no need to be insecure. Jesus could hear the insecurity behind Peter's question but Jesus confirmed that he would be rewarded despite his uncertainties. The same applies to us. If we give ourselves to him, even if we are not sure about how it will all work out, we should hang in there because we will be rewarded.

**A sense of calling**
I believe, as kingdom people, that we need a sense of rightness about where we are. It doesn't matter if other people think we could be doing so much more somewhere else. If you feel in your heart that this is what God has called you to do, you stay there. Many who thought they were first will be last, and many who thought they were last will end up first.

When we get to heaven we may begin to understand how the topsy turvyness of the kingdom turns the world the right way up. There'll be a lot of surprises, because we will have discovered that some people who were on the side of the poor who we thought were in the wrong place were in the right place. We may find that some people who had been passed over in society, who we thought, were “riffraff” and didn’t really count, were very highly favoured. When we work with those who are excluded and marginalised we do it not just because it gives us a buzz but because God is on their side. In God’s economy and in kingdom principles, even if it doesn’t seem like it, the first can be last and sometimes the last will be first.

## 2. LIVING OUT THE LIFESTYLE

I want to continue looking at our theme of "the first shall be last" by reminding ourselves of some broad principles of God's topsy turvy value system. Firstly, the story of the workers in the vineyard tells us about God's ability to be almost indiscriminately generous with his own resources. Secondly, it demonstrates a radical alternative value system that is not just about giving to get, but is about God's graciousness and His ability to turns things upside down to bring a totally different approach to the way we see things. The story of the rich young ruler indicates how a person may do all the right things but miss out on what is really valuable in life. Thirdly, Jesus underlines for us the need to see the eternal perspective. Christians without a sense of the bigger picture of final accountability are likely to get overtaken with the immediacy of present needs.

**The distinctive of hope**

We can bring something to our work which non Christians are unable to bring and that is a touch of eternity, the reality of a sense of hope. I suspect that what our world needs today is a framework of hope to bring to our communities. In the Middle Ages people spoke about redemption in terms of ransom. Jesus as a ransom was a concept that actually helped to communicate the gospel of redemption at that time. People understood because it fitted within the cultural context of society and the current world views. In other times people spoke about the substitutionary sacrifice of Jesus, and that fitted in with the cultural context of its day because it was about the honour of God and the preservation of the dignity of God. People understood that dignity was a very significant thing. But now in our fragmented and spiritually relativised society nobody is quite sure who is to say what is right or even whether there is such a thing as truth.

So what is the contemporary cultural framework which will make sense in order to help them understand the story of redemption? I think there is a need for a new application of an understanding of hope in so many hopeless scenarios. There is a difference between optimism and hope. Optimism comes from circumstances. Hope comes from God. Hope steps outside of the madness of our situation, does not deny the problems or play them down, is not superficial or naive, but brings the perspective of eternity to bear on the situation. If you and I have nothing to offer beyond the immediacy of our work environment then we are missing out on one of the greatest gifts that God has given as people of the kingdom.

Jack Hayford once said that we are the people of the horizon. I like that. He spoke about the place on the horizon where we cannot quite see where the sky begins and sea ends - just a tip of the horizon where the sky and earth meets. That is where we live - we are the people of the horizon. I think that is a really beautiful image. The people of the horizon who bring hope to very desperate situations. We do that as we see the bigger picture which God has given us which is about final accountability. In the gospels and the Book of Acts the apostles speak in equal measures about hope and about judgement, about hope and about accountability. The final accountability is the culmination of history where Christ will reign and where everyone must give an account of the deeds that they have done on earth.

Human history moves towards God and anyone who resists that is going against the flow. It is called disobedience and is spiritual anarchy. Whether it is whole dynasties, prime ministers, nations, communities or an individual, those who resist the flow towards accountability are in a state of rebellion. God's topsy turvy value system only has genuine and real meaning in our world today if there is accountability to God. Otherwise we are the final arbitrators of right and wrong and we become humanists not Christians.

When I worked as a Probation Officer what I found most jarring were sloganised responses to sexism, ageism, and racism. We are right to battle against these things, but if we lose the divine backdrop, we are only offering human aspirations. If there is a God who will call everyone to justice, we can speak against racism, ageism and sexism from a framework of divine principles not just from a human social and political standpoint. Going against God himself is a much bigger charge than simply disputing a human enterprise. I hope that when we challenge the police about racism that we don't just do it because it is politically correct but we do it because we have a sense of the horizon. We're not being politically naive but we are offering a bigger picture.

This emphasis on our eternal accountability indicates a seamlessness in God's expectation of us in our homes, in our work places and in our churches because it is the same God who calls us to obedience to Him.

This affects the way we work and the way we become husbands and wives and parents. It takes us to the heart of the matter. It challenges our motivation. The rich young ruler wasn't prepared to pay the price. His motivation was good but it wasn't good enough. The biblical sense of future accountability, which the young man did not seem to appreciate, is the fuel that drives our activities.

When Jesus called his disciples to leave everything to follow Him, he was inviting them to God's topsy turvy world where the last shall be first. In our attempt to understand social exclusion the assumption must be that God is committed to push people who are at the back to the front. The disciples, by leaving all to follow Jesus, could be seen as marginalised and disadvantaged but they were to receive a hundredfold. Jesus' teaching in the Sermon on the Mount in Matthew 5 is also about this reversal of roles. "Blessed are the poor", "Blessed are those who hunger and thirst", "Blessed are those who are persecuted". The whole topsy turvyness of kingdom values is presented in such a way that Jesus gave his audience a severe culture shock.

**Miracles and social security**

It's worth looking at Jesus' miracles from the point of view of social exclusion. At the wedding of Cana was he just demonstrating his power or was he making a very profound social comment on a very important social event? Or consider the woman of Nain whose one and only son had died. Jesus stopped the funeral procession, restored this boy to life, and gave him back to his mother. That was a very profound act. It was not just about the resurrection of a dead boy, but is also about the restoration of the woman's social security system. What about the leper who Jesus touched and released back to the community? That is surely a statement against social exclusion because if you were a leper you stayed outside the walls of the city. Consider the blind man who begged and had no economic independence. Consider the young man let down from the roof of the house who was restored to health. All of these are not just miracles of a restoration of health – they are also the restoration of people's social and economic independence. These were people who were socially excluded within the first century community of Judaism.

**Christians in the minority**

Jesus demonstrated that he was committed to the socially excluded in both word and deed. How does this commitment impact on our social and political realities? How is God's policy on social exclusion to be implemented where Christians are the minority lobby? We cannot ignore the power of the ballot box and we must recognise that the popular vote rather than principles often shape policy. Even where we have self-confessed Christian leaders like President Chiluba in Zambia, it is still patently clear that the majority of the nation must agree with the consensus of Christian values for Christian policies to be implemented. We Christians are a minority group. We may have a Christian heritage but there are very few people who have an active commitment to Christian values.

I often describe the UK as Tattooed Jim. The tattoo says "I love Jane" but he and Jane separated 25 years ago and Jim is not quite sure what to do with the tattoo. We can talk about Christian values and Christian heritage but the vast majority of the population are dancing to another tune. They have very different value systems that guide their actions and attitudes. How do we, therefore, bring Christian values and God's policy for social exclusion into this kind of environment? The Bible is not a private memo for Christians, even though we sometimes behave like it is. It is actually God's commentary on human relationships. How do we apply its radical topsy turvy philosophy to our context?

Where does it fit between the political philosophy which says "To each according to his need and from each according to his ability" and the other political value which suggests, "To each according to his ability". Between those two extremes is a philosophy about the first being last. It doesn't sit very comfortably with either of those extremes but it is the kingdom of God on earth seeking to be actively influencing people's behaviour.

**Living the lifestyle**

This topsy turvy kingdom has to be communicated primarily through our own personal lifestyle. The Bible never gives us the impression that it promotes systems at the expense of personal lifestyle. The power of the gospel to tip things upside down has always been through the people of God and their lifestyles. I was asked some time ago whether using the law was the best way to change church and society's attitude to racial justice. Certainly the law of the land has to reflect rightness and justice. But imagine a million people who are actively committed to Christian values on the street, in their homes and shops, in their offices and sports clubs. That kind of army can make a very powerful impact.

The book of Daniel demonstrates that Daniel was a very influential figure but part of his influence wasn't just his political clout but his personal integrity and lifestyle. He was uncompromising in his principles even when it meant foregoing promotion, which it did at least twice in his career. This seems to me to be something that faces us on an individual basis in the harsh world in which God has called us to live. I have a good friend who has a very influential position doing a job that actually cuts against the grain of all his Christian principles. His boss does not know that he is a Christian. He has to choose whether to disclose his principles and take the risk of getting fired or keep quiet and keep his job. If we are committed to this topsy turvy philosophy then we may have difficult choices of our own. Are we prepared to really live out Christian principles? We do not need to be cut-throat even if we do have to be competitive, because we are committed to a principle of humility. We may be in the rat race but we can operate with some long term principles about valuing people and remembering the poor.

**The Church's role**

This is a challenge for the Church. How do we bring the principles of the kingdom into the real world around us? Sometimes we've got it terribly wrong, and the Church has many atrocities of which we should be ashamed. We have subjugated other cultures in the name of Christ and sought to perpetrate violence and impose our superiority on others in the name of truth. But there are some good things as well. The Church has attempted to find ways in which to bring the topsy turvy values of the kingdom into cultural and political realities. The Church has always been at the sharp end of education and social work.

The probation service, for example, developed from Christian initiatives although my social work training did not mention this. In fact during my two years training I felt like an alien, bombarded as I was with secular humanism. Christians in social work are the true heritage, not intruders. We need not be apologetic about our role. The Evangelical Alliance is proud to have around 700 societies whose tasks range from evangelism and creative ways of communicating the gospels to social action on the ground.

Why? Because we are committed to God's policy against social exclusion not only in word and personal lifestyle but also in deed. We are increasingly recognising that it won't happen if we hide behind the walls of church buildings, but we are seeking to meet people where they are and make a difference.

I would love to see greater attention paid to the quiet work that goes on within church communities up and down the country. There are numerous caring initiatives that don't make a lot of noise or razzmatazz but continue to care for the elderly, visit prisoners, raise funds, offer accommodation to those under stress, provide food for the hungry and work for the unemployed. We have got a long way to go and a lot more to do but there is the quiet commitment that the church continues to have. Some colleagues and I have been wondering about the possibility of carrying out a survey of all the social action that churches are involved within the UK. I would like there to be a greater recognition of all these activities.

**Principles rather than policies**

However, despite all of this Christian concern for the excluded and disadvantaged there is no evidence that some of the social ills in the Bible were attacked in biblical times. There is nothing in the Bible that categorically lays out an anti-racist or anti-slavery policy. It is clear that there was slavery, women were abused, and children were marginalised and neglected. But it would be hard to find a coherent social policy in the Bible that you could put in front of a Prime Minister to say this is the chapter and verse that spells out a policy against such things. And yet it's there in the mood of the Bible.

It shows itself primarily through radical subversion. There is no way that the first century could sustain slavery if it looked carefully at the principles in Paul's letter to Philemon. Paul asked Philemon to treat the slave Onesimus like a brother or a son. That was radical language – an inconceivable concept!

There was no way that superior attitudes to women could remain unchallenged when men were told to love their wives as their own bodies. I have a vivid picture in my mind as Paul's letter to the Ephesian church was read out. "Wives, submit to your husbands." No surprises here they thought. But then they heard, "Husbands love your wives." Now this is new language for the first century. "Fathers, do not exasperate your children." That's subversive. This is the policy of subversion, and it's written in the heart of the good news.

Good news to the excluded is that God has an inclusive policy and the nature of the church is to challenge itself to be inclusive of all people. The journey is painfully slow and over the last 2000 years we haven't got it right, but the principle is there. The principle is that we are inclusive to those who are marginalised. It is a policy against social exclusion that is meant for the whole community and not a private memo to the Church.

There is evidence that God's inclusive policies work. I have been to prisons where they are trying to operate a person centred approach on biblical principles and finding that the recidivism rate is significantly reduced. A recent report suggested that church based schools turn out better pupils than those which are not church based.

In order to present the topsy turvy radical kingdom principle that "the last shall be first", we must demonstrate through our lifestyle and attitudes that we have integrity. We need to show that we are consistent with what we say and what we do in the workplace. Then we can say to our neighbours, to policy makers and governments that there is a radical upside down philosophy which comes from a God who is inclusive of all people, who wants to see a world which recognises that the first can be last, and the last may sometimes be first.

## 3. GOD'S POLICY ON SOCIAL EXCLUSION

As I was thinking about social exclusion I was reminded of the caste system in India and the concept of "the untouchables" which seem so alien to us in the West. But we have our own untouchables, don't we? Our social security system and some of the voluntary sector activities may minimise the marginalisation that goes on within our own society, but it's there nonetheless. Jesus reminded us that the poor would always be with us (Matthew 26 v 11). It is a sobering thought. In fact economists and social analysts suggest that the poor will become poorer and the rich will become richer.

**Bias to the Poor**

God, the friend of the friendless, exhorts us to be on the side of the excluded. In fact some of the strongest denunciations in scripture are reserved for those who don't take the poor, the marginalised and the disenfranchised seriously. God very seldom had harsh words for poor people, but he certainly made clear what was expected of those who are privileged or powerful.

> *"Do not ill-treat an alien or oppress him, for you were aliens in Egypt. Do not take advantage of a widow or an orphan. If you do and they cry out to me, I will certainly hear their cry. My anger will be aroused, and I will kill you with the sword; your wives will become widows and your children fatherless." (Exodus 22v 21)*

This is a strong message against exploitation. If the Bible has a policy on social exclusion, it is, to quote David Sheppard[1], a bias to the poor. The Bible tells us,

> *"Do not deny justice to poor people in their law suits." (Exodus 23 v 6)*

However, God's bias to the poor is not a prejudicial bias. He does not absolve the poor of their own responsibility. Exodus chapter 23 verse 3 reads,

> *"Do not show favouritism to a poor man in his law suit."*

[1] David Sheppard (1983) "Bias to the Poor" Hodder and Stoughton, London

God's bias is not prejudicial bias. The poor and marginalised are also accountable. God's policy of social exclusion does not pander to an unprofessional subjectivism that exempts or excludes people who are struggling from their own personal responsibility.

**Responsibility**

When I worked as a Probation Officer there was often a tension between the police and ourselves. Those who were responsible for catching the criminal often felt that we did not take the responsibility of the criminal sufficiently seriously. The police seemed to feel that our entire focus was to produce reports calculated to undermine personal responsibility. But the Bible does not undermine our responsibility. Whatever we make of Labour's "New Deal", it is trying to wrestle with the issue. I get very impatient with cries on behalf of black people that make us less than human, because they also take away our responsibility in terms of crime or dysfunction within the community. Sometimes those speaking on behalf of disadvantaged groups suggest that they have no kind of responsibility for their own development or contribution to the wider society.

We certainly do not want to relieve the police of their responsibility for some of the things that have come to light recently, but neither do we want to ignore individuals within society whose behaviour is manifestly irresponsible. We have a very tough and difficult role in promoting justice on the one hand, and on the other hand insisting that we all take some element of responsibility for who we are and what we do. Any policy or practice that treats the excluded entirely passively eventually becomes counter-productive, paternalistic and potentially patronising. It is important to recognise the principle of mutuality that is illustrated by the text in Exodus and demonstrates the responsibility of rich and poor alike.

**Equality**

Another principle we find in the Bible is that of equality. Rich and poor are both of equal value. In Exodus 30 verse 15 we read,

> *"The rich are not to give more than a half shekel and the poor are not to give less when you make the offering to the Lord to atone for your lives."*

In other words the poor and the rich pay the same amount because the offering relates to the value of their lives. This is a principle of equality before God. Our lives are not to be measured by economic differences. It is the same value that is at the heart of the American Declaration of Independence – the truth that all people are created equal.

This equality should run through our attitudes and actions as well as our institutions and processes. There should not only be legal protection of the excluded but also a radical change of attitude. Institutionalised exclusion often results in attitudes that then interpret legal frameworks. If the attitude is not one of respect and equality then a legal framework can only restrain, but not fundamentally change people and communities. At the end of the day we tend to respond from our own attitudes to those who are of a different group. Laws may restrict injustice against excluded people but right attitudes build inclusive communities.

One of my probation colleagues had a cartoon in his office. It was a picture of a judge leaning over his bench to an offender, as he was about to pronounce his sentence, saying "I know that you committed these offences as a result of **your** background. I am sentencing you as a result of **my** background." It refers to the way our attitude towards other people can shape what we say and do even when interpreting legal requirements.

This biblical understanding of mutuality and equality is basic to our work with the disadvantaged. It reminds us that we are all made in God's image and this can give us the tenacity, the strength and the endurance to deal with the idiosyncrasies of those who are marginalised. People who have been marginalised and discriminated against over a long period of time can develop patterns of life that will sometimes jar with our own. We can move beyond those idiosyncrasies by remembering that whatever side of the desk we sit we are created in God's image. There were times at work when I looked at other black youngsters, much like myself, and I would think "There but for the grace of God go I." I continue to find it helpful, when I come across situations and attitudes that irritate me, to remember the principle of mutuality and equality – to recognise that we are all made in God's image.

**Being poor**

We also need to examine our assumptions about what it is to be poor. The Bible gives us an alternative definition of poverty.

> *"Blessed are the poor in spirit, for theirs is the kingdom of heaven."* Matthew 5 v 3

Poverty may not be exclusively about economic empowerment or employment although we must not minimise their importance in the battle against injustice. Jesus challenged the Christian community in Laodicea on their understanding of being rich and poor. They thought they were rich but they were told they were actually quite poor because their values were wrong.

I have travelled to places where people are very impoverished economically such as Nigeria, South Africa and The Philippines. I had to confront my own poverty. It was clear that people I met in these countries had a humanity and personhood that was far richer than some of those who are materially comfortable. The human spirit can rise above very severe economic deprivation and display considerable riches in terms of character and personality.

So how do we measure poverty and wealth? Do we recognise that we can all give and receive something from each other? We need to understand the mutuality that prevents the paternalistic approach whereby the privileged give something to the excluded that they cannot repay. My wife works with an employment project for people with a learning disability and she spends a lot of time supporting, and training people to be able to hold down a job. It is often very intensive support where she may spend hours enabling people to carry out a relatively simple task such as using a photocopier. She enjoys her job because she gets something back from working with people with disabilities. It is not a one way street. This is the message of the Bible. We are people that have the image of God inscribed in us, and we give to and receive from one another.

In dealing with social exclusion God is profoundly concerned about our attitudes to one another. If we lose this understanding of mutuality we may get overwhelmed with political concerns, and then we risk being no different to those who work outside of a kingdom paradigm.

**Government policy on exclusion**

In the 1980s government policy raised the profile of economic criteria in the caring professions. During my time as a Probation Officer I was very aware that the service was moving away from a caring ethos to a controlling ethos. The value of our work was being measured by other criteria than our ability to professionally care and assist in the area of the criminal justice system. Care in the community has partially foundered because the economics card has trumped the principle of mutuality.

We now have a different government with a commitment to tackling social exclusion. Social exclusion is a short-hand label for what can happen when individuals or areas suffer from a combination of problems such as unemployment, poor skills, low incomes, poor housing, high crime environment, bad health and family breakdowns. It means being cut off from the things that most of us take for granted such as a job, qualifications, a home and a safe environment.

Poverty and unemployment may be aspects of social exclusion but they are not synonymous with it. Not all unemployed people on low incomes are socially excluded and not all socially excluded people are poor and unemployed. We have a responsibility to make sure that the government maintains a breadth of concern that is integrated across departments and various aspects of social deprivation. Many of us welcome the approach to joined-up work across departments, bringing the private and public sector together, including the Church and other faith groups. There is a challenge to us as a Church to seek opportunities to combat social exclusion. There are great opportunities for the Church to actually get on board and to be a part of what the government is doing.

I welcome what the government has been saying in terms of the emphasis on education but to miss out the importance of spiritual values will not be a step forward. I do not think it is an accident that many of the top primary schools are church schools. Attitudes and values are crucial to developing a community of inclusion. I know from experience that my two children were at ease with themselves culturally until they went to school when they began to ask whether they were really inferior? In the wider area of community relationships I applaud the signs of decisive statements on institutional racism following the Stephen Lawrence Enquiry. But we must make sure that values aren't left out of the political rhetoric.

**Christians social policy and politics**

There are many other areas of concern. How will the government balance the issues of rights and responsibilities, of low taxation at the same time as high employment, of centralism and devolution. What outcome will there be for those who are poor and marginalised? To apply God's policy on social exclusion to all of these issues we must start where Jesus did - with the incarnation. As Eugene Peterson expresses it in The Message,

> *"The Word became flesh and blood, and moved into the neighbourhood."* John 1 v 14.

Jesus was born as a baby, grew up, lived and died among the people. In his death his proximity to the poor was very clearly shown as he died between two thieves, even though he was buried in a rich man's grave. The responsibility of the church is to continue to seek ways to apply kingdom values to social policy, and to ensure that economics are not placed above the value of people and the community. We need to continue with the prophetic vision of the Council of Churches report on Unemployment and the Future of Work[2] and the Catholic bishops lead on The Common Good.[3] There are going to be further opportunities to engage with policy makers from a Christian perspective on how to deal with those who are excluded. As social workers you have a very important role to play because I don't think it's going to be the rarefied pronouncements of people in the pulpit which will do this job alone. We need both Christian practitioners and academics who have something to say and who insist on marrying biblical principles with social policy. We also need more Christians in politics. Together we will seek to demonstrate God's policy on behalf of the socially excluded through the various mechanism of government.

We also need to consider how we support those Christians in politics. At a recent Evangelical Alliance Council meeting for church leaders we had a number of Christian MPs who felt that they did not always get the support or understanding as Christians. They felt that they were seen as party politicians before they were seen as fellow Christians. There is often a huge gulf between a political understanding of social exclusion on the one hand and the activities of the local church on the other. Somehow we need to narrow the gap between those who are on the sharp end of political and social enterprise and those who direct and participate in church life.

---

[2] Council of Churches for Britain and Ireland (1997) "Unemployment and the Future of Work"

[3] Catholic Bishops Conference, England and Wales (1997) "For the Common Good"

We need to develop a posture that makes it increasingly clear that we stand on God's side of the argument for those who are excluded. There is a risk that the Church may drift away from this understanding of being alongside the poor and excluded. The Church is sometimes in danger of promoting a lifestyle that lifts people economically and culturally out of their disadvantage but them leaves them detached from their communities.

Increasingly there is an emphasis on a kind of prosperity teaching that suggests that Christians should not have economic problems. I am concerned when I see churches that become wonderful centres of celebration but have not yet found ways to make an impact in the community on behalf of the poor. I have been challenged by a book entitled Transforming the World[4] that suggests for the last two or three hundred years there has been a huge gulf between the Church and the poor. We rightly celebrate the work of Wilberforce and Shaftsbury but there is still a tremendous work for us to do to ensure that we work on God's side on behalf of the poor.

Our main task is not just to go to church. At the end of the day our main task is to see God's policy for the excluded coming to effect in such a way that we are agents of change and transformation.

## PRAYER

"Holy Spirit of God, we thank you for the work you are doing in our lives and for the way you challenge and change us. We thank you for the way you gently minister to our rough edges and hard places. Be with us as we focus on the work you have called us to do that we may be effective ministers of your love and care to those we meet day by day. We pray that we may be wounded healers bringing wholeness as we are being made whole. May we be channels of your grace as you bestow your ongoing grace upon us. We ask these things through Jesus Christ our Lord, Amen."

[4] David Smith (1998) "Transforming the World" Paternoster Press